Play Practice

The Games Approach to Teaching and Coaching Sports

Alan G. Launder

Human Kinetics

Library of Congress Cataloging-in-Publication Data

Lander, Alan G., 1934-
    Play practice : the games approach to teaching and coaching sports / Alan G. Launder.
       p. cm.
    Includes bibliographical references and index.
    ISBN 0-7360-3005-0
      1. Sports--Study and teaching. 2. Physical education and training--Study and teaching.
    I. Title.

    GV363 .L39 2001
    796'.07'7--dc21

                                      00-053521

ISBN: 0-7360-3005-0

Acquisitions Editor: Scott Wikgren; **Developmental Editor:** Jennifer Clark; **Assistant Editors:** Laurie Stokoe and Maggie Schwarzentraub; **Copyeditor:** Barbara Walsh; **Proofreader:** Pamela S. Johnson; **Indexer:** Betty Frizzell; **Permission Managers:** Courtney Astle and Dalene Reeder; **Graphic Designer:** Fred Starbird; **Graphic Artist:** Denise Lowry; **Photo Manager:** Clark Brooks; **Cover Designer:** Nancy Rasmus; **Photographer (interior):** Tom Roberts, unless otherwise noted; **Illustrators:** Craig Newsom and Tom Roberts; **Printer:** Versa Press

Printed in the United States of America   10 9 8 7 6 5 4 3 2

Human Kinetics
Web site: www.HumanKinetics.com

United States: Human Kinetics, P.O. Box 5076, Champaign, IL 61825-5076
800-747-4457
e-mail: humank@hkusa.com

Canada: Human Kinetics, 475 Devonshire Road, Unit 100, Windsor, ON N8Y 2L5
800-465-7301 (in Canada only)
e-mail: orders@hkcanada.com

Europe: Human Kinetics, 107 Bradford Road, Stanningley
Leeds LS28 6AT, United Kingdom
+44 (0) 113 255 5665
e-mail: hk@hkeurope.com

Australia: Human Kinetics, 57A Price Avenue, Lower Mitcham, South Australia 5062
08 8277 1555
e-mail: liahka@senet.com.au

New Zealand: Human Kinetics, P.O. Box 105-231, Auckland Central
09-523-3462
e-mail: hkp@ihug.co.nz

To all sport educators in every land, be they friends, parents, teachers or coaches who give their time and enthusiasm to help young people appreciate the joy of sport and so contribute to the creation of more civilised societies.

Therefore Junuh, love your opponents. When I say love, I don't mean hand them the match. I mean contend with them to the death, the way a lion battles a bear, without mercy but with infinite respect. Never belittle an opponent in your mind, rather build him up, for on the plane of the Self there can be no distinction between your being and his. Be grateful for your opponents' excellence. Applaud their brilliance. For the greatness of the hero is measured by that of his adversaries.

—Bagger Vance to Rannulph Junuh in ***The Legend of Bagger Vance***
(Pressfield Steven, Avon Books, NY 1995)

Contents

Foreword

Len Almond
Loughborough University

I am pleased to write this foreword because over a number of years I and many others have encouraged Alan Launder to commit his ideas to print. As a distinguished coach of both talented young people and elite performers, and as a firm believer in the importance of good teaching for all young people, he brings an excellent pedigree and thoughtful intellect to the promotion of sport education. This book is essential reading for the perceptive and thoughtful teacher or coach because it represents a real education in its own right. It will likely have a far-reaching impact in physical education as well as in the coaching world, adding another dimension to the much-needed debate on the important role sport can play in the education of young people and their teachers and coaches.

Though much of the previous thinking about learning in sport has focussed on games teaching, Alan Launder opens our eyes to the notion that his ideas can apply equally to such dissimilar sports as athletics and skiing. His insights have tremendous value in promoting our own understanding of the richness and potential of sport in young people's lives. *Play Practice* requires careful reading because it contains significant pedagogical principles embedded within a sound philosophy of sport education that needs to permeate both the teaching and the coaching worlds. *Play Practice* challenges us to rethink how we represent sport to young people, whether they are learners or elite performers. Finally, I recommend *Play Practice* highly to teachers, teacher educators and coaches of young people because it encourages careful observation, critical reflection and the exploration of ideas in our own practice. Its aspirations are to inform and promote intelligent practice.

Preface

The aim of this book is to improve the quality of sport education so that more young people choose to make a lifelong commitment to sport. Its objectives are to clarify the nature of skilled performance in a range of sports and to introduce the innovative Play Practice approach to teaching and coaching them. While it will be especially valuable for sport educators at the beginning of their careers, it should also prove a useful resource for experienced teachers and coaches who are looking for sound and interesting alternatives to their usual methods.

I have carefully chosen the term Play Practice to describe an innovative approach to sport education that harnesses the immense power of play to create challenging learning situations. It represents a new direction for sport education, with a potential limited only by the enthusiasm, knowledge and imagination of teachers and coaches.

The Play Practice method was initially driven by a need to find worthwhile alternatives to traditional approaches. With deep and diverse roots, it has taken shape over many years of reflective tinkering in which ideas have been developed, borrowed, trialled, modified, discarded, accepted and improved. This pragmatic process has led to a very practical approach to sport education that is in line with modern research findings into the instructional process.

This book is heir to both the liberal humanistic tradition of British physical education and the pragmatic, goal-directed methods employed by coaches worldwide. Like many worthwhile innovations, it is a working compromise between two apparently conflicting ideologies. This means that once the principles that underpin Play Practice are understood, coaches can apply them with equal effectiveness to teaching beginners as well as elite players across sports as diverse as skiing and table tennis.

Play Practice may prove to be a very valuable tool as sport challenges the sedentary amusements of television and computer games for the hearts, minds and bodies of young people. It replaces mindless games and mechanistic training methods with a joyous and challenging process through which beginners, young and old alike, can play their way to understanding and competence.

This approach is also important at the elite level because as training volumes increase in the drive toward excellence, play becomes work, enjoyment diminishes and the motivation inherent in joyful participation is lost; as a result, many talented individuals stop playing. Play Practice counters this by providing a framework for the development of a vast range of realistic practice scenarios that can simulate the demands of high-level competition while retaining the crucial element of play.

Although Play Practice has a coherent theoretical framework, it is not necessary for coaches to understand and apply it as a complete package. You can start by making one small adjustment to a practice situation or one simple modification to a game, using a working model of technique or trying a fantasy game. In this way it is possible to move gradually toward the Play Practice approach to teaching and coaching sport. Ultimately this may prove to be this approach's greatest strength: history is littered with good ideas that were not successful in practice.

Finally, the template that the principles of Play Practice provide makes it easier for sport educators to understand the relationships between different sports and to appreciate the ways in which their players can transfer good ideas and methods from one to another.

Play Practice is underpinned by a very simple philosophy based on two apparent contradictions. While it accepts the long-held view of the British that a game worth playing is a game worth playing badly, Play Practice also holds that a game worth playing is a game worth playing well! The primary task, therefore, is to help youngsters become competent and enjoy participating in physical activity. They are then more likely to maintain their involvement in the future as players, officials, teachers, coaches or informed spectators. In addition, the sense of mastery gained from increased competence may also generate the feelings of self-worth that enable individuals to cope with life in our increasingly complex world. This simple tenet clarifies and expands the role of the sport educator and takes it far beyond the mere teaching or coaching of sport, important as both those tasks are.

However, helping young people meet and overcome challenges, even those as apparently simple as controlling a ball, is a complex undertaking. It is a craft in which an instructor's professional and personal skills may be stretched to the limit and where a very fine line exists between the relative importance of process and product. Play Practice can play a vital role here as it combats the drudgery of repetitive playing and practicing and brings joy and humanity back to the sport experience.

To this end, part I of this book looks at the immense potential of sport to contribute to the lives of young people around the world, details the limitations of traditional methods of teaching them and suggests how a clearer understanding of the nature of skill in sport can lead to more effective teaching and coaching through the Play Practice approach. Part II provides a vast array of practical examples of this innovative approach in action and details specific approaches to improving technical ability and developing game sense. Part III looks at broader issues related to the role of the sport educator.

A sage once observed that there is nothing new under the sun, and that is certainly true in this case. Many experienced sport educators will quickly identify similarities between Play Practice and the methods they have devised for themselves to help solve the problems alluded to here. For them Play Practice will simply provide a framework that will help them clarify and expand their own ideas. For example, the terms shaping, focussing and enhancing, introduced in chapter 6, are only new definitions for processes that effective instructors have always used. When they are defined precisely in this way, however, the concepts they represent are easier to understand, employ and improve on.

Some readers may find the specific examples that are provided to be of the greatest value, whereas others may find greater satisfaction in developing and applying their own ideas around the general theme of practicing while playing. I hope that both the intellectual aspect of this approach and the insights it offers will prove both challenging and stimulating for those who try it.

Play Practice has immense potential, but this potential will be realised only when more sport educators begin to apply it in their own work, thus expanding the possibilities of this interesting innovation.

Reprinted, with special permission, of King Features Syndicate.

Acknowledgments

John and Chris Halbert for their part in dragging this book out kicking and screaming.

Wendy Piltz for her unfailing and enthusiastic support of all of my ideas and especially for this project.

John Gormley for his penetrating critiques of the final drafts and his invaluable assistance in finding pertinent quotes.

Len Almond for helping to clarify the evolution of Games for Understanding and for his encouragement and friendship over many years.

Rod Thorpe and Dave Bunker for sharing their ideas.

Dave Eldridge, Harley Simpson, Trevor Cibich, and Chris Deptula for their help in developing specific elements of *Play Practice*.

John Elwin who has acted as a sounding board for many of the ideas outlined here.

Darryl Siedentop for his willingness to support a heretic.

The late Deane Pease for his friendship and his encouragement to pursue different directions.

Jennifer Clark for striving hard to make sense of what must have initially seemed to be an impossible task.

Scott Wikgren for supporting the project.

Rainer Martens for allowing the project to go ahead.

My doctor, Peter Barnes, for helping to keep me alive long enough to finish it!

And finally to all my family and especially my wife, Jennifer, who have had to cope with the irritability and stress attendant on producing this work.

The Play Practice Approach

The Social Impact of Sport

*To develop a society of players and a culture devoted to play
is to contribute to a civilised humanistic future.*
—Darryl Siedentop

● ● ● ● ●

Anthropologists of the future may well be astounded by the complex and turbulent nature of life on Earth during the 20th century. As they study the phenomenon of sport during this period, will they conclude that it was merely a low form of entertainment similar to the circuses of Rome two thousand years earlier, or will they decide that sport helped lead mankind toward a golden age? We may fast be approaching a watershed, a point from which sport will go forward to make a wonderful contribution to the development of our species, or one where it will be highjacked and exploited by an increasingly avaricious "third party".

Sport as Entertainment and the Impact of the "Third Party"

Since its birth in the 19th century, modern sport has become the most significant element of

mass entertainment on the planet; and its nexus with the electronic media has made it an almost ideal vehicle for the promotion of a vast range of goods and services. Given the real-life, real-time drama of modern sport and the intensity with which it is both promoted and presented, this is hardly surprising, especially in those comfortable societies where the daily challenge and struggle to merely survive has been eliminated. Athletes can now aspire to almost obscene wealth and to adulation bordering on worship; it is quite possible that the most recognisable faces on Earth during the past 30 years have been those of Pele, Muhammad Ali and Michael Jordan.

In Australia, probably the most committed of all sporting countries and arguably the most successful on a per capita basis, legions of sportsmen and women have become national heroes. Among these, Sir Donald Bradman is, by a very large margin, the greatest batsman in the history of cricket and the first sportsman to be knighted by his sovereign for services to sport. In 1998, on the occasion of the 90th birthday of "The Don", Prime Minister John Howard observed, "Sir Donald Bradman is the greatest living Australian. He was a beacon of hope for a generation. He gave Australians something very tangible and something enjoyable to believe in, and they saw him as a repository of what was valuable about the Australian character."

Writing at the same time in what was virtually a eulogy, Don Watson wrote, "We think of gods when we contemplate Bradman because his deeds suggest the conquest of mortal limitations. He annihilated the barriers between mind and body, art and science, prose and poetry. He took his bat and forged a marriage between pragmatism and something sublime ("A Demi God Called Don," *The Australian,* August 27, 1998).

There is very little doubt that many hundreds of sportsmen and women around the world have had and continue to have a major impact on the countries and communities in which they live.

© Action Images

Courtesy of the Bradman Museum

Michael Jordan, the greatest basketball player in history, grew up in Brooklyn, but went to high school in North Carolina. While the essence of his talent derived from his amazing agility and athleticism, the thing which most aficionados will remember is his incredible ability to take the crucial shot. He was the archetypical clutch player, the go to man when the basket was needed. However what many will forget is that in his freshman/sophomore year at Laney High School in Wilmington, North Carolina he did not make the cut! Michael Jordan was a failure! Clearly he could have been an outstanding performer in many sports and his love of golf and baseball testify to a broader vision of sport.

Sir Donald Bradman, "The Don", grew up in the small town of Bowral, Australia. He went on to become the greatest batsman in the history of the ancient game of cricket, to captain Australia, a position which has often ranked ahead of that of Prime Minister in that sports-crazy nation, and to be knighted by the King of England for services to cricket. As a boy he developed his hand eye coordination with a unique play practice—continuously keeping a golf ball in play while hitting it against a corrugated iron water tank with a cricket stump—the diameter of a baseball bat handle. He was a fine sprinter and long jumper, an excellent tennis and squash player and continued to play golf to the age of ninety.

This has come at a cost, however. Because of sport's potential to reach people, there now exists a greater emphasis on winning and a consequent erosion of the very qualities that make sport valuable as both a human and a humanising experience. Also, because sport interacts with all elements in society, it reflects the vast technological and cultural changes that society has undergone in the past two hundred years.

One major consequence of this is that sport has been used as both a political and ideological weapon and is increasingly abused and exploited by what U.S. Senator Bill Bradley, erstwhile Rhodes Scholar, professional basketball player and presidential candidate, called the "third party". This third party includes self-serving politicians; avaricious owners, agents and promoters; cynical businesspeople; an ever more intrusive and sensationalist media and, of course, fanatical supporters. Each group has its own agenda, and it clearly does not always include the best interests of sport or the participants.

Among the most damning comments on modern sport was that of iconoclastic writer George Orwell (cited in Green 1982, p. 344), who observed, "... serious sport has nothing to do with fair play. It is bound up with jealousy, hatred, beastliness, disregard of all rules and sadistic pleasure in witnessing violence. In other words, it is war minus the shooting." While this is clearly an extreme position, daily events in sport around the world tend to bear out his views. Surely the wild popularity of professional wrestling, which precisely matches Orwell's comments on hatred, beastliness, disregard for the rules and covert sadism with its Hollywoodian theme of deadly violence, must point a warning. Of course, we can choose to view it as merely high-camp comedy, but remember, many saw Hitler as a comic figure until it was too late.

The people who can best ensure that sport retains its value as a humanising experience are those who should care about it most. This includes participants, both former and current, as well as all the teachers, coaches and parents who are committed to helping young people develop. We certainly need to see more high-profile players and coaches express support for all that is best in sport to counter the negative influences. One who has done so is Danny Blanchflower (former captain of the Irish soccer team), who said in 1968, "Sport is a wonderful thing. One of the few honorable battlefields left. It is a conflict between good and bad, winning and losing, praise and criticism. Its true values should be treasured and protected.... They belong to the people." (p. 341)

Sport educators at all levels are especially important because of their high status, their continuity of experience and their role as a bridge between athletes and administrators. Equally important, they can, by their every word and deed, demonstrate a sound philosophy of sport in action.

Indeed, as technological and cultural changes come apace, sport educators may hold in their hands the future of sport as a worthwhile human activity. And who better to be charged with this task? Most have enjoyed a lifetime of involvement in sport. Often their whole lives have been changed by their participation in sport; it has brought them many of their best friends, their most cherished memories and their most significant achievements.

While participants now have an immense range of sports and pastimes to choose from, games involving a ball are clearly the most popular. The great invasion games of basketball, field and ice hockey, lacrosse and the varied football codes seem to provide an immense attraction for all ages, and billions of people around the world play and watch these sports. Their attraction lies, paradoxically, in both their simplicity and their complexity: simplicity in the sense that ball possession and position clearly indicate the balance of play at any instant, complexity in the sense that games of this type present the players with challenges that they can resolve tactically and technically with a wide range of responses. In the same way, a vast array of racquet games such as tennis and badminton, target games such as golf and bowling and the striking/fielding games of cricket, baseball and softball all present innumerable technical, tactical and psychological challenges to participants.

At the highest levels, the great players display such skill that their body movements and control present the spectator with images of perfection that become an ephemeral art form. As Cozens and Stumpf (1953) stated, "Sports belong with the arts of humanity because they are as fundamental a form of human expression as music, poetry and painting." (p. 9) Arthur Steinhaus (1963) supported this idea when he said, "Players paint a picture for hundreds of thousands of people, in which the theme moves constantly and each second the scene changes completely. They are creating a picture of the highest form of art, neuromuscular control." (p. 32)

At the same time, the tactical aspects of many ball games call to mind the magnificent game of chess. The players must employ both intelligence and intuition, often under enormous pressure, often without letup, throughout the course of an entire game to solve the problems and challenges posed by their opponents.

Most importantly, when played in the true joyful spirit of competitive sport, games allow young people to begin the process of extending and defining themselves, thus expanding their awareness of their own potential. Michael Novak (1988) captured this notion beautifully when he wrote,

> *If I had to give one single reason for my love of sports it would be this: I love the tests of the human spirit, I love to see defeated teams refuse to die. I love to see impossible odds confronted. I love to see impossible dares accepted. I love to see the incredible grace lavished on simple plays—the simple flashing beauty of perfect form. But, even more, I love to see the heart which refuses to give in, refuses to panic, seizes opportunity, slips through defenses, exerts itself far beyond capacity and forges momentarily of its bodily habitat, an instrument of almost perfect will.*
>
> *All my life I have never known such thoroughly penetrating joys as playing with an inspired team, against a team we recognized from the beginning had every reason to beat us. I love it when it would be reasonable to be reconciled to defeat but one will not, cannot; I love it when a last set of calculated, reckless, free and impassioned efforts is crowned with success. When I see others play that way I am full of admiration or gratitude. (p. 150)*

Sport flourishes because in one way or another it engenders emotions such as these in millions of spectators and in participants of all ages and abilities throughout the world. Indeed, often forgotten amid all the hype about the importance of winning is that the vital attraction

Edson Arantes Do Nascimento, known to the world as Pele. Pele, sometimes called "Perola Negra" or "the black pearl," rose from a poor background in Brazil to become an icon of world soccer and the Minister of Sport for his country. A relatively small man at 5'8" and 160 pounds, Pele was initially rejected by major clubs, but once he got his opportunity he soon demonstrated great technical ability and a well-developed games sense which allied to his natural athleticism and made him the greatest player in the history of the game.

of games is the pleasure that players experience when a movement task is done well. The sweet feeling of clean contact when hitting a ball properly, of mastery when controlling or catching it, of satisfaction when intelligent teamwork produces a goal or thoughtful defence snares an interception; these are the magical moments we remember long after the result is forgotten, and they, more than any other factor, are the reason we continue to play even when our bodies can no longer sustain our dreams.

Though it is clear that we can enjoy games at this purely emotional level, the philosophy of Play Practice holds that true appreciation is linked to understanding. In fact, without a deep understanding of the challenges involved, it is impossible to fully appreciate or enjoy the five days of a cricket test match or even the "simple" game of baseball.

The sport educator—teacher, coach or committed parent—who undertakes the task of introducing young people to these kinds of experiences can play a vital part in helping to create a better, fairer and happier world. As Darryl Siedentop wrote in his highly acclaimed book, *Developing Teaching Skills in Physical Education* (1983), "To teach people how to play and to want to play is to enhance their potential for humanistic experience. To develop a society of players and a culture devoted to play is to contribute to a civilized humanistic future." (p. 131)

Novak further extended this notion when he wrote,

> *Sports are the highest products of civilization and the most accessible, lived, experiential sources of the civilizing spirit. In sports, law was born and also liberty, and the nexus of their interrelation. In sports, honesty and excellence are caught, captured, nourished, held in trust for the generations. Without rules, there are no sports. Without limits sport cannot begin to exist. Play is the essence of freedom: The free play of ideas. Play is the fundamental structure of the human mind. Of the body, too. The mind at play, the body at play—these furnish our imaginations with the highest achievements of beauty the human race attains. (p. 43)*

Finally, it is vital to understand the place that sport increasingly can play in the lives of young people growing up in our complex and potentially soul-destroying modern society. Fifty years ago, 15-year-olds could enter the workforce and begin productive lives. Today, many people may never find permanent work. In fact, both developed and developing nations already face this major challenge, and it is one that will not be easily resolved. It has been estimated that at the beginning of the new millennium, 60 million young people between the ages of 15 and 24 were looking for work around the world. Even those fortunate enough to find productive work, perhaps in the professions, must wait many years before they gain the recognition they seek. Only in the fields of entertainment and sport is it possible for young people to reach the pinnacle of success.

In the sporting arena young people can compete on even terms with the best in the world. For some this will bring huge financial rewards, but at the very least it should give all participants a chance to feel competent and worthy and help them begin a lifelong commitment to sport and a healthy lifestyle. It can also introduce them to the varied roles of player, official, recorder, coach, trainer or even spectator.

Sport Education: An Undervalued Facet of Modern Life

Despite the immense potential of sport to contribute to the all-round development of young people, improvements in sport education have not kept pace with the phenomenal developments in coaching and training methods at the elite level. There, in a professional and performance-driven environment, cross-fertilisation takes place between sports and nations to ensure that any successful innovation is copied and applied almost immediately.

There are several reasons why developments in sport education have lagged behind the rapid improvements at the elite level. One of the most significant is that in most countries a vast gulf still exists between university academics and practitioners in the field. Sadly, this dichotomy ensures that innovations remain rare, because, like the most significant developments in the fields of science and technology over the past thousand years, they are generated only when the searchlight of reflection is applied to pragmatic experimentalism and tinkering in the workplace or laboratory. As Donald Schon

(1987) implies in his book *Educating the Reflective Practitioner,* academics have tended to remain on high ground, solving relatively unimportant problems according to prevailing standards of rigor rather than descending to the swamp of important problems and nonrigorous inquiry. True, their work over the past 30 years has at least confirmed why the largely intuitive behavior of many good teachers is effective and also provides the foundation for a scientific understanding of the process of instruction. However, crucial questions have been left unasked, and this has ensured a dearth of innovation from those institutions charged with engendering it.

The Problems of Junior Sport

Because little innovation has occurred at the junior level, traditional methods of teaching games have survived even though they often do not meet the needs of ordinary children and do little to help even talented and enthusiastic youngsters play more effectively and enjoyably. Above all, these methods do not cater to reluctant learners who are unwilling to undertake the repetitive practice often associated with becoming proficient at sport.

> *T*raditional methods of teaching games do not cater to reluctant learners who are not willing to undertake the repetitive practice often associated with becoming proficient at sport.

Even worse, recent history has shown that it is possible for overambitious coaches and parents to drive talented children to extraordinary levels of performance in sports such as gymnastics and swimming using methods that few elite senior athletes would tolerate. Perhaps the most chilling example of the abuse of young people in sport was detailed in the February 14, 2000, issue of *The Australian.* In an article entitled "Cycle of Success Sentences Young Stars to Burnout", Lynne O'Donnell, after making a comprehensive study of sport education in China, writes,

[T]here is no room for shame in the mean, competitive environment of Chinese athletics. With a population of 1.3 billion and a demographic bulge between the ages of 15 and 35, China offers conditions far more difficult for a hopeful sports star than most countries on the planet. This, coupled with an excruciating training regimen, is what experts point to when explaining the short careers of Chinese swimmers. They start early, they peak early, they burn out fast.

The Chinese start their training very early, at 5 or 6 years of age, and they train 7 days a week. There is such a huge pool of juniors to choose from that those who can survive the rigorous training are indeed elite athletes ... intense competition from hopeful up-and-comers means that coaches have enormous choice and switch interest from current champions to those they see as future stars, according to Zhang Qiuping, Vice Chairman of the China Swimming Association. Women dominate swimming because they are better-equipped to endure the training, Mr. Zhang said.

It is the same in many sports—weightlifting, gymnastics, soccer, volleyball, athletics. These sports do not generally appeal to Chinese men, but the women 'HUI CHIKU'", he said, using a Chinese phrase which literally means "women can eat bitterness". In other words, they can be encouraged to sacrifice everything in the pursuit of success in sport.

Similar problems have occurred around the world in the teaching and coaching of games where a strong desire to win on the part of many adults overshadows a commitment to sensible and sensitive sport education programs for all children. Even in a balanced and sports-loving society such as that of Australia, the phenomenon of "the ugly parent" who hurls abuse at officials and players alike is all too common.

To date, no nation, even the most liberal and supportive, has been prepared to put in place the comprehensive programs recommended by the unending inquiries into sport and physical education that all nations undertake. In addition, and perhaps inevitably, while governments tremble at the cost of providing adequate health services for their citizens, physical education programs, which could play a major role in preventive medicine, are allowed to wither. For example, in the United States, sport is the dominant feature of the culture and a multibillion-dollar industry, yet elementary school physical education is starved of funding.

> *The physical education programs, which could play a major role in preventative medicine, are allowed to wither.*

Perhaps the biggest disappointment is the state of sport education in the United Kingdom, the country where modern sport began. Driven by the ethos of what has been termed "muscular Christianity" in the public—but quite private!—schools of England in the early 19th century and supported by the massive wealth generated by the industrial revolution, sport rapidly became a major element of Britain's culture. Indeed, Britain exported sport to all corners of the globe as readily as it exported the industrial, managerial and financial infrastructure that enabled other countries to develop their economies.

Unfortunately, the United Kingdom did not build on its head start and is now a relative minnow in terms of world sport. While the reasons for this are clearly very complex, there can be little doubt that the inability of successive governments to develop and support forward-looking policies for sport at any level has been a major contributing factor. This has especially been the case in the education sector. Indeed, the greatest tragedy has been the virtual collapse of the traditional system of school sport and physical education in the government sector because of successive governments' unwillingness to provide essential funding and staffing. The government has reduced funding to schools and refused to increase salary levels, so many teachers have opted out of school sport, which, as a result, has withered.

Ironically, the countries that came closest to an ideal model of sport for all were the Communist nations of Europe during the period between 1950 and 1985, when governments spent large sums on developing a sports infrastructure for all citizens, training coaches and funding elite athletes. Unfortunately, despite the free-flowing rhetoric, this effort was not intended to lead to a civilised humanistic future but was merely part of the overall struggle for ideological supremacy in the cold war.

Even in Australia, which has made a commitment to improving sport at the junior level, a haphazard approach still dominates that is not fully supported by government or by the business community with sponsorship. Vast numbers of young people grow up with their potential talent undeveloped or even unrecognised, often because they are never exposed to the sport they could potentially excel in. Programs the government has initiated are inevitably bureaucratised and concerned more with delivering resources of doubtful quality than providing quality experiences for children.

Finding Solutions

Yet in most countries it would be relatively easy to make significant improvements and ensure that sport fulfills its potential to contribute to positive educational, developmental, social and health outcomes. All that is needed is for communities, schools and clubs to make as big a commitment to providing opportunities for all young people as they do in supporting their "sports entertainers". This may seem idealistic, but it only needs a few committed individuals with basic political skills to change even entrenched positions—if their cause is just. And what could be more just than ensuring that every child has the opportunity to play sport?

A first step would be simply to ensure that all community sporting facilities, including those in schools, are made available for every possible minute of the day. In addition, informal competitions and pickup games should be encouraged at every possible venue, with equipment provided where needed. Here it is important to remember that sport flourished long before coaches, sport administrators or even officials came on the scene.

Any dedicated sport educator who understands and applies the Play Practice approach to teaching sport can play a vital role in developing a society of players and a culture devoted to play (Siedentop 1983). For with Play Practice, young people can play their way to understanding and competence. With competence comes confidence, two qualities that may help develop the feelings of self-worth individuals need to cope with the slings and arrows of outrageous fortune that are so much a part of life in our increasingly complex world.

CHAPTER

2

The Emergence of Play Practice

The barber learns his trade on the orphan's chin.
—Arabic proverb

● ● ● ● ●

The Play Practice approach could not have evolved if earlier sport educators had not dedicated their time and thoughtful reflection to the field of sport education. This chapter presents a brief summary of some of this early work that enabled the development of Play Practice.

Games for Understanding

It would be impossible to write a book in the field of sport education without acknowledging the work of the talented team of Len Almond, Dave Bunker and Rod Thorpe at Loughborough University in England. Their Games for Understanding approach, initially outlined in a series of articles entitled "Games Teaching Revisited" in the spring 1983 issue of the *British Bulletin of Physical Education,* has been a seminal influence for many in the field of sport education.

The initial stimuli for the Loughborough group were the mindless "games lessons" they often

observed during their visits to schools to supervise student teachers. These talented teachers were not just concerned with merely improving the teaching of games, however; they wanted to change the entire games curriculum in English schools. It had become increasingly clear to them that with the time allotted for physical education steadily diminishing, the games curriculum was under increasing pressure, and it was impossible to deal with every aspect of effective play.

The Loughborough group's emphasis on understanding led them to identify the key tactical elements of different families of games and to use these as the basis for simple game forms. They believed that when the technical demands of a game were reduced or modified, players could then concentrate on learning the tactical components of effective play. In their view, the teacher's task was to introduce game forms that were simple enough for beginners but which could be developed progressively to allow players to move toward the adult version of the game. To facilitate this process the Loughborough team also introduced alternative approaches to lesson planning for games.

Although they emphasised the importance of tactical awareness, the team never questioned the importance of technical ability in effective play. They simply believed that given the limited time available, it is better to help children understand the nature of games rather than try to teach the techniques of a vast range of complex, "major" games ineffectively. They believed that sport instructors should introduce techniques in the later stages, or if the game is breaking down because of weaknesses in this area. A basic tenet of their approach was that with a love and an understanding of games, youngsters could become involved in many different ways—certainly as players, but also as officials, administrators, coaches or simply as informed spectators.

The Games for Understanding approach brought a fresh direction to sport pedagogy and excited considerable interest as a potential alternative to tired and meaningless traditional methods. Unfortunately, despite this as well as the fact that it has become a hot topic at conferences and has provided the basis for many articles, Games for Understanding has yet to have a major impact on the way games are actually taught or coached at the junior level around the world. There has certainly been a vast difference between the enthusiasm with which these ideas have been greeted by academics and sport administrators with a special interest in this area, and their uptake by teachers and coaches.

The Evolution of the Games for Understanding Approach

In a personal communication Len Almond clarified the evolution of the Games for Understanding approach. He wrote:

During the 1970s the climate at Loughborough College was reflective and innovative. The interaction between many faculty members, especially those involved with major sporting bodies, meant there was constant flow of ideas. Developments in one area were reflected back into teaching and vice

versa. Eric Worthington (soccer), Rod Thorpe (racquet games), and Jim Greenwood (rugby) were all key players in this process.

When Len Almond, with his interest in curriculum development, joined Rod Thorpe and David Bunker, both of whom had strong backgrounds in teaching games, a concerted team effort was made to formulate ideas and practical suggestions. Drawing together the ideas of experienced games players and practitioners from other institutions, they developed the notion that games were problem-solving activities where it was important to identify the major tactical challenges. This was a major debate because they were forced to address the issue of the role of techniques in understanding how to play the game.

Questions were posed about the best ways of representing games in their basic form. Representation, key principles of play and ideas about modification became key issues. Teaching games through games became a major focus and, with a significant contribution from Margaret Ellis, modification principles emerged in the form of reducing the technical and tactical demands of a game. This was vital because all those involved in the development process believed that every child was important.

Len Almond, as editor of the British Bulletin of Physical Education, *saw the need to publicize these new ideas and generate reactions from the profession. He saw critique as necessary for any innovation and the Loughborough team was anxious to entertain alternative interpretations and expose weaknesses in their thinking and practical suggestions. As with many innovations, their proposals were seen as too theoretical at first, yet they had emerged from a practical base and retained a strong focus on 'doing'. They certainly represented a major challenge to current thinking at the time.*

The biggest problem was that the implementation of these ideas demanded a thorough practical knowledge of a wide range of games and a willingness to set up small-sided games to create learning laboratories where questions could be asked and practical solutions sought. While many teachers were excited by this concept, they were unprepared for the teaching demands of this approach.

The Problems of Innovation

While the failure of any innovation to impact on practice is always a complex matter, the most likely reason in this case is that this innovative approach to teaching games requires advanced instructional skills and a deep understanding of the activities involved if coaches and other sport educators are to use it successfully. This is a problem that faces any innovation presented to a highly conservative audience such as that in sport education. Certainly educational gymnastics, perhaps the single most important innovation in the history of British physical education, suffered from the ignorance and intransigence of teachers when it was introduced following World War II. In the hands of committed and highly skilled practitioners, educational gymnastics provided a magical vision of the potential of our field to contribute to the total development of young people; in the hands of ordinary teachers, however, it was little more than groups of children rolling aimlessly around on gymnasium floors. As with educational gymnastics, perhaps the Games for Understanding approach is an aeroplane that only a test pilot can fly.

● ● ● ● ● ● ● ● ●

Traditional gymnastics, or "Vaulting and Agility" as it was often called, was a major component of the physical education curriculum of British schools both before and after World War II. The agility element was based around the teaching of a vast array of specific challenges, beginning with forward and backward rolls and moving on through headstands, handstands, headsprings, handsprings, fly springs and so on, toward ever more complex and difficult stunts. The vaulting element progressed in a similar manner, with both the complexity of the challenge and the height of the vaulting equipment continually rising. Under the direction of a highly skilled and sensitive teacher, it was possible for some children in a class to attain very high levels of performance. The nature of the challenges involved, however, meant that while mesomorphs flourished, ectomorphs and endomorphs were virtually condemned to failure or even humiliation, no matter how hard they might try.

● ● ● ● ● ● ● ● ●

The educational gymnastics approach, which many hoped would solve the problems with the traditional methods outlined in the special element box, was the product of many factors operating in British education in the period following World War II. It drew on Laban's notion of a movement notation and was essentially an understanding approach to the teaching of gymnastics in which the teacher used open-ended challenges to give each child a chance to create a unique physical response within the limits of his or her ability. This gave every child a chance to be successful and to develop a fundamental understanding of the nature of movement.

Similarities and Differences Between Play Practice and Games for Understanding

Many similarities exist between the Games for Understanding approach and Play Practice. This is hardly surprising. In both cases the innovators were immersed in the English tradition of physical education and coaching, had strong links with coach education programs and combined an ongoing practical involvement in sport education with wide-ranging experience and the time for continuing reflection. Importantly, both groups were in a position to experiment and tinker with ideas and practice, which is the key to innovation in many fields of human endeavour. The ideas of the Loughborough group certainly influenced Play Practice and in fact provided a "play practice" solution to the teaching of striking/fielding games.

A common thread that connects these two approaches is the emphasis on understanding. This should not be unexpected, since even a cursory analysis of any sport will confirm the importance of understanding the rules, the tactics and even the strategies in skilled performance at every level.

However, important differences exist between these two innovative approaches. These are due in part to the slightly different backgrounds of the innovators involved but mainly to different circumstances and objectives. The initial aim of Play Practice as it evolved was to give beginners the chance to really enjoy sport and help them become competent enough to

Played with minimal equipment in any available space with no officials, uniforms, time limits or prizes, pickup games give anyone a chance to play. It is probable that at any instant, more people around the world are playing in informal games of this kind than in official competitions.

One of the key concepts that emerged from analysing pickup games was the notion that if a learning situation is to be really useful, failure must be legitimised. The very informality of pickup games means that even when participants are playing with great intensity, mistakes are not crucial. This gives players the freedom to experiment, to try out moves and tactics, to try on roles, all without the threat of criticism from authority figures if they fail. This idea is so powerful that it can be stated as "Nothing succeeds like failure," because while early success may lead to the dead end of stagnation, failure encourages continued experimentation.

Other significant influences were the ideas and methods that English soccer coaches developed in the 1950s. Under the leadership of Alan Wade, director of coaching for the English Football Association, they introduced the use of small-sided games in which they could emphasise the principles of tactical play, thus laying the foundations for both Play Practice and Games for Understanding.

go on with an activity if they wished. In Australia, however, there was also a need to develop an approach that could bring the joy back into sport at all levels and could improve both games teaching in schools and sports coaching in both the schools and the community.

The Evolution of Play Practice

As with many innovations, Play Practice has diverse and surprisingly deep roots. One seminal influence was the worldwide popularity of pickup games, which are found wherever there are at least two people and a ball of some kind.

One of the key concepts which emerged from analysing pickup games was the notion that if a learning situation is to be really useful, failure must be legitimised.

Other factors also played a part. One was the poignant story of an intellectually impaired child who got a potential base hit in baseball but ran toward third base instead of first. Nothing could have highlighted his disability more than this. To strike out is a minor tragedy but is infinitely better than hitting the ball and not knowing where to run. This story was an important element in the evolution of Play Practice because it hammered home the fact that it is as important for children to understand the game and its rules as it is for them to become technically proficient.

A study trip behind the Iron Curtain in the 1970s led to the surprising discovery that in early gymnastics training in these countries, talented youngsters were allowed free rein on all the equipment and foam pits in large, well-equipped halls. Here they frolicked and played, challenged and copied each other, gradually building their confidence along with the physical qualities necessary for later success.

The Effect of the "Swamp of Reality"

The concepts and methods that underpin Play Practice first began to evolve in the "swamp of reality" I faced in my first experience as a sport educator at a secondary school in England. Here it is worth remembering the immortal words of George Napper, an American policeman, who said, "When you are up to your ass in alligators, it is hard to remember that your original purpose was to drain the swamp." (Green 1982, p. 31)

This swamp of reality quickly exposed the limitations of traditional methods of teaching many activities, and I had to develop alternative approaches. As I had no mentors to learn from or to share ideas with, it was the children's responses that increasingly drove the change process. If the children liked an idea and it motivated them to play or practise more purposefully, then I recycled it; if they did not accept it, I put it aside, to be either tinkered with or junked.

The change process was increasingly driven by the responses of children.

The whole future of Play Practice depended on these early days, when the children's ready acceptance of new ideas, limited and ill defined though they were at the time, contrasted strongly with their negative reaction to traditional methods. First applied to the teaching of cross-country running and then to track and field, neither of which is easy to develop in a school environment, the principles of Play Practice slowly began to emerge.

The whole future of Play Practice depended on these early days when new ideas, limited and ill defined though they were at the time, contrasted strongly with their negative reactions to traditional methods.

In the beginning I had no theoretical basis for the ideas and methods being developed. The process involved simply going with what appeared to work with children and continual reflective tinkering to ensure gradual improvement. At the same time that Play Practice was evolving to replace traditional methods of teaching sport, I was developing the "Ps" model of pedagogy, which is detailed in chapter 7, to fill a vacuum in instructional theory, a vacuum that has been filled only in recent times. Gradually, as theory has caught up with practice, it has been integrated with Play Practice, both to legitimate an approach that has simply evolved pragmatically and to provide a sound basis for further development.

No Formal Research Base—But...

At a time when it appears that no innovation can be presented, far less accepted, unless it is supported by a sound body of reviewed scientific work, it may seem damning to admit that neither the Games for Understanding approach nor Play Practice has a specific research base. Both of these approaches to the teaching of sport have evolved through a process of reflective tinkering in which ideas have been generated, trialled, discarded, accepted or improved on. In both cases the process has been driven by a need to find better ways of inducing young people to make sport an integral part of their lives. This is a here-and-now task, one that is far too important to await any seal of approval.

This situation has developed because until very recently there has been a vast gulf between researchers in universities and practitioners in the field. As Donald Schon suggested, the former tend to "go to mountain tops" to conduct research, where it is easy to meet required standards of academic rigour. But such lofty surroundings are irrelevant to the "swamp of reality", where the really important problems arise. This is the main reason why there has been little worthwhile research into the teaching of games, a topic not particularly amenable to measurement by a stopwatch nor one especially valued in the hierarchy of research.

Not so long ago, many universities were assessing their students' "skills" in practical courses with skills tests that in fact had little or nothing to do with skills used in a game. Though some might argue that a correlation existed between these tests and the players' observed performance, for many years the use of these tests inhibited serious inquiry into the real nature of skill in games. It also led many in the profession down a dead-end track of misunderstanding and thus contributed to ineffective teaching and coaching.

Another charge into a dead end was led by academics espousing the virtues of "individualised instruction". This approach, while eminently suitable for individual activities such as weight training, was completely inappropriate for the teaching of games in which skilled performance is a composite of many elements and not based solely on technique. Though it is possible to individualise the practice of some aspects of technique, it is clearly impossible to individualise the more critical elements of team play in games. So this too contributed to a misunderstanding of the nature of "skill" in games by emphasising only the obvious but less important aspects of effective play.

Interestingly enough, elite coaches often seem to be closer to understanding the real issues, or at least they behave as though they do. This is probably because their methods are driven by the need to achieve results in the real world and not by the pressure of educational philosophies or academic politics. While many academics will find it difficult to accept, the best teachers of anything, but especially of physical activity, have often been coaches.

Fortunately, researchers are now addressing these issues in a way that should lead to a dramatic improvement in the understanding of games and ways to teach them. Darryl Siedentop at Ohio State University has initiated this work; he has driven forward the notion of "sport education" as an adjunct to or even a replacement for the traditional physical education curriculum. His book *Sport Education* outlines an organisational and administrative framework for the development of sport education and its incorporation into the physical education curriculum. One inevitable consequence of this will be a greater interest in sport pedagogy by researchers. They have much to do to catch up with practice.

A Ready Acceptance by Teachers and Coaches

While Play Practice has never been tested in a formal sense, it has been accepted and approved by practitioners and the young people they teach and coach. Teachers and coaches, especially novices trying to come to terms with the enormity of the task they face, are consumers. They do not readily accept novel ideas, nor will they persist with something that clearly does not work for them or their peers after a fair trial. They intuitively understand the truth of Bronowksi's (1973) statement: "But the test…, of a technical practice, the test of a scientific theory, is 'Does it work?'" (p. 133) The evidence to date suggests that novice instructors can make use of many of the ideas suggested in this book and that many experienced coaches have been applying the principles of Play Practice, albeit unwittingly, for years.

Play Practice and Novice Instructors

The work of several generations of students at the University of South Australia in Adelaide first confirmed and then extended the value of the Play Practice approach. This was made possible because a major element of the four-year course to prepare specialist teachers of physical education was a comprehensive curriculum and teaching studies strand. This strand included a six-week teaching block in a high school at the end of the third year of the course and culminated in an eight-week block in a different high school at the beginning of the fourth year.

Intensive periods of planning and preparation preceded both teaching blocks. One of the most significant elements preceding the third-year teaching experience was labeled simply "a directed study". This became a learning laboratory for Play Practice in which sports activities, which the students had not previously covered in their course work, were analyzed with a view to developing teaching approaches for them. In this way the teaching of touch was completely revised while at the same time a viable method of introducing Australian children to the complexities of American football was developed. In addition, new approaches to teaching activities as diverse as archery and cricket were examined.

When the experiences of each third-year block were detailed, analysed and summarised, the advantages of Play Practice were increasingly highlighted, especially by those student teachers placed in what might be termed difficult schools—that is, those with a higher-than-usual percentage of resistant learners. This gave the approach immense credibility with young teachers, who are always looking for ideas their peers had successfully applied in the crucible of real teaching. So as student teachers prepared for their final teaching block, they had a "strong set to learn" and were prepared to consider a broader range of possibilities.

During the final teaching block, the students were required to plan and teach at least one innovative unit of work. The level of innovation could range from merely something they had never attempted before, to ideas their supervising teacher had never seen, to approaches not used by any student teachers previously and, most significantly, to "ideas which had never been used before on the planet"! This led to the development of a vast range of innovative teaching ideas, including many based on the principles of Play Practice.

Play Practice and Coaching

As suggested in the preface, many experienced teachers and coaches will quickly recognise similarities between Play Practice and their own methods. For them, the great advantage of this text may be that it will provide a coherent framework that will help them to clarify and further develop their ideas.

For over 40 years, soccer coaches in England have been using small-sided, conditioned games to emphasise tactical principles. More recently some field hockey coaches have begun to use the same approach; for example, Ric Charlesworth, coach of the Australian women's hockey team, undoubtedly the most successful international side over the past decade, uses what he has termed "designer games".

Many volleyball coaches have also begun to replace drills with conditioned games to ensure that athletes maintain their training intensity through the months or even years of purposeful practice needed for success at the top level. Even track and field coaches have their own version of Play Practice in the form of field tests, which are used to deal with the challenge of maintaining commitment and intensity through long periods of preseason training.

Summary

Work undertaken at the University of South Australia has shown that student instructors can use the Play Practice approach effectively to turn practice into play by using games and challenges in some form or other to create realistic and enjoyable learning situations for beginners. At the other end of the performance scale, anecdotal evidence suggests that many elite coaches use variations on this approach to ensure purposeful, pertinent practice.

Traditional Approaches to Teaching Games

To think of football as merely 22 hirelings kicking a ball is merely to say that a violin is wood and catgut, Hamlet is so much ink and paper.
—J.B. Priestley

• • • • •

While there are many reasons why old-fashioned, inappropriate methods and ideas survive in the field of sport education, a key factor is the complex and demanding nature of the sport educator's role. So before attempting any critique of traditional methods, we must first both fully understand and value the nature of this role. A key concept here is that in the ultimate, teaching and coaching sport are not so much about "knowing" as about "doing".

These are two aspects of a complex craft in which a vast array of skills, information, knowledge and even wisdom are brought to bear on an array of problems that can encompass virtually all aspects of the personal, professional, academic and sporting lives of individuals or teams. This craft involves a range of processes that may require careful observation, thoughtful analysis, precise diagnosis, accurate prescription and effective communication.

Above all, as they deal with the unending and problematic challenges of helping young people strive for excellence, sport educators must be masters of the "instantaneous response". Here they fuse their professional and personal skills to ensure an immediate and effective response to every one of the interactions with their players. This is demanding because usually little time is available for reflection and crafting a carefully considered response. But the nature of this instantaneous response is crucial because in that instant of communication, an instructor's true values and motives may be revealed. In a flash, youngsters may discover what their mentor really thinks about them and their performance, no matter what words are spoken.

The role requires tremendous enthusiasm, energy and commitment, and good sport educators are so completely immersed in their work that they often have little time for reflection. As with professionals in many fields, their behavior is often intuitive; as Donald Schon would say, their knowing is in their actions. In other words, they cannot always conceptualise or verbalise what they do, even when they do it superbly.

The problem is that if their knowing lies only in their actions, sports educators may be unable to provide a rational and coherent explanation as to why they do what they do. It also means that they may not appreciate the limitations of their methods, or may not see a need to change them. Sport educators are not unique in this respect. In his seminal book *Crisis in the Classroom,* Charles Silberman (1970) wrote, "Professionals must act on incomplete knowledge because science does not, and as a rule, cannot directly generate rules of practice, and certainly not rules to cover the almost infinite variety of behavior a teacher will experience." He quoted Dean Harvey Brooks, who stated, "To the professional goes the responsibility of using existing and new knowledge to provide services the society wants and needs. This is an art because it demands action as well as thought, and action must always be taken on the basis of incomplete knowledge." (pp. 388 and 427)

It is therefore not surprising that most sport educators hang on to what they know and feel comfortable with, especially if they have little or no access to new ideas or to mentors who might help them improve. This is even more likely if a shaky theoretical background leaves them unable to critically analyse ideas and practices. In this situation they will often fall back on the methods they experienced when they themselves were taught and coached as young players. These experiences can have a powerful and long-lasting impact on both the philosophies and methods of sport educators, but it can also lead to the continued use of old ideas and practices.

Another important issue, which Silberman (1970) raised several years ago, is that many universities have abrogated their responsibility for the promotion of effective teaching across the whole spectrum of education, including their own faculties of education. They have, in many cases, ignored the university's history as an institution dedicated to promulgating knowledge and turned instead to churning out banal research papers, often merely replicating rather than extending the seminal work of others.

Theoretical Concepts

As a result of all of these factors, the teaching of games has been dominated by three approaches. The first of these is the "let's have a full game" approach where teams are picked and the ball is thrown out by the instructor who then either joins in as a player or simply stands and watches play. The second is the use of "minor games" which usually bear no relationship to the real game, while the third is the "coaching" approach which typically emphasises the development of technical ability. While the limitations of all three of these approaches have been apparent to perceptive observers for many years, it is now possible to analyse and critique them more objectively using key theoretical concepts developed or clarified over the past 30 years. These concepts are outlined below.

Academic Learning Time

The first of these concepts is academic learning time—physical education, or ALT-PE for short. The notion that ALT-PE is a valid indicator of effective instruction has underpinned much of the research in the field over the past three decades. Although ALT-PE is a relatively crude measure of instructional effectiveness, studies based on this concept have at least confirmed that a direct relationship exists between the amount of learning that takes place and the amount of time learners are practising. Plenty of practice does indeed tend to make perfect—or almost!

Armed only with a stopwatch, an observer can determine how much time in any session is devoted to active learning, compared to how much time the instructor spends instructing, managing or organising. This information at least provides an initial guide to the overall effectiveness of a practice session.

Maximum Individual Participation

The second theoretical concept is that of maximum individual participation, or MIP. MIP is a critical extension of ALT-PE because although it is easy to determine the amount of time a group is involved in a learning task, there is no way of knowing whether any or every individual is actively involved during this period. To establish the level of MIP an observer must either watch specific individuals throughout a session or employ a sampling procedure.

Although MIP is a slightly more sophisticated assessment tool, it too measures only the amount of activity, not the quality of that activity. Even this, however, enables an instructor to appreciate that it is better to give every child a ball to perform a series of basketball dribbling practices than to use relays where four or five youngsters share one ball.

Transfer of Training

The third concept is that of transfer of training. The theoretical bases for this area were established even before the emergence of a credible knowledge base for sports pedagogy. Unfortunately, researchers initially concentrated on the simple issue of transferability of skill between body parts or from one movement pattern (technique) to another. They virtually ignored the "swamp", in this case the far more important area of transfer from one practice situation to another or from a practice situation to the real activity. As a result, there has been a singular lack of understanding of the importance of transfer of training in sport education. This is arguably the major reason that instructors continue to use mindless minor games and dead-end drills in the teaching of games.

*T*here has been a singular lack of understanding of the importance of transfer of training in sport education.

In an attempt to clarify the issue of transfer of training in sport education and to separate it from its historical baggage, this text introduces the concept of alignment. Educators have commonly used this term to describe a direct relationship between planned outcomes, the learning situations designed to achieve those outcomes and the procedures used to assess the efficacy of the overall process. For the purposes of this text, however, alignment in sport education occurs when many similarities exist between one practice situation and another, or between a practice situation and the real game or sport. In figure 3.1 a series of soccer practices and games shows that the closer the alignment—that is, the greater the similarities between any practice situation and the real game—the more likely it is that new learning will transfer from one to another.

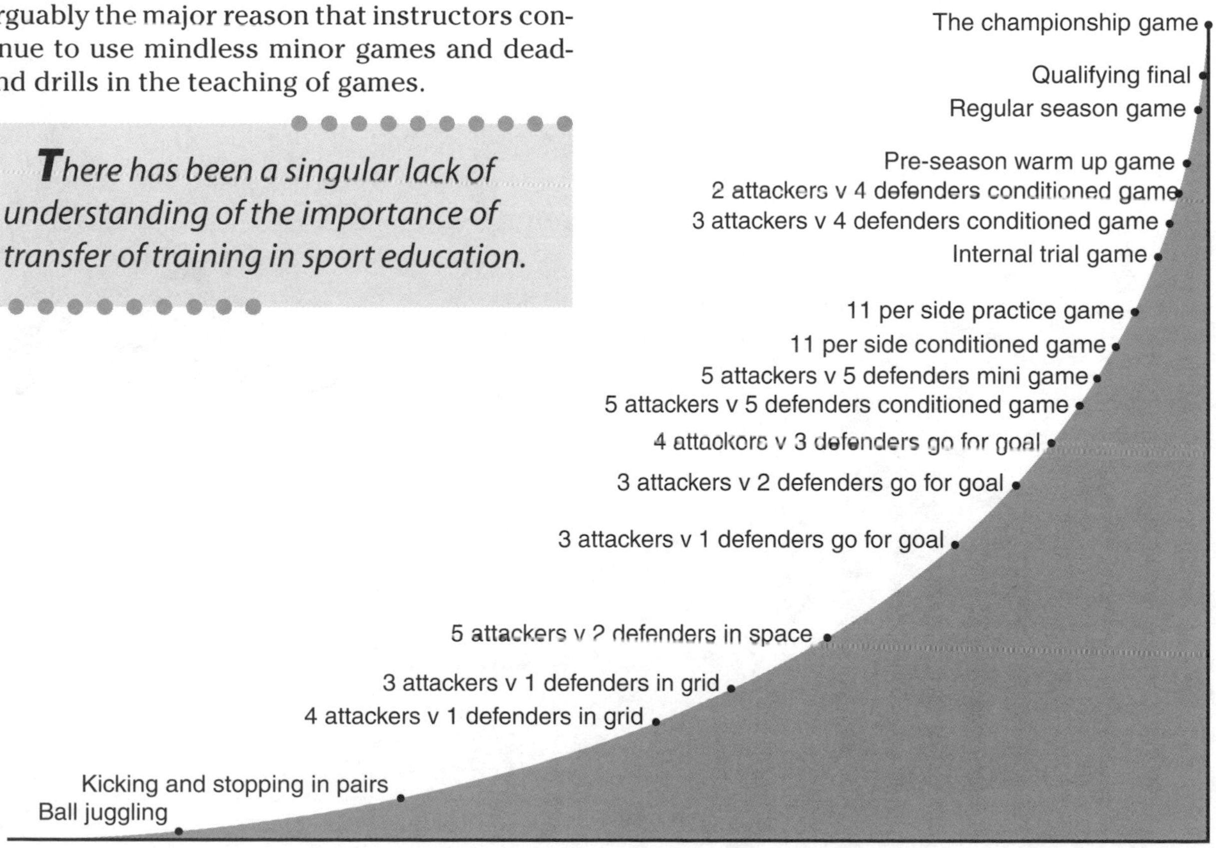

The championship game
Qualifying final
Regular season game

Pre-season warm up game
2 attackers v 4 defenders conditioned game
3 attackers v 4 defenders conditioned game
Internal trial game

11 per side practice game
11 per side conditioned game
5 attackers v 5 defenders mini game
5 attackers v 5 defenders conditioned game
4 attackers v 3 defenders go for goal
3 attackers v 2 defenders go for goal

3 attackers v 1 defenders go for goal

5 attackers v 2 defenders in space

3 attackers v 1 defenders in grid
4 attackers v 1 defenders in grid

Kicking and stopping in pairs
Ball juggling

Figure 3.1 This diagram shows that the closer the alignment between a practice situation and the real game, the greater is the possibility of transfer of skill from one to the other.

> **I**n sport education, alignment occurs when there are many similarities between one practice situation and another or between a practice and the real game.

Conversely, if little alignment exists between a practice and the game, any useful transfer between them is unlikely to occur, and as a result players will not improve. As shown in the medium-shaded area of figure 3.2, this is the case with many of the drills and unrelated mi-

nor games that instructors have traditionally used in sport education. In fact, in extreme cases these may be so different from the real game or activity that they interfere with learning and thus have a negative effect. Practices or games of this kind would fall into the zone below the baseline.

The three concepts just outlined are drawn together in the "Ps of Pedagogy" model of instruction outlined in chapter 7. It is summed up by the truism "Train as you play and play as you train," and by the Play Practice mantra, "To become an effective performer, a learner needs plenty of perfect practice under conditions as similar as possible to the environment in which the new learning will subsequently be applied."

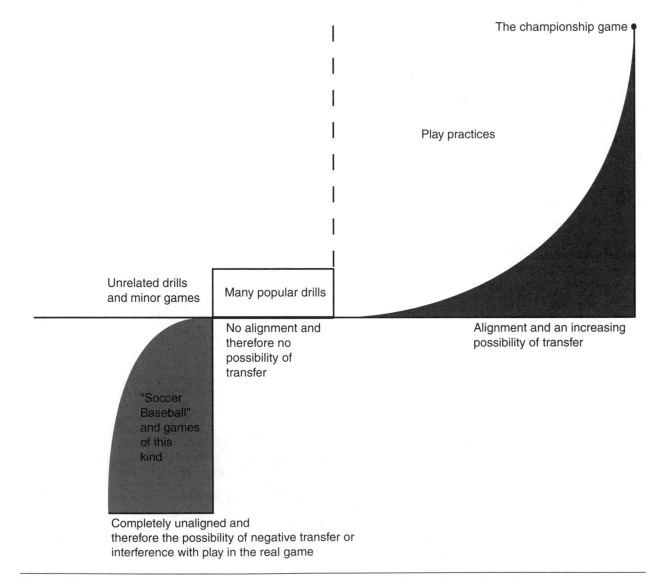

Figure 3.2   Many popular drills have nil alignment, pertinence and transfer to the real game.

> *T*o become an effective performer, a learner needs plenty of perfect practice under conditions as similar as possible to the environment in which the new learning will subsequently be applied.

Although transfer between closely related—aligned—situations may occur automatically, it will be enhanced if the instructor points out to learners the similarities between them, as well as any significant differences. In addition, though it has yet to be confirmed by research, it is reasonable to assume that transfer is more likely to occur when practice and application are closely related in time.

The Three Commonly Used Methods of Teaching Games

The theoretical principles that underpin ALT-PE, MIP and transfer of training, or what I have termed alignment, deal a death blow to the commonly used approaches to teaching games, which are described next.

The "Let's Have a Full Game" Approach

As suggested earlier, the group is divided into two teams, and the children are thrown into a full game straight away—even when there are more players than would be the case in a "real" game. Team captains, nominated by the instructor, often pick the teams, a process that not only wastes time but also is demoralising for the less able youngsters.

This demeaning, soul-destroying process entered popular culture many years ago through Janis Ian's (1975) bittersweet song "At Seventeen," where she sings, "To those of us who knew the pain / Of Valentines that never came / And those whose names were never called / When choosing sides for basketball..."

These games are inevitably dominated by the more aggressive, more experienced players, while children with limited ability hover on the fringes, trying to make sense of the apparently chaotic whirl of play going on around them. These children rarely touch the ball and quickly learn how to position themselves to stay out of the way.

The soccer scenario that includes a wet and muddy pitch, a heavy ball and an insensitive instructor develops into the kind of games experience that many Englishmen have recorded with passion and hatred in their autobiographies. Of his school days, the English poet John Betjaman wrote, "... the dread of beatings! Dread of being late! And, the greatest dread of all, the dread of games!" (Cohen 1980, p. 40)

A brilliant depiction of such a game is shown in the feature film *KES,* directed by Ken Loach, who is renowned for his biting social commentary. We watch a young schoolboy suffer extreme humiliation as a result of the damaging, unjustifiable and unnecessary method of picking teams alluded to earlier. When it becomes clear that neither side wants him, he is forced to tag along, unnoticed, behind one of the teams as it moves off to begin the game. Interestingly, the screenplay for this superb film was adapted from the book *A Kestrel for a Knave,* now republished as *KES,* by Barry Hines, who originally trained as a physical education teacher at Loughborough College in England. However, we must remember that the scene in the film is fictional and depicts an extreme situation that is not typical of all games lessons in most present-day English schools.

Softball, baseball or cricket sessions often follow a similar pattern. Some children never touch the ball as fielders, while children on the batting side sit lined up, patiently awaiting their turn. This approach survives because it is easy for the instructor and popular with the better players who enjoy dominating play. Clearly, there is alignment—after all, they are playing the real game! ALT is also high, but the crucial weakness is in the amount of individual participation, especially by the weaker players, who in fact may never be in contact with the ball.

The Minor Games Approach

Well-meaning but untrained helpers often introduce minor games. They often select a minor game because of its title, such as soccer baseball or circle soccer, and because the game uses a soccer ball, with little consideration for its value as a lead-up game for real soccer. Unfortunately, the instructors are sometimes influenced by physical education texts that recommend such games.

Two examples selected from a popular text on the teaching of physical education illustrate the limitations of minor games. Note that the following games are **not** recommended for use and are simply described to explain the lack of alignment.

Soccer Dodgeball

Formation and playing area: One-half of players form a large circle while the other half scatter inside the circle.

Equipment: One soccer ball

No. of players: One-half of class on each team

Skills: Kicking and trapping

How to play

1. The players forming the circle attempt to hit the players inside the circle by kicking the ball at them.
2. A player who is hit below the waist must join the circle.
3. The winner is the last player out.

Clearly this game has little in common with soccer, and there is no alignment. While few players may get the opportunity to kick the ball, even fewer will have an opportunity to trap; it is clear that individual participation will be low. A key issue is that few novices will be able to control a bouncing ball and kick it low and accurately, so one suspects that instructors who use this game spend considerable time comforting children who have been hit in the face!

Soccer Softball

Formation and playing area: Use a softball diamond and arrange teams as in softball.

Equipment: One soccer ball

No. of players: 10 to 30

Skills: Kicking for distance and trapping

How to play

Play the game using the same rules as softball, with the following exceptions:

1. The "batter" (kicker) stands with one foot behind the plate.
2. Pitched balls must be below the batter's knees; a ball is called if the pitch is not over the plate or below the knees.
3. A ball hitting the batter above the knees is a dead ball. A base runner cannot advance on a dead ball.
4. A base runner hit by a thrown ball while off base is out.

This game does nothing to help youngsters become better soccer players because once again far more differences than similarities exist between the two games. There is no alignment. Players will not learn the rules of soccer or gain any understanding of it—although they might learn something about the structure of baseball. It is unlikely that any child will get more than one at bat during the session, and with the large number of fielders, few are likely to have more than one or two touches, so individual participation is low. In fact, it is unlikely that many of the "pitched" balls will even be close enough to home plate for the batters to kick them and so get a "hit". Clearly many youngsters will get on base via a walk!

The key issue is that a structured play experience must have a purpose, and that is to help children learn something of value about the game or about themselves. A game or a drill cannot be justified simply because it has been used in the past and because the children enjoy it. Children enjoy it because sitting in the sunshine talking to friends while waiting for a turn at bat is always better than sitting in a classroom, but instructors must not fritter away valuable time like this. They must help children become competent players who understand the nature of sport because it is an important part of their culture, and because for some it may open a critical window in their lives.

> *A* structured play experience must have a purpose, and that is to help children learn something of value about the game or themselves.

Clearly minor games, along with a large range of other games of low organisation, have a place in elementary school physical education programs. Even very simple games such as rats and rabbits, or red rover, chain tag and freeze tag can be useful in developing agility in young children. However, instructors must have a clear understanding of why they are using a particular game and must avoid setting objectives a game cannot achieve.

Lead-Up Games

If minor games are carefully chosen or structured so that they share many similarities with the real game, they can be classified as lead-up games. Instructors can use such games with younger children who may not be ready for even scaled-down versions of the real game. Games such as matball, skittleball, benchball and goalball, which are virtually identical to each other, can introduce children to the initial concepts of passing games such as netball, basketball, korfball and team handball.

One reason that Play Practice is effective is that it encourages instructors to try to create their own lead-up games—in the form of "mini games". This is not an easy process, so as an aid to instructors, the practical section in part II of this text provides many examples of such games. Experience shows, however, that with growing confidence and improved teaching skills, instructors can learn to carefully assess

their groups, decide what most needs to improve and then build games suitable to achieve their goal.

> **T**here must be many similarities between a minor game and the full game if it is to be a useful lead-up game.

Relays

Relays in various forms are very popular with children and instructors. They are easy to organise and can be used to keep large numbers of children active and involved for an hour or more. Relays are perfect for those days when sport educators find themselves looking after 80 children with little time for planning or organising the session.

Unfortunately, instructors often use relays as skills practices to teach children the fundamentals of major games. While some might claim

This photograph was taken on the famous Melbourne cricket ground, one of the great sporting arenas of the world. It can, and often does, hold up to 110,000 fanatical spectators watching cricket test matches, Australian rules football, and Olympic soccer. But here we have a group of very young boys taking part in a soccer-coaching clinic in April 2000. Almost everything is wrong about this scenario! At a simple level it is clear that there are too many players involved and that the ball is too big for them to use effectively. Indeed one wonders how it managed to get through the legs of the tiniest child. However, the real problem is that tunnel ball, as this drill is called, bears no relationship to soccer. So, no matter how well the boys "play" it, it will not help them become better soccer players. Ultimately the real issue is, are they ready for a "sports coaching experience" of this kind.

that these relays at least teach ball control, the fact is that children would get far more practice if they each had a ball.

Other relay formations, such as those used for corner spry or captain ball, are commonly used to teach children passing in preparation for the games of basketball, netball, korfball or team handball. If they teach or reinforce anything, it is the simple techniques of throwing and catching, not the far more complex skill of passing.

The problem, as with poor minor games, is that no alignment exists between a relay and a ball game such as soccer or basketball, so once again there will be no transfer. Another weakness is that although there appears to be a lot of activity, most children spend much of their time waiting for their turn. So relays do not create favourable situations for new learning, and therefore serious sport educators should not use them except in an emergency. The biggest problem with relays, however, is that despite their many limitations, children love them, and as a result young instructors will continually be sucked into the soft option they provide.

The Coaching Approach

The coaching approach is the most professional and structured of the three approaches and is favoured by many committed sport educators. With its emphasis on organisation, structure and control, this approach can be an efficient way of developing some aspects of skilled performance. It can certainly convey a vision of positive professionalism.Careful analysis will show, however, that though this approach may seem efficient, it is not always effective, and the vision of professionalism is often an illusion. It is easily misused by untrained "wannabe" coaches who tend to focus on the development of the so-called "fundamentals" or "basic skills" of the game.

In soccer the major emphasis would be on teaching the techniques of kicking, controlling, heading and dribbling the ball, whereas in basketball it would be on throwing, catching, dribbling, shooting and rebounding. A typical session would start with a warm-up, proceed to isolated practice of these techniques (often using drills of various kinds) and finish with a full game.

In this sense, isolated practice is practice in which the sole emphasis is on the development of technical ability—the ability to control and direct the ball. This practice occurs completely outside any real game context and invariably without any defenders. Though isolated practice has its place in the initial stages of learning any technique, it is important that players move quickly into more realistic practice scenarios. This is essential because techniques practised in isolation, that is, outside the context of the game, are unlikely to transfer into the real game, where the combination of pressure from defenders and the need to make appropriate decisions while receiving, controlling and directing the ball will lead to a rapid breakdown in whatever technical ability the players have gained in the calm of isolated practice.

With the coaching approach, drills are commonly used. Drills are a simple form of repetitive practice in which players execute specific techniques or movement patterns again and again. Unfortunately, all too often coaches select particular drills either because they have always used them or because they are recommended in some 30-year-old text. These drills are often not aligned with the real game.

Drills that are carefully chosen or, better still, created to achieve specific objectives and actually represent what happens in a real game can be valuable in ensuring the repetitive practice essential for players to learn techniques. However, instructors must make sure that players always understand the game context of any drill. The coach can do this by showing the move in its game context first and pointing out the similarities or differences between the drill and the game—such as the fact that there are no defenders in the drill.

> **D**rills are often not aligned with the real game.

The give-and-go in basketball is one of the simplest and most effective tactical moves in the game; indeed, under other names it is fundamental to attacking play in many invasion games. The player with the ball passes to a teammate and cuts to the basket for a return pass and, ideally, an easy layup. This simple tactic can be turned into a drill that can help players improve several elements of technique (see figure 3.3).

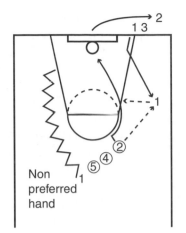

Figure 3.3 Player 2 passes to the outside hand of Player 1, cutting out to the free throw line extended, then cuts to the basket for a return pass and layup. Player 1 follows the pass to rebound the ball and dribble out to the guard spot. Player 2 goes to the baseline and gets ready to break high to continue the drill. Meanwhile, Player 4 passes to 2 cutting high and continuing as stated above.

Applying the Play Practice approach to this situation, youngsters would be taught the general principle: After you pass, if the defender swivels the head—or even just the eyes!—to watch the ball, cut to the basket blind side, that is, behind your defender; if the defender allows a cutting lane, cut ball side. In this way players will quickly understand the concept involved and will be able to generalise it throughout their playing careers any time the situation occurs. This practice can take place through half-court games—naturally, after players have been taught the importance of balancing the court—or through continuous 3-v-3 games. Once youngsters begin to understand and apply the principle, the instructor can then introduce drills to tidy up the technical elements of play.

The fundamental problem with many drills, however, is that they teach a stereotyped response to situations that in the real game demand flexible responses. For example, to ensure that the drills run smoothly, the coach often has the players practise them without opponents. But most ball games are interactive! What a player does in a game is almost always influenced in some way by an opponent, who is not always predictable. This means that when youngsters try to apply what they have practised in a drill to the scramble of a game, both technique and

skill often break down because players cannot anticipate the defenders' reactions.

> *T*he real problem with many drills is that they teach a stereotyped response to situations that in the real game demand flexible responses.

In fact, drills can be more effective with experienced players because they *do* know where their opponents should be in a game. This is because they know where they would be if they were defending and can use their understanding to predict defensive responses. So as they carry out the drill they always have an image of the defender with them. Even here coaches would be well advised to continually remind players during a drill exactly how it fits into the total context of the game and how defenders are likely to respond.

Beginners, on the other hand, usually have little or no idea where defenders should be. Even if they understand the basic principles of defence, they are unable to use this knowledge to create imaginary defenders. So when they move from drill to game, the intervention of defenders often causes them to forget everything they have learned.

Because of the vast difference between a drill without defenders and the game, instructors who use drills must continually stress the way in which defenders are likely to respond. However, the quicker the coach moves the players from drills to play practices, the more likely it is that transferable learning will occur.

Drills that are properly structured and executed can create valuable learning situations for some aspects of skilled play. Others, however, have no place in the curriculum of any professional instructor. One drill that represents all that is bad about this form of practice is the so-called pepper pot drill used in basketball. Another major problem with drills is that they tend to overemphasise technique over other aspects of play, such as understanding. Drills are abused partly because sport educators do not always understand their limitations and also because they meet the needs of many coaches to completely control the practice environment.

Obviously, it is possible to create good drills. The drills must be aligned with the real game, however, and must simulate or replicate a specific aspect of that game. Ideally, they should gradually become more complex and gamelike as the players progress. An example of such a drill in basketball is shown in figure 3.4. Here O3, guarded by X3, sets up low on the edge of the key; O1, with the ball, is initially unguarded to ensure that the drill will achieve its objectives. The drill begins as O3 makes a sharp cut to the wing, looking for a potential pass from O1. However, X3 overplays to deny the ball on the wing and O3 now makes a backdoor cut, with X3 again covering the move. This in-out-cut is repeated a second time without O1 attempting a pass.

Clearly the initial objectives are

- to improve the specific movement patterns and footwork of both O3 and X3,
- to teach O3 how to use hand signals to indicate where and when the pass should be thrown, and
- to teach X3 how to deny the first pass and still be able to cover a backdoor cut.

The drill continues with O3 cutting to the wing a third time. Now X3 allows the pass, and O3 immediately attempts to drive to the baseline. Now O3 is learning how to take the pass, square

to the basket and drive while X3 must learn how to rapidly adjust from overplaying to deny the ball, first into a position to stop the baseline drive and then to draw a charging foul. At this time the instructor can focus on small but important aspects of footwork if he or she feels it necessary or appropriate.

Because this is a drill, O3 is allowed only three bounces when driving to the baseline and cannot take a shot. O3 "wins" the game if he or she can get one foot into the key.

The drill now continues (figure 3.5) with O3 passing the ball out to O1 from the low post area and then breaking hard to the top of the key to receive the ball back in the high post position. Naturally X3 tries to deny this, so both players can continue to develop important elements of agility and position. The drill continues with O3 rolling away across the lane, with X3 now forced to find a balance between covering O3 while also helping out against the ball. Finally O3 flashes back toward the ball for a pass, which can now lead to a shot or a move to the basket.

Gradually this drill can become more and more gamelike, with O3 introduced to, or allowed, more and more offensive options while X3 learns how to counter them. Finally the drill can become a two-on-two game with various conditions applied to shape play in the direction the instructor desires. For example, at first the game can follow the original pattern of the drill with O3 allowed only one-on-one moves after receiving the ball; then, following an unsuccessful backdoor cut by O3, O1 is allowed to drive to the basket. Finally, while still operating from the initial set and in only one-half of the front court, the drill becomes a play practice in which the instructor focusses play on whatever is needed to help players move to the next level.

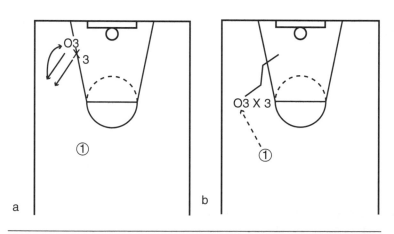

Figure 3.4 (a) This drill with gamelike qualities can be used to develop both offensive and defensive ability. Player O3 sets up low defensively covered by X3. Player O1 is unguarded. Player O3 cuts to the free throw line extended, while X3 overplays to deny the pass. Player O3 goes back door and Player X3 opens up to deny. This is repeated three times. (b) Now Player O1 passes to Player O3 who immediately tries to drive the baseline to get one foot into the key to "win a point".

Problems With Traditional Approaches

The fundamental problem with all three traditional approaches is that they are based on a facile analysis of games and what is required to play them effectively. Because of this, they

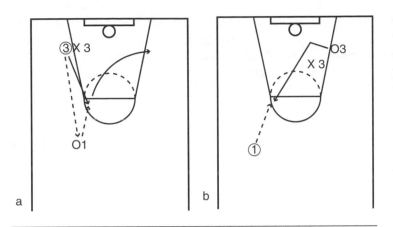

Figure 3.5 (a) Player O3 passes the ball out to Player O1 and flashes to the high post to try to get the ball back against defensive denial from Player X3 to "win a point". Now Player O3 returns the ball to Player O1 and rolls away to the opposite post. (b) Finally, Player O3 flashes back to the high post to receive the ball and shoot or drive to the basket. This drill can be turned into a 2-v-2 game very easily by incorporating give and go moves where Players O1 and O3 exchange positions.

focus almost entirely on the development of technical ability and virtually ignore other critical aspects of effective play. In some sports, especially the racquet games, technical ability is crucial, and instructors must emphasise it from the very beginning. In invasion games, however, technical ability is only one of a number of elements a person must develop to become an effective player.

An emphasis on developing technical ability has other weaknesses. In most sports the ability to control and direct a ball takes hours of repetitive practice. Coaches at the elite level have almost unlimited time to spend developing and refining their players' technical ability, and elite athletes often spend hours of their own time practising. It is not unknown for table tennis players to practise eight hours a day or basketball players to take over five hundred jump shots a day simply to maintain their performance level. For example, many years ago in Crystal City, Missouri, a young boy named Bill Bradley practised seven hours a day to refine his moves and improve his shooting on the way to becoming a college All-American and a great professional basketball player.

This has several implications. Where technical ability is crucial, children should be introduced to the fundamentals of technique in the formal sessions but then encouraged to prac-

tise on their own time. In games where technique is not so important, it is better to spend valuable time teaching youngsters critical aspects of play that they cannot learn for themselves. The key is understanding! Whereas developing technical ability takes hours of repetitive practice, and increasing one's fitness takes weeks of training before improvement occurs, **understanding—of rules or of tactics—can come in an instant.**

The following example confirms the relationship between understanding and the effective use of techniques in a game. In basketball, attempting a three-point shot with a hand in your face is a difficult challenge for even the great players. By using games sense, however, a player can continually get open shots from the same spot. This can be done

- by coming off a pick set by a teammate,
- by shooting from behind a screen,
- after receiving a pitchout from a teammate whose drive to the basket has sucked perimeter defenders in to help out,
- after receiving a skip pass when a zone defence flexes toward the ball, or
- after receiving a pass from a teammate who has used the "dribble draw" tactic to pull a defender away from the shooter.

All of these require understanding—of the rules in the first two examples and of tactics in the others. A final example of using understanding to create an open shot was evident in the final basket of Michael Jordan's illustrious career. With six seconds to play and the game in the balance, Jordan faked a drive to the basket to force his defender back, and then stopped and calmly hit the long jumper. He *knew* what his defender would do and simply exploited this knowledge.

The issue here, however, is something the traditional approaches neglect—that the importance of understanding games goes far beyond becoming a better player. Without a deep understanding of sports, young people will never be able to take on any of the varied roles associated with this important aspect of our culture, nor will they wish to do so. At the very least, helping young people understand the real nature of games prepares them for a lifetime of enjoyment as intelligent spectators who can more fully appreciate the nature of a contest and can recognise the skill and commitment of the participants.

The Nature of Skill in Games

The beginning of wisdom is when things are given their proper names.
—Chinese proverb

● ● ● ● ●

To answer the question "What competencies do children need to play a sport effectively?", a sport educator must understand the nature of skilled performance in that sport. Though this may seem obvious, traditional methods have endured because as sport educators we have been unable or unwilling to critically analyse our methods, understand our sport or even to define key words in the vocabulary of sport.

All three of these issues are tightly linked, for as philosopher Herbert Spencer observed at the beginning of the 20th century, "How often misused words generate misleading thoughts." (Collins 1996, p. 383) **In sport education the problem begins with the careless use of the words "skill" and "skillful", which are central to understanding the nature of sport.**

The following scenario illustrates this idea.

With 15 seconds left in the deciding game of the NBA finals, the crowd erupts as Michael Jordan drives down the court against great defensive pressure to put up a perfect fadeaway jumper for yet another three-pointer.

On the surface it seems a simple situation: a great player has demonstrated his amazing talent yet again. It might seem ridiculous to wonder whether Michael was being skillful when he took that shot. But what if his side was ahead by two points with 20 seconds left on the shot clock? Under those circumstances, was he being skillful?

Michael was clearly skillful at shooting the ball, but his coach and his more perceptive teammates might question whether he was skillful in taking a relatively low-percentage shot at a time when the wiser thing to do would be to run the clock down. So was he skillful or not?

An invasion game such as soccer introduces yet another level of complexity to the meaning of the key words skill and skillful. With 22 players on the field at the same time, each individual can be directly involved with the ball for only two or three minutes in a game. Clearly a player must be skillful in controlling and directing the ball. But how does an individual play skillfully *without* the ball for the remainder of the game?

An example of how it is possible to play skill-fully without the ball appears on pages 84 and 85 of the excellent book *Soccer Skills and Tactics* by Jones and Welton (1978). The authors analyse a brief passage of play in one of the greatest soccer games ever played—the European Cup final between Real Madrid of Spain and Eintracht of Holland in 1973. As shown in figure 4.1, Real incomparable Di Stefano breaks downfield, repeatedly interpassing with several other players in a move that leads to a shot at goal by the great winger Gento.

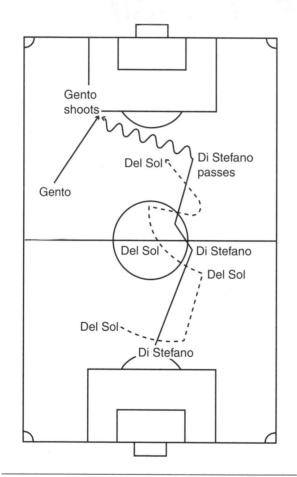

Figure 4.1 Del Sol playing skillfully without the ball.

Unnoticed except by those who really understood skillful play in soccer, his teammate Del Sol ran almost the whole length of the pitch, continually moving into excellent support positions to be available for a pass from Di Stefano. Although Del Sol never touched the ball in this move, his selfless running and good position-ing continually distracted defenders who expected the ball to go to him because of his great reputation. Del Sol's highly skilled play off the ball meant that Di Stefano always had easier passing options to other players, and a strike at goal was the result.

The meaning of skill in games is further complicated by the fact that in American football, highly skilled professional players are paid millions of dollars a year but may not touch the ball in a game throughout an entire season. And in both American football and Australian rules football, games with a shared heritage, it is possible for a player to be skillful by scoring points for the opposition! In American football this happens when a player chooses to concede a safety instead of risking a turnover in the end zone. Similarly, in Aussie rules, a player in a tight situation will deliberately concede one point, called a behind, by knocking the ball through his own goal if doing so robs the attackers of a chance for a six-point score.

> *In American football and Australian rules football it is possible for a player to be skillful by scoring points for the opposition.*

Interactive games, that is, games in which the performance of one player or team directly influences that of their opponent, introduce yet another element to the discussion. In such games it is possible for a highly skilled player to be made to look very unskillful by an even more skilled opponent, or even by an inferior player who plays a career-best game on a particular day.

Skill Versus Technique

Clearly, skill in games is a complex phenomenon. The word skillful is commonly used to describe both a player who is totally effective in every aspect of the game and also one who is merely expert at controlling the ball. Are they both just skillful, or should a distinction be made between the two?

This is not simply a matter of semantics. Misused words do indeed generate misleading thoughts, which in turn may lead to misguided actions. One of the major weaknesses of traditional approaches to teaching games is that they are based on the belief that skill in ball games is the skill of controlling and directing the ball. This becomes the focus of instruction, and other important elements of skilled play are ignored.

Given the high profile of sport in modern societies, such a situation is as surprising as it is potentially misleading. A principle of philology holds that the greater the importance of any aspect of a culture, the more words that are associated with it and the more precise the distinctions made between those words. The Inuit have over one hundred words to describe the differing qualities of snow, for when it concerns a matter of life and death, misused words cannot be allowed to generate misleading thoughts or misguided actions.

It might be possible to clarify this issue if the actions of controlling and directing the ball are defined as techniques. Within this framework, kicking and heading in soccer, dribbling and shooting in basketball and the serve and volley in tennis would be defined as techniques—not "skills". Even this simple distinction would begin to resolve some of the problems that now exist. Though it is obvious that the ability to control and direct the ball is of critical importance to players in most ball games, instructors who appreciate that technical ability is only one aspect of skilled performance are more likely to include other critical aspects of skilled play in their practices.

> *It might be possible to clarify this issue of skill versus technique if the actions of controlling and directing the ball are defined as techniques.*

If, after defining technique in this way, we could clarify the crucial term "skill" as it applies to sport, there would be enormous benefits:

- It would be easier to understand the fundamental nature of specific sports and to analyse players' performance more objectively.

- It would be possible to conduct a more rational critique of traditional approaches to teaching and coaching sports and so better understand the limitations of the methods used.

- It would be possible to fully appreciate the advantages of the Play Practice approach.

The answer to the question "Was Michael skillful?" provides a clue. Clearly his technique was excellent, but his decision to take the shot was a poor one in the context of the game. His team was ahead by two points with only 15 seconds left in the game, so with 20 seconds on the shot clock he did not need to shoot! If he missed, he would have given his opponents a chance to rebound the ball and take it downcourt for the winning basket. The skillful thing to do, and what the real M.J. would have done, would be to run the clock down until there is no time left for the other side to score. In this situation

Reprinted, with special permission, of King Features Syndicate.

How important is technical ability in checkers?

Michael made a bad decision that could have cost his team a championship trophy.

All of this suggests that in many sports, skill is based on a combination of technical ability and effective decision making. An analysis of a range of sporting activities may help clarify this further.

Gymnastics and diving demand absolute body control and perfection in movement; they are absolute tests of agility. The decision making involved is usually carried out weeks before the competition as athlete and coach determine what routines or dives to prepare. The challenge for the competitor in both sports is to ensure a performance on the day of the event that is technically perfect.

A golfer may make decisions minutes before playing a shot. First the golfer computes the distance to the hole, analyses the probable effects of any wind, decides whether to play it safe or take a risk, selects a club and then at last plays the shot. The challenge is to hit a tiny ball often a considerable distance to a specific spot using a relatively long lever, all this while under the pressure to perform in front of between two and two hundred million or more critical eyes.

Clearly, technical ability is crucial to success in golf. It is possible, however, that as many major tournaments have been lost because of poor decisions at critical moments as have been won by great shot making. In his superb book *Ultimate Golf Techniques,* Malcolm Campbell (1998) says, "There are many players with limited ability as pure ball strikers who have been highly successful on the course when it matters. Much of this is because they have had the ability to make the right decision at the right time; they have been able to assess correctly what is possible and stick with the decision." (p. 176) He goes on to repeat the truism, "Golf is not about how, but how many!" (p. 176)

Among the examples he provides to make his point is Ben Crenshaw's play at the 13th hole at Augusta National in 1984, where a sensible decision helped him to a great win. As Campbell says, "...the 13th is a part of the course where many a Masters has been won and lost and where strategy plays a crucial part." (p. 178) Crenshaw arrived at the par five 13th in the lead. After a long drive off the tee, he was faced with the decision of whether to try to reach the green in two by driving over a difficult water hazard called Rae's Creek or to play safe and take the

route favoured by lesser players. He chose the latter. He hit his second shot short of the creek and went on to get a par for the hole. By choosing what many observers felt was a safe but soft route instead of the more challenging one, he laid the foundations for the first win of his professional career.

While technical ability and good decision making are important components of skilled play, their relative importance varies from one game to another. The key factors seem to be the number of players in a game and the degree of variability in the playing environment.

In soccer, for example, the ability to control and direct the ball is clearly important, and at the highest levels of play, where one perfect strike can win a game, it becomes critical. However, with 22 players on the field and only one ball, each individual can be "on the ball" for only approximately two minutes and must play off the ball for the remainder of the game. Another factor is that soccer is a game of fluid, almost continuous movement and frequent unexpected changes of possession, so decision making is crucial.

This low percentage of time on the ball compared to the amount of time off the ball, along with the extreme variability of the playing environment, means that decision making is a vital component of skilled play in the World Game. In Rugby Union with 30 players and one ball, the on ball/off ball ratio is even lower, especially for players in certain positions. This, allied with the game's tactical complexity and the draconian penalties for rule infringements, means that the ability to make sound decisions in the heat of the game is also of vital importance in this rugby code.

The on ball/off ball ratio is taken to extremes in American football, where only the quarterback and chosen receivers usually touch the ball.

Even where the player-to-ball ratio is one to one, as in tenpin bowling and golf, the relative importance of technique and decision making varies enormously. In these games the ball must be repeatedly delivered or struck with absolute precision, so sound technique is crucial. However, whereas the bowling environment is absolutely stable and critical decisions are needed only when dealing with splits, the golf environment varies with virtually every stroke, so sound decision making is an essential element

How important is technical ability in Viking soccer?

of skilled performance in this game.

In racquet games, too, players need technical ability to hit a small, fast-moving object often to a precise point in an opponent's court. With one ball between two players, both have to be completely committed to tracking and directing the ball for each of the hundreds of shots made during a long match. As players improve, however, decision making becomes increasingly important because the challenge is not just to hit the ball properly but to outwit an opponent in a kind of mobile chess game. A player must make decisions—whether to "go for it" or to keep the ball in play, which stroke to use, where and how to hit the ball—instantly, in real time, with little opportunity to reflect. Then, after executing a stroke, a player must again try to anticipate the opponent's reaction and move early into the best possible position to deal with a return. In racquet sports, good positioning by a player not only increases the pressure on one's opponent to make a good return but also reduces the movement, perceptual and technical demands of the player's own response.

All of this confirms that technical ability and decision making are key components of skilled play in ball games. Although technical ability is easy to comprehend, the concept of decision making in games is more difficult. The key lies in the term "games sense", a concept Rod Thorpe developed during the dialogue following the publication and promotion of the Games for Understanding approach. Since then it has been given several different connotations, none of which seems especially appropriate or helpful in clarifying the nature of effective play in games.

Games Sense

In an attempt to apply the Chinese proverb at the beginning of this chapter, I have defined games sense as

The ability to use an understanding of the rules; of strategy; of tactics and, most importantly, of oneself to solve the problems posed by the game or by one's opponents.

Defined in this way, the term games sense bridges the gap between understanding and action and incorporates the process of decision making. It could even be defined as "understanding in action". This is important because, except in games such as chess, mere understanding in a cognitive sense is not enough for a player to be effective.

In the often chaotic and frenzied atmosphere of competitive games, players must be able to react and respond instantaneously, almost instinctively, to rapidly changing situations. To do this they must access and interpret stored data in the form of an understanding of the rules, tactics and strategy and simultaneously factor in a vast range of real-time data. In invasion games this might include the score, the time left in the game, who has the ball, the field position, the importance of a specific result, substitution patterns, the flow of the game, time-outs remaining, player injuries and player matchups.

The real challenge is that even while new data is pouring in, players must be responding to decisions already made. This overlap of accurate data retrieval and acquisition, rapid interpretation and prediction, clear decision making and precise physical execution, all carried out in milliseconds, often while the players are fatigued, emotionally stretched, or both, is what makes ball games both challenging and interesting. It can severely test even the human brain, still pound for pound the best computer on Earth, and it is why even the greatest players make mistakes and why the play of beginners is often chaotic. Games sense is the overt way in which players demonstrate their ability to cope with this challenge. At its simplest level, however, games sense merely means that players can get into the best possible position at the right time and make sensible decisions about what to do next.

Games sense is the overt way in which players demonstrate their ability to cope with the constant challenges posed by the game and by their opponents.

The Rules

Knowing the rules is obviously important to successful play and is therefore a critical component of games sense. Here it is important to distinguish between the primary and secondary rules of games. Whereas the former, such as the handball rule in soccer, determine a game's basic structure and cannot be altered without completely changing the game, secondary rules, such as soccer's throw-in, could be changed without creating a major impact.

Nowhere is the impact of the rules on a game's strategy and tactics better illustrated than in the rugby codes played around the world. Here, the offside law, which prevents forward passes, leads to a tactically complex game in which the players' ability to withstand heavy body contact is at least as important as technical ability.

In fact, it was changes to the offside law in 1906 that altered the entire nature of the rugby-style game being played at that time in the United States. This change eliminated tactics such as the "flying wedge", which was one of the major factors in the increasing incidence of death and serious injury in the college game; it also gradually led to the development of American football as a unique game. Perhaps of even greater importance was the fact that these changes saved football in the United States at a time when many university presidents were considering eliminating their football programs because of the dangers involved. But for the intervention of President Teddy Roosevelt, who arranged for a commission to come up with rule changes to create a safer game, many more might have followed the example of the prestigious University of Chicago, which dropped its football program and which has never reinstated it.

Applying Tactics

Tactics are often regarded as a highly complicated aspect of ball games and therefore considered important only at the elite level. This is not the case. Tactics are part and parcel of play at every level in all games, even when the players themselves do not know they are applying them. For example, in team games tactics are simply the ways in which attackers combine with teammates to keep possession of the ball and try to score, as well as the way in which defenders maneuver to regain the ball.

In most invasion games the simplest tactic is to get there, as Confederate general Nathan Forrest was fond of saying, "fustest with the mostest"—in other words, to outnumber the other team at the critical point. Here the moment of transition, that instant when the ball changes possession, perhaps through a steal or an interception, is critically important. In an instant defenders must switch roles to become attackers and begin to counterattack. The fast break, counterattack or rebound from defence are all names for this highly effective tactic that usually leaves defenders outnumbered, because only great teams fast-break into defence as effectively as they rebound into attack.

Once the defence is organised, other simple tactics are needed. The give-and-go in basketball, the wall pass in soccer and the one-two in Aussie rules football are all different names for the same tactic—passing the ball to a teammate

Good teams fast break into attack. Great teams fast break into defence.

and then exploiting any defensive error that results from the ball movement. The passer usually does this by cutting ball side or blind side into the space behind the defender to get the ball back and continuing the passing sequence or taking a shot.

As defenders counter these moves and make it difficult for attackers to get open shots close to the goal, the tactical complexity of a game increases. In basketball, for example, "clearout", "pick", "screen", "penetrate and pitch out" and "drive and dish" are simply shorthand terms for specific tactics devised to beat increasingly competent defenders. In this game as in many others, tactics evolve from a simple process of exploiting basic defensive mistakes into a complex system based on exploiting the predictability of a defender's response.

While a rules-based approach to tactics is well suited to a high-speed game such as basketball, it is not as comprehensive and logical as the approach developed by the coaches of the English Football Association in the 1950s. By carefully observing and analysing what good players did, the coaches developed a coherent series of principles that they could use to help players, including beginners, understand how to position themselves and move intelligently during a game. Players and coaches can also apply these principles, which are outlined in the soccer section of chapter 9, directly to other invasion games such as field hockey and lacrosse.

The notion of a games player creating space and time might seem far-fetched. Yet by using the principle of mobility they can do just that! Figure 4.2 shows a soccer scenario in which each attacker is marked and the crucial space is being covered. However, if A1 and A2 make diagonal runs to the ball side of the pitch and take their defenders with them, they create space for A6, sprinting late and fast from a deep position to arrive unmarked with the time needed to ensure a skillful strike on goal. Basketball players can use this same principle of mobility to create space, using the clearout against man-to-man defences and the replacement tactic against (zone) ball defences.

This tactic of mobility is also used in many plays employed in American football. Here the limited time a quarterback has to make decisions means that the offence must determine its tactics before putting the ball in play. The

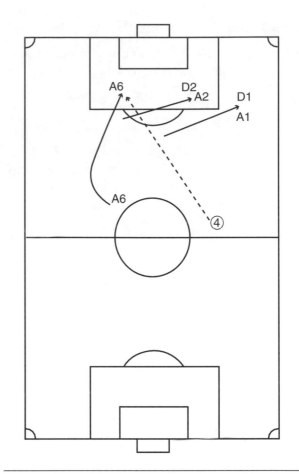

Figure 4.2 Players A1 and A2 "create space" for Player A6 by making diagonal runs that pull their defenders away from critical space in front of the goal.

decision-making process is easier, because the quarterback knows exactly what the other players on the team will be trying to do and what pass routes they will be running. In defence, as players read and react, games sense is more important, especially in the key defensive position of middle linebacker.

An understanding of tactics is the glue that holds a team together. When every player understands and applies key tactical principles, a team becomes more than the sum of its parts, and cooperation and teamwork become easy. This can generate an almost telepathic understanding between teammates that builds trust, which in turn can foster that most powerful yet intangible of motivational forces, team spirit.

In racquet sports, tactics are based on intelligent positioning to make it easier to cover the court in defence and the use of clever placement, speed and spin in the attack. Badminton players, for example, use the clear, the smash and the drop shot in combination to force opponents into mistakes as they try to deal with the long/short tactics that the effective use of these techniques permit. In striking/fielding games, tactics are based on hitting the ball into the defender's territory in such a way that allows the attackers enough time to seize a base or score a run.

Strategy

While good tactics will help players win many of the skirmishes in a game, they need sound strategy to win the match. As a good example, some basketball coaches base their strategy around full-court pressure defences. For a team with no great height or individual stars but with a group of athletic, quick and determined players, such a strategy makes sense. Properly executed, it leads to a full-court, high-tempo game in which agility, fitness, hustle and teamwork are as valuable as silky outside shooting and slick one-on-one moves. This strategy can disrupt an opponent's well-coached half-court game and expose limitations to their fitness and mental toughness. "Stars" who are made to work hard for every possession and who are not getting their normal quota of shots may even lose their cool as the pressure mounts.

Though such a strategy may seem to be essentially defensive in nature, it is a total package. This is because the pressure causes steals and turnovers that lead to many easy baskets scored against broken defences. In this strategy the offence is not only built on a good defence, it is driven by it.

As long ago as 1964 the great John Wooden won the first of many NCAA basketball championships at UCLA using this strategy. As he relates in the 1971 book *Sports Illustrated Basketball,*

This particular defense was used for several reasons. First, I thought the individual talents of the starting personnel fitted it very well; second, some method was needed in this West Coast area of ball control teams to prevent our fast break minded boys from being lulled into a slow tempo; third, I thought our quickness would enable us to play this type of defense quite well; and fourth, I felt this type of game would help to neutralize the advantage in height that all the other opponents would have.

Furthermore I must point out that this type of defense was not designed to take the ball away from the opposition nearly as much as to force them into mental and physical errors on which we hoped to capitalize. We also felt that if we kept constant pressure on them they would be forced to hurry their offense, which would be in direct contrast to the style of the game they normally played, and, perhaps, this would keep them from executing it as well as when they were able to control the tempo. (p. 31-32)

Because a strategy is based on the strengths of a particular team or individual it is usually constant throughout a season or, in the case of individual sports, throughout a career. Many coaches, however, believe in developing a specific plan for every game. This game plan complements a team's basic strategy to ensure that the opposition's weaknesses are targeted and their strengths countered.

In individual sports, too, players can overlay their basic strategy with a game plan. A tall,

Reprinted, with special permission, of King Features Syndicate.

powerful tennis player with a great serve will usually base his strategy on a serve volley game. However, the game plan he employs against a fine ground-stroke player might also aim to keep rallies, and games, as short as possible to prevent the opponent from finding his rhythm and therefore getting into the match. To achieve this he contests critical points but deliberately concedes others quickly. A game plan like this may also counter an opponent's superior fitness and gradually lead to psychological capitulation as he finds himself unable to get into the match.

Sometimes, apparently sound tactics make for a bad strategy. A tennis player may win many points through the tactic of pounding an opponent's weaker side, perhaps the backhand, but the practice she is providing her opponent may gradually strengthen that stroke during a long match so that when crunch time arrives, the opponent can take the pressure and no longer yields easy points. A player with a strategic vision will exploit a weakness of this kind only on critical points. In the same way, a table tennis player will hold back his most devastating serves so that his opponent will be unprepared to deal with them when the crucial moment arrives. So, with strategy it is important to plan for the whole game or even the campaign and not be distracted by early setbacks.

Though strategy might seem the sole province of coaches, it adds another layer of complexity to games and therefore makes them even more interesting for all participants. Certainly, very few teams will be successful without at least one player with strategic vision who can ensure that everyone follows the game plan. Schemers, quarterbacks and playmakers are all names for this player who is essential to every team and who, when getting the job done, can make a coach's task infinitely easier.

Reading the Game and Applying Games Sense

While an understanding of the rules, tactics and strategy provides a foundation for games sense, players must also process a vast amount of real-time data as they make the decisions that bridge the gap between knowing and action. To do this they must be able to "read" the game.

Reading the game is another aspect of effec-

Photo courtesy of News Limited

This photograph provides an excellent example of "reading the play". With head up and eyes attentive to the surrounding action, this field hockey player is ready and able to make a quick and responsible play.

tive play that researchers have not studied in depth. In essence, a player must be able to see and interpret the complex display, or picture, of the game as players and ball continually move around the playing area. This process is complex because the player who is reading the real-time display is also already in the process of

- reacting to inputs received milliseconds before,
- deciding what to do on the basis of earlier inputs,
- responding to even earlier inputs, and
- possibly controlling or delivering the ball.

Top-class players can instantly compute where the ball is going and do not have to watch it throughout its flight. This allows them to read the game even as they prepare to control the ball. Beginners, on the other hand, find it very difficult to track a moving ball and anticipate its flight path even when they watch it carefully. They can begin to read the game only after they have the ball under control. Clearly this has significant implications for the way in which coaches must structure practice for players at different performance levels.

Other Elements of Effective Play

Important though it is, games sense must not be overvalued, because playing games is not merely an intellectual exercise. Skilled performance involves the melding of games sense with other elements of effective play. For example, players must be able to get into good positions at exactly the right moment. This requires agility. So although games sense is important, the fundamental bases for success in all ball games are sound body control and balance allied to good footwork. The movement skills of running backward, sideways and forward; accelerating; stopping; changing direction; turning; jumping and landing—which, taken cumulatively, are what coaches label "quickness" or "athleticism"—are crucial to success in ball games. Agility enables players to move quickly into position; to be first to the ball, even when it is high in the air; to cut past or break away from defenders when attacking or to pick up, cover and pressure opponents when defending.

At the highest levels of play, agility separates the great players from the merely good. Andre Agassi in tennis, Pele in soccer, and Michael Jordan in basketball are all great examples. Indeed Jordan allied sound but not outstanding technical ability, and a great drive for excellence, with outstanding athleticism or agility to become the greatest player in the history of the game.

Athletes in many sports also need fitness to keep on getting into good positions throughout the game and to ensure they maintain a high level of concentration and technical expertise. They may also need to communicate with teammates. A call of "man on!", "turn!" or "time!" in soccer will often give the ball player the information and the time necessary to be skillful, whereas in volleyball the call of "mine!" or "ball!" will minimise confusion when several beginners attempt to play the ball simultaneously.

To be really effective, players need to be physically, psychologically and morally resilient and ready to play at all times. The ability to focus completely on the task at hand is crucial to effective performance in sports. For the elite performer the ideal state of readiness is to be "in the zone", where no distractions of any kind occur and where perfect performance seemingly flows without effort.

Given the importance of each of these elements, one could argue that skilled performance depends on all of them. For example, if a player with superb technical ability and games sense is always beaten to the ball because she lacks the agility she needs to get into the right place at the right time, can she be skillful? What about a player whose performance drops off toward the end of a game because of poor fitness? Or the player who always pulls out of a tough challenge because of lack of confidence? With this in mind it is tempting to define skill as simply the ability to do whatever is required to get the job done!

Although all of these elements underpin effective play, ultimately games are won or lost by the ability to control the ball (or shuttle) and direct it accurately enough to score a goal, a run or a point or simply to get it into a small hole in the ground. So in most games players must be technically proficient. Therefore, for the purposes of this text, I have defined skill in interactive games as the combination of games sense with technical ability sufficient to achieve a specific desired outcome.

Skill in interactive games is defined as the combination of games sense with technical ability to achieve a specified desired outcome.

With skill clarified in this way, then, it is easy to see that skill in these games is always contextual and that what constitutes skilled performance depends on the circumstances at any instant. Sometimes games sense is the dominant component, sometimes technical ability is more important and sometimes the two must be completely melded.

So, in soccer a player

- relies on games sense to play skillfully without the ball for the majority of the game. The players are like mobile chess pieces, countering the moves of opponents while maneuvering to create scoring opportunities.

- demonstrates great technical ability when bending a free kick around the defenders into the corner of the goal. In this situation the player is like a golfer, with time to choose his target and the opportunity to concentrate completely on striking the ball perfectly.

- reacts almost instinctively as a ball is unexpectedly deflected into her path and she gets the opportunity for a reflex strike at goal. In this situation technical ability is stretched to the limit as she responds like a car driver braking hard to avoid an accident.

- melds games sense and technical ability as he receives the ball under various degrees of pressure from opponents. Now he must read the play, control the ball, decide what to do and then play the ball accurately. Here the simple equation

*space (distance from an opponent) =
time (to read the play and decide what to do) =
skill (a sound decision combined with precise
execution)*

indicates the importance of context in skilled performance in games.

Although it is convenient to separate games sense and technical ability to better understand them, in practice there is continual interaction between technique and tactics/strategy in both individual and team sports. In tennis, it is obvious that serve and volley tactics can be effective only if a player possesses technical ability in those areas. In basketball, an individual or a team with limited outside shooting ability will find defenders sagging off them to clog up the key and stop inside scoring. Conversely, good shooting, especially from three-point range, pulls defenders out and creates space and scoring opportunities inside.

Sport educators should never lose sight of the fact that all of the elements necessary for skilled performance are inextricably bound together so that deficiencies in any one area will impact on others. With beginners, especially, the nexus

between technical ability and agility is as important as that between technical ability and games sense.

> *S*port educators should never lose sight of the fact that all of the elements necessary for skilled performance are inextricably bound together so that deficiencies in any one area will impact on others.

The preceding analysis has not been a mere intellectual exercise. Figure 4.3 shows a scenario where on receiving the ball Michael is faced with a range of options. He must decide whether to

- immediately shoot the three pointer;
- pass to any of the four possible receivers, who may be in a better position than he is;
- drive past the defender;
- drive down the middle toward defensive help but a possible foul on a key opponent;
- drive along the baseline away from defensive help and an open shot; or
- fake the drive and force the defender back to open up the jump shot.

If he chooses to go to the basket, he will face even more decisions. As defenders move to help out against the drive, Michael must decide whether to take the shot, dish off to open teammates close to the basket or pitch the ball out for the outside shot.

He must consider all these options within an overall framework provided by

- the strategic game plan that reflects the coach's philosophy,
- the tactical situation at that moment,
- the score, and
- the time remaining in the game.

Michael's decision will also be influenced by his shooting percentage from that spot and the way he matches up with his opponent. In addition, factors such as how many fouls he or his immediate opponent has, his level of fatigue and even psychological considerations will play a part. If

Figure 4.3 The composite shows the different offensive decisions a player has while being guarded up close. The player has the option of shooting, passing off or driving to the basket. A player must be composed and knowledgeable enough to make this split-second decision.

he is playing well and is confident, he may choose one option; but if he is lacking confidence, he may choose a different one. Even the relationship between the player and the coach may influence the decision.

This process, in which games sense and technical ability are integrated with other elements of skilled play, is repeated every time a player receives the ball during the game of basketball and is replicated in other games of a similar nature.

Thus, the relative importance of technical ability and games sense along with other key elements of effective play has enormous implications for the way different sports should be taught. To be fully effective, then, sport educators need to think carefully about the nature of skilled performance in every sport they teach. The challenge for all sport educators is to better understand the nature of their sport, assess the needs of their group and then plan suitable play practices to take their athletes to the next level. The following chapter indicates how they can do this.

Play Practice: The Theory

*If I had to give one single reason for my love of sports it would be this:
I love the tests of the human spirit.*
—Michael Novak

● ● ● ● ●

The essential premise of this text is that every child, not merely very talented children, should have the opportunity to participate in enjoyable and challenging sporting activities. Not only will they learn fundamental truths about themselves and about life, but in the future they may also become more tolerant supporters of sport and those who play it, as spectators, parents or coaches.

Play Practice evolved in a search for better ways to introduce young people to the joys of sport and help them to become competent, confident players. As the term implies, Play Practice turns practice into play by using games and challenges in some form or other to create realistic and enjoyable learning situations. The object is to remove the idea that play must become work if children are to improve, so challenges replace technique practices, and drills make way for carefully structured games. Here we must emphasise that throughout its evolution, Play Practice has always been driven by young people's responses to the ideas being trialled.

● ● ● ● ● ● ● ● ●

*P*lay Practice turns practice into play by using games and challenges in some form or other to create realistic and enjoyable learning situations.

● ● ● ● ● ● ● ●

Three Strands of Knowledge

Play Practice interweaves three critical strands of knowledge to create a very practical approach to teaching sport. These strands are based on the following questions:

1. What do young people want from a sport experience?
2. Under what conditions do young people best learn?
3. What competencies do young people need to participate effectively and enjoyably in a sport?

Let us consider each question in turn.

What do young people want from a sport experience?

This question has always been the driving force behind Play Practice. It is a complex issue that boils down to a number of precepts. These precepts hold that most young people

- would like to be good at sport;
- prefer to play a game than to practice;
- like playing real games or trying the real activity;
- like to play in teams or groups;
- prefer to play with their friends;
- prefer central roles;
- want challenges where they can be successful;
- prefer competition to be evenly balanced;
- do not want to lose or be embarrassed;
- would like significant others to see them as skillful; and
- see practice as a means to an end, not an end in itself.

Under what conditions do young people best learn?

We have distilled this complex and much-researched issue into the following precepts. Young people learn best when

- they really want to learn something;
- they know that a significant other really cares about their development;
- they have a very clear model of the learning task;
- they feel that the task is challenging but attainable;
- they have many opportunities to practice in a positive environment;
- they clearly understand the relationship between the practice and the real activity;
- they get feedback about the quality of their performance;
- they are not threatened by immediate or continuing failure;
- significant others, especially their peers, recognize their efforts, improvement and successes; and

- they quickly apply what they have learned in what they see as real situations.

What competencies do young people need to participate effectively and enjoyably in a sport?

Chapter 4 confirmed the complex nature of skill performance in sport. Clearly, sport educators must understand the fundamental nature of the sport or sports they are involved with. However, they also need to consider the following two questions:

1. How is effective participation defined?
2. What is the difference, if any, between fun and enjoyment?

The first question is a difficult one because what one person defines as effective participation must always be relative and is determined by a vast range of factors, including national and local cultural influences. The importance of distance running in Kenya, soccer in Brazil, javelin throwing in Finland, skiing in Austria, swimming in Australia, basketball in Kentucky or ice hockey in Canada are manifestations of how powerful these influences can be. That said, it is likely that the key to effective participation will be the attitudes and expectations of the young person's significant others such as the instructor, peer group and parents. In many situations, especially in schools, a struggle may develop between elements of the peer group and the instructor, which can cause major complications. However, there is little doubt that a dedicated and energetic sport educator can create a microculture in a school, club or community, especially if there is support from other key elements.

The second question is important because although people often use the words fun and enjoyment interchangeably, in fact major differences in meaning exist between them. Clearly children can have "fun" when simply playing, no matter their level of performance, but below a certain level of competence, players will gain little enjoyment and will sensibly move on to other things. Beginners who spend all their time sprawled in the snow, or picking tennis balls out of the net, or waiting for passes that never come will neither enjoy the experience nor want to continue with it. Nor should they.

However, anyone who has ever participated in sport knows that on certain occasions one would rather not face a new challenge. Fear of injury, of failure, of making mistakes in front of one's peers can block any one of us from even attempting the next step. But every experience in life presents a challenge that we must face and deal with if any personal growth is to occur. For this reason the important notion of "challenge met and challenge mastered" runs as a coherent theme throughout the philosophy of Western physical education. It was an especially powerful force in the development of outdoor activities as educational and developmental tools in Great Britain during the 1930s and now appears to underpin the philosophy of those who participate in extreme sports.

However, helping young people meet and overcome new challenges, even those as apparently simple as controlling a ball, is a complex process. The sport educator must motivate, encourage, urge and even insist that youngsters make a determined effort to master a task without ever putting them at risk or creating a situation that might alienate them and drive them away from sport. This is an art in which an instructor's professional and personal skills may be stretched to the limit. It is a process through which the instructor can encourage young people to look for the enjoyment and satisfaction that comes from facing a challenge rather than always just looking for fun. The dilemmas inherent in this situation will be resolved not by mere rhetoric from either side of the behaviourist-humanist divide, but only through the genuine efforts of individual sport educators to commit themselves to the all-round development of young people.

> **U**ltimately, the test of the effectiveness of a sport experience is whether young people continue or even expand their involvement in the future as players, officials, teachers, coaches or informed spectators.

Play Practice Advantages

Play Practice has many advantages. The first is that it harnesses the powerful forces that play

releases to introduce young people to the joys of sport. Because a play element almost always promotes a more positive commitment to any activity, with Play Practice youngsters are far more likely to be actively and purposefully involved. This gives the instructor a powerful weapon in the struggle toward excellence, and it may also seduce even resistant learners, first into participation and then into commitment. Once youngsters begin to play, the skilled sport educator has an opportunity to interact with them positively on a personal level, potentially changing their perception of both the activity and themselves.

As an illustration, consider how an instructor can use Play Practice to introduce lacrosse. At the very beginning of the first session, beginners play mitt ball, a game that is virtually identical to lacrosse except that instead of trying to use a crosse to control and direct the ball, players catch with a softball glove and throw with their free hand. Because this is far easier, youngsters can experience the joy of playing a game at the very beginning of the lacrosse experience.

A positive early play experience such as this may motivate youngsters to quickly master the techniques of lacrosse so that they can move on to play the real game. So one of the keys to Play Practice is to get beginners playing a game, although not necessarily the real game, as quickly as possible and to continue playing as much as possible throughout every session. This initial experience also provides an opportunity to establish the real entry level of players and so determine which elements of effective performance need to be emphasised to ensure both short- and long-term development.

If the instructor is able to film or objectively record in some way the play in this initial game, the resulting evidence may be useful in helping novices, especially young adolescent males with "attitude", realize that they have much more to learn. It also provides a useful datum against which the instructor can measure progress at the end of a season or unit.

When beginners play the real game at the start of a session, they have a chance to appreciate the fundamental nature of an activity. Even if they play badly, it is easier for them to understand the relevance and importance of rules, tactics, techniques and skill and even the concept of being a good sport when these elements are introduced in subsequent play practices. In this way the crucial issue of alignment, or transfer of training, is more easily resolved. An additional benefit is that if youngsters can clearly see the need to improve as well as the relevance of new learning, they may even be more willing to practice purposefully and persistently until they have reached new levels of mastery or understanding.

Educators can use this approach with many sports. Clearly, the closer the initial experience is to the real game the better, but this will depend on the nature of each sport. The practical sections of this text outline a series of initial play experiences, but note that carefully chosen film of great games can also provide an overview and introduction to a game. In addition, many children grow up immersed in the culture of a particular game so that even before they are participants themselves, they understand how it is played.

The second major advantage of Play Practice is that it is not necessary to understand and apply it as a complete package. **Instructors can pick from a wide range of possibilities and choose those ideas that are easiest to integrate into their normal instructional methods.** They can start with one small adjustment to a practice situation, one simple modification to a game or the use of a working model of technique, or by trying a fantasy game. In this way it is possible to gradually move toward the Play Practice approach to teaching and coaching sport.

Play Practice has many other significant advantages over traditional methods. These include the following:

1. The principles and pedagogy of Play Practice are in line with modern research findings. For example, academic learning time, physical education, maximum individual participation and alignment are all terms used to describe concepts that instructors have employed, if only intuitively and pragmatically, in the Play Practice approach for many years. However, as chapter 2 suggests, Play Practice has been driven by a process of pragmatic reflective tinkering in the real world of teaching and coaching instead of by researchers' findings. As Deng Xiaoping (1979), a Chinese leader in the last century, observed, "Practice is the only norm for verifying truth." (cited in Green 1982, p. 373)

2. The Play Practice approach encourages a holistic view of effective sport performance. It is clear that proficiency in sport involves many complex and often interacting elements. In the past instructors and coaches have tended to forget the holistic nature of sport and focus on individual elements such as technique to the detriment of both enjoyment and performance. Play Practice continually brings the instructor back to the bigger picture, that is, players' overall performance in the real activity.

The process of reflection will also encourage sport educators to consider the fundamental nature of their sport and force them to begin to clarify what the terms skill, skilled and skillful really mean when analysing performance.

3. Play Practice is supported by the clearly defined action plan for instruction detailed in chapter 7. This action plan, labelled "The Ps of Perfect Pedagogy", is a working model of instruction designed to simplify the complex task of instruction into component parts that novice sport educators, for whom the global task of teaching may initially seem incomprehensible, can more easily recall and apply. Always remember, however, that the instructional process is totally integrated and that each element interacts with and complements every other element. At its highest level, instruction is an almost intuitive process as science and art meld seamlessly.

While the Ps model is essentially a working model of instruction designed for novice sport educators, potentially it can expand to meet the needs of highly experienced instructors. Most importantly, it provides a coherent framework for the many intuitive teachers working in the field and enables them to understand why they are effective. This is the first step in their becoming reflective practitioners who are able to initiate improvements in their own instructional behaviour.

4. Using a process that involves shaping, focussing and enhancing, instructors can develop Play Practices that expedite the development of virtually any element of effective performance.

For example, if limited technical ability is holding back development, that element must be improved as rapidly and efficiently as possible. By varying the task and using many different progressions, as suggested for the teaching of dribbling in basketball, or by creating play practices, such as those suggested for the teaching of table tennis, it is possible to motivate youngsters to practice seriously for long periods. Examples of how to ensure plenty of persistent, purposeful practice are outlined later in this book.

5. Play Practice is complemented by the notion of working models of technique, which evolved in parallel with the Play Practice approach. In fact, the use of simplified models of technique is essential because they enable learners to begin playing the real game quickly—a key element of Play Practice.

Many sports require working models because the techniques elite players use are often advanced technical models. These advanced techniques exploit biomechanical principles; usually require special physical qualities such as strength, flexibility, excellent body control or superb hand-eye coordination and often depend on the use of specialized and expensive equipment. Mastery often requires years of high-quality practice and training.

A good example of an advanced technique is one used by a world-class pole-vaulter and shown in figure 5.1. Many youngsters would never be able to master such a technique, and even talented youngsters would have to undertake years of specialized training to even approach such a performance. On the other hand, figure 5.2 shows a working model of technique that would enable any reasonably talented youngster to begin clearing a bar above his or her own height with only 30 minutes of practice.

In simple terms, a working model is technique stripped to the bare bones. This concept was expressed beautifully by the great harmonica player Larry Adler (1957), who said, "Even Bach comes down to the basic suck-blow-suck-suck-blow!" (cited in Green 1982, p. 164) Working techniques in common use include the sliding wedge in skiing, the pat-a-cake tennis serve, the scissors high jump technique in athletics and the dog paddle in swimming.

A working model must always provide the framework for continued development toward the advanced model. In other words, it cannot be a dead-end technique—one that allows participants early success but then blocks them

Figure 5.1 An advanced pole vaulting technique with a flexible pole and a carefully measured run-up.

Reprinted, by permission, from International Amateur Athletic Federation, *Techniques of athletics and teaching progressions.*

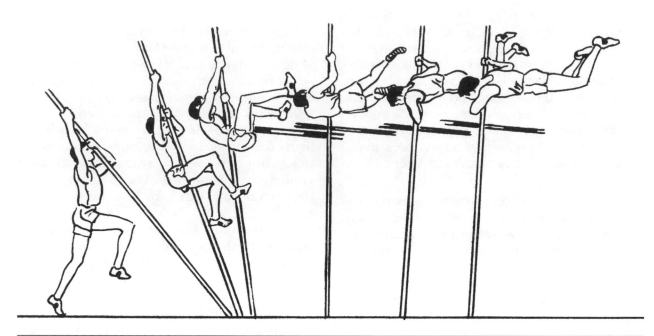

Figure 5.2 A working model of technique for the pole vault that allows less experienced athletes to begin competing very quickly.

Reprinted, by permission, from International Amateur Athletic Foundation, *Techniques of athletics and teaching progressions.*

from further progress. A good example of a dead-end technique is often seen with beginners playing table tennis. Youngsters with a good eye who use an exaggerated backhand grip will find it easy to block the ball back almost indefinitely. In the early stages they will be very successful against opponents who are struggling to master the techniques necessary to impart topspin and who inevitably will make many unforced errors. While the latter are building the techniques required to move to the next level, however, the blocker will stagnate.

> **A** working model cannot be a dead-end technique.

The major advantage of working models is that they enable young players to take part in the real activity much sooner than if they have to wait for mastery of more advanced techniques. Working models also make it possible to delay the introduction of advanced techniques until novices are better able to cope with their complexity and thus less likely to fail or to develop bad habits.

6. Though the driving force behind Play Practice was to find better ways to introduce sport to beginners, the basic principles can be applied at the elite level as well. For example, an international basketball team preparing for a tough match against opponents renowned for their pressure defence can play practice games in which two additional defenders step in against them every time they gain the ball. Now, both the ball handler and the next logical receiver are double-teamed, and there is still no one else free! This replicates the pressure the team is likely to face in their next game; as Russian General Suvarov once observed, "Easy training, hard battle; hard training, easy battle."

7. Instructors can use Play Practice to introduce youngsters to sports as varied as track and field, swimming and skiing. For example, traditional approaches to teaching skiing focus on the repetitive practice of isolated techniques in a specific area. With the Play Practice method, the students are taken on a trek across carefully chosen terrain and the techniques of skiing, including how to get up after a fall, are introduced and practiced at appropriate points along the route.

This approach is effective because learning takes place in a real environment and the set to learn is very high. Another advantage is that youngsters learn to read a slope and choose a suitable route down or across it, important competencies at all levels of recreational skiing.

8. Play practices can help players overcome negative transfer from one activity to another. For example, in most invasion games a ball carrier facing defensive pressure is often encouraged to carry or pass the ball backward so the team retains possession. In the rugby codes, however, giving up ground is usually a mistake, one that novice players naturally make quite often.

To counter this and to encourage correct tactical play, a coach can structure play practices for the rugby codes to emphasize the importance of carrying the ball forward at all times, to accept a tackle rather than running backward and giving up hard-won ground. In this way it is possible to change, if only gradually, established patterns of behavior.

9. The Play Practice process encourages youngsters to cooperate with each other, to become supporters, "feedbackers", even teachers and coaches. An emphasis on a "helping" attitude in sports is long overdue. If it can be nurtured from the beginning, it may be possible to help young people appreciate that sport is as much about cooperation and personal growth as it is about competition. To encourage this helping attitude, I developed the term feedbacker as a shorthand name for any student who provided positive and useful feedback to their peers. The role is built into many play practices in which players take turns and make positive use of what otherwise might be wasted time.

10. Play Practice lends itself to innovation of all kinds. "Action fantasy games" and "play like Hingis/Davenport games", which are described in chapter 15, evolved quite naturally through the pragmatic reflective process suggested earlier. As sport educators themselves play with the concepts and principles of this approach, they will almost inevitably create something unique and exciting to add to the range of effective ideas.

Perhaps the most innovative application of the principles of Play Practice was the "Tour de West Lakes" that turned a routine high school curriculum unit on cycling safety and maintenance into an exciting, dynamic learning experience for the children involved. How this was achieved is outlined in the fantasy game section of this text.

11. With the Play Practice approach, the ongoing interaction between instructor and student tends to develop reflective sport practitioners who learn from every experience and every student. It also engenders a learner-centered view of instruction. This is important because any instructional process should be based on a revolving, expanding analysis of student needs that in turn depends on the instructor's continuous, perceptive observation.

This process involves higher-order instructional skills such as accurate observation, perceptive analysis and sensitive intervention that develop only through a process best termed reflective experience. While this process may take many years, these skills are essential components of any really effective strategy of instruction and sport instructors must master them if they want to attain Jedi status!

Once mastered, however, these skills can be relied on throughout a long career and, most importantly, can be put to good use in other ways. For example, a common problem that every sport educator faces is the effect that a very rapid growth spurt can have on a child's physical capacities. As muscles struggle to catch up with bones, a youngster may begin to look and move like a baby giraffe, with all of the attendant problems of poor coordination and the loss of the power necessary for agility. **The trusted, empathetic and observant sport educator is one of the few individuals capable of helping young people pass through this most difficult phase of life.** If they achieve nothing else, sport educators who help young people make it through this period with their confidence and optimism undimmed have more than done their job.

12. The emphasis on small-sided games and on competition provides numerous opportunities for youngsters to take on other roles such as referee, timekeeper, feedbacker, coach or even commentator. In this way, when teams or

individuals are waiting for their turn to play, youngsters can pass their time more profitably. Not only will individuals gain further insights into a sport, but having people fill these roles also ensures that play practices run more smoothly; for example, in teaching the game of touch (rugby), the role of the student referee is crucial.

Though all of these roles are important and clearly have immense potential to generate continued involvement in sport, young people are usually particularly drawn to the roles of feedbacker, coach and commentator.

13. One of the great strengths of Play Practice is that it is continually evolving. In some cases this evolution results from an instructor responding intuitively and pragmatically to the students' needs in the early stages of the approach. In other cases improvements occur through an ongoing, reflective process on the part of the sport educator, and some arrive through moments of sheer inspiration!

In most sports, the potential of Play Practice has barely been exploited, so if sport educators or coaches connect with each other and share their ideas and experiences, the possibilities are unlimited. This is a completely open-ended process, for once those involved understand the basic principles, they can apply them to all levels of participation and to almost all sports.

Summary

Play Practice is not a panacea for all of the problems concerning the teaching of games, and it has its disadvantages. The first is that it can place far greater demands on instructors than traditional methods of games instruction. To accurately observe and analyse play, and then to select, modify, condition or even create a progressive series of play practices for students, requires a very clear understanding of the fundamental nature of the activity as well as good instructional skills.

A second disadvantage is that play practices will often appear chaotic compared to the orderly formations of drills or relays. A sport educator needs confidence and patience to accept this apparent chaos as normal for beginners learning to play complex games and to work patiently toward improvement. In fact, even coaches working at the highest level must be prepared for continual performance breakdowns when players are working to master new techniques or tactics. Almost certainly, the players will experience what Vince Lombardi termed "game slippage" as they transfer new techniques, tactics or skills from practice into a competitive game.

These reservations aside, Play Practice does have the potential to provide every child with the kind of experiences that Novak describes so beautifully. To maximise the educational and developmental possibilities when children play games, it is important that sport educators harness the intense feelings of pleasure and satisfaction a child experiences when a movement task is well done. The sweet feeling of

© Terry Wild Studio

Children around the world enjoy games and sometimes unofficial pickup games with other children are the best way to try out new moves and abilities without repercussion from others.

clean contact when a ball is properly hit, of mastery when it is controlled or caught, of satisfaction when intelligent teamwork produces a goal or thoughtful defence snares an interception must all be highlighted and savored. These are the magical moments that children can remember long after the result is forgotten, and these are, more than any other factor, the reason that we continue to play even when our bodies can no longer sustain our dreams.

If any further support for this innovative approach is needed, we can find it in the tremendous upsurge in interest in sports such as surfing, skateboarding and snowboarding. The sole driving force behind these sports are youngsters searching for a freer, more joyous involvement in challenging physical activities, and they represent the natural application of the philosophy of Play Practice.

So the first task for sport educators is to commit themselves to helping young people make sport a major element in their lives. Armed with little more than this commitment and large reserves of energy, sport educators can make a major contribution to the well-being of their communities.

The second task is to become lifelong students who improve, if only gradually, their understanding of the three strands of knowledge outlined in this chapter, because it is clear that the greater their knowledge, the more effective they will become.

The third task is to learn how to draw these strands together through an instructional process that seamlessly blends applied science and artistry to create play practices that shape, focus and enhance learning. This is in itself a process—a complex, enjoyable process that will take the reflective sport educator on a great journey of discovery and fulfillment.

Play Practice in Action

When are we going to play a game?
—Any child, anywhere, any time

● ● ● ● ●

Chapter 4 indicated the components of effective play in ball games. The challenge is to help youngsters become more effective players by using play practices that retain the essential feel of the real game but are carefully planned to ensure specific outcomes. The key phrase that sums up the Play Practice method is "Teach through the game and in the game."

Teach through the game and in the game.

Because sport functions within a given sociocultural context, certain games have far more importance and support in some countries or in a specific community than others. Throughout Brazil, for example, soccer rules supreme; in Cuba it is baseball and in New Zealand it is Rugby Union. This fanaticism also is evident in regions or even small communities within a nation. Kentucky and Indiana have traditionally been basketball-crazy at the high school level in the United States, whereas Ohio and Pennsylvania emphasise American football. Basketball has been called the "city game" because of its immense popularity in U.S. inner-city areas.

In these places even beginners who have had no previous formal instruction may already be quite skillful players or at the very least have a general understanding of the game. We must recognise that peers, parents and television can all be effective instructors. This has immense implications for sport educators in communities in which specific games are highly popular. Most 14-year-olds in these communities are already likely to be competent players with a clear understanding of the game, so the task of an instructor in this environment is completely different from that of someone taking a game into a community or school where it has not previously been played. It is therefore important for the instructor to quickly establish the entry level of groups or individuals in terms of their attitude, knowledge and ability.

Gus Macker basketball is an example of small, community-based games in which members of the community come together with a safely prepared area for local youth to participate in competition at their level.

dition of the 24-second clock and the three-point shot.

In fact, most games go through a continual change process as rules are altered to make the game fairer, more exciting or even more marketable. The process of creating play practices is similar except that the instructor can manipulate far more variables and develop far more extreme-learning situations. In this way it is possible to create practice environments that shape play in such a way that will more easily improve specific elements of effective performance. This is teaching *through* the game. For example, two-touch soccer is a game in which a player receiving the ball is allowed to touch it only twice. In other words, the player can control the ball with the first touch and then pass it with the second. This rule or condition immediately begins to shape play because it eliminates dribbling and encourages players to control the ball quickly and make the easy pass.

Although we can most easily apply the concept of shaping to the teaching of team games, we can also apply it in various ways to many different activities. For example, in the teaching of skiing, the practice environment the instructor selects will have a powerful effect on the speed of learning. Even with an activity like dancing, in all its varied forms, careful selection of the music will make it much easier for beginners to learn. In both of these examples, the instructor can shape learning by controlling and manipulating one critical variable.

Play practices can also shape performances at the simplest level. In swimming, for example, a horizontal body position is essential. However, beginners find this impossible to achieve because they are unable to control their breathing when the face is close to the water. Playing

Play Practice in action is based on three fundamental processes, which are

- shaping play,
- focussing play, and
- enhancing play.

These processes can be applied in the teaching and coaching of most sports. This chapter, however, concentrates on the way instructors can use Play Practice to improve instruction in team games; specific practical sections later in the text will outline its application to individual sports.

Shaping Play

Every team game is shaped by the rules, the size and shape of the playing area, the nature of the goal and the number of players. James Naismith manipulated these variables to create basketball at the end of the 19th century to meet a specific need for a game that people could play indoors during cold winters in Springfield, Massachusetts. Since that time basketball has evolved with a continually expanding keyway, the change to the centre jump rule and the ad-

simple games in which they have to compete at blowing a table tennis ball across the surface of the water can help to resolve this problem.

> *T*he notion of shaping play by manipulating specific variables can readily be applied to other sports.

Focussing Play

Sport educators cannot, however, simply set up play practices such as the ones discussed here and let them run without any intervention, hoping that the children will teach themselves key concepts or develop necessary technical ability. Nor can they expect youngsters to appreciate the similarities and differences between a specific play practice and the real game—a crucial element if the instructor expects positive transfer from one to the other. So the second task is to focus play by teaching *in* the game. Instructors can also use this focussing process to point out the similarities and differences between a specific play practice and the real game.

Using this focussing process, the instructor can take the simple game of two-touch soccer and help players develop or refine very sophisticated skills. They might begin by stressing the importance of supporting the ball player to give her many easy passing options. Next, they could show how intelligent calls of "man on", "hold", or "turn" can help alert the ball player to how much space and time she has and so enable her to be more skillful in her distribution. Finally, they might begin to encourage players to read the play even as they prepare to control the ball—a high-level skill indeed. The focussing process is vital because it determines both the quality and the direction of the practice and helps ensure positive transfer from the practice to the real game.

This process is also important because sometimes a particular condition may lead to results the instructor has not anticipated. The instructor must therefore be prepared to take advantage of any situation and focus it in a positive direction. For example, a half-court basketball play practice in which players are allowed to score only from outside the three-point line could shape play in several directions. First, it may lead to many off-balance shots as players try to shoot from outside their usual shooting range. This in itself could be a valuable learning experience as players discover that they may not be as good as they believed they were in this aspect of the game. More importantly, it is likely to lead to many rebounds initially, which will give the perceptive instructor the opportunity to focus on positioning and blocking out. Without intelligent intervention of this kind, a coach will lose many valuable learning opportunities.

This practice can then be developed to focus on the importance of teamwork as players help each other get completely open shots, emphasising simple tactical moves such as the quick reverse pass, the dribble draw, the pick and roll, and the penetrate and pitch out. Finally, this practice can be focused on helping defenders deal with these offensive moves by finding a balance between putting pressure on the ball when it is in the hands of a defender's direct opponent and helping out when it is not.

Enhancing Play

The third task is to enhance learning by making improved performance appear to be important and meaningful. Many ways exist to achieve this. Clearly, the sport educator's personality and skills and the respect players have for him or her is a major factor, but it is possible to further enhance player commitment and performance by presenting challenges, using time constraints or action fantasy games and handicapping individuals or teams.

The Freeze Replay

The ability to focus and enhance performance will depend on the instructor's intelligent intervention. The instructor must create and exploit "teachable moments", those times when the learners are completely receptive to new ideas and concepts. The freeze replay is a critical element in this process, especially in the teaching of understanding. Choosing the moment carefully, the instructor gives an agreed-on signal to "freeze" the players, who must immediately stop moving. Play is then "rewound", as in a television replay, back to the critical point and then the guided discovery process can be used to help the players "replay" the scenario backward and forward to draw out key elements of good play and to consider alternatives.

Carefully handled, and certainly not overused, the freeze replay enables the instructor to capture great teaching moments and use them to help players better understand the game. It is also a highly effective way of controlling the chaotic scramble that occurs at the beginning of many play practices and of reducing the high error rate that is inevitable as young beginners try to come to terms with the challenges any sport poses. Freeze replays can be a key element in raising the quality of performance at any level of play. With motivation high, with play shaped by the real learning environment and with learning focussed and enhanced by the instructor's intelligent intervention and input, youngsters can make rapid progress.

The Process of Shaping Applied to Invasion Games

Because the structure of the learning environment is critical to the shaping process, it is important to understand how it is possible to achieve desired outcomes by manipulating specific variables. The two-touch soccer game outlined earlier is one example of how a simple change to the rules of play can lead to improvements in both technical ability and games sense.

Invasion games are the most tactically complex of all sports and are often the most poorly taught. Therefore, the following section focusses on how it is possible to manipulate many different variables to create a vast range of play practices so that each becomes a learning laboratory for the real game.

The key variable in invasion games is the number of players involved. This is an important variable because a good learning situation is one that encourages maximum individual participation. Clearly, the fewer players in any game, the more opportunities exist for each individual to be involved. The challenge is to work out the optimum number of players for each game.

In games such as basketball, korfball and netball, 3-v-3 games ensure a good balance between improvement in technical ability and the development of games sense. 5-v-5 games are almost perfect for teaching field games such as soccer, hockey and lacrosse and are virtually learning laboratories for them. Even in their simplest forms, such mini games ensure that all children are actively involved in playing and learning. The sport-specific sections in part II of this book will show how mini games can range from 1-v-1, 2-v-1, 3-v-1, 3-v-2, 3-v-3 and 4-v-3 up to a maximum of 7-v-7 for a game such as Australian rules football.

It is not always easy to sell the idea of small-sided games to children, who usually prefer to play the real game even though many of them know, if only intuitively, that the stars will dominate and that they themselves will hardly touch the ball. This may be the result of cultural pressures they do not understand, but they know what they want.

One way to overcome this is to show a video of a great game, with the camera zooming in to demonstrate that even the real game is made up of a linked series of small-sided or mini games. Once children become accustomed to mini games and get the satisfaction of being positively involved in them and contributing to team play, they quickly accept them.

The Attacker/Defender Ratio

At any instant in a real game, either the attackers or the defenders may—if only for an instant—hold the numerical and tactical advantage. The classic fast break in basketball pits three attackers against a single defender and, with good passing, usually results in an easy score.

So if the objective is to encourage beginners to pass the ball and to help them develop both technique and games sense as well as to build confidence, attackers must always be given the numerical advantage. In basketball, where the ball is easily controlled, a one-player advantage is enough. In games such as soccer, hockey and lacrosse, where controlling the ball is more difficult and where the ball player must continually switch focus from ball to opponent, it may be necessary to begin with four attackers against a single defender, or perhaps five against two.

As quickly as possible, however, the instructor should move toward the continuous 3-v-1 "go for goal" games shown in figure 9.2d in the soccer section. Three attackers (O) are confronted by one defender (X) as they go for goal. After a score or a change of possession, X's teammates join in to break forward to attack the lone defender, Y. In turn, Y's teammates join in so that play moves backward and forward continuously. While these games give players many opportunities to control and direct the ball, they can also introduce the basic tactical principles of width and depth in attack and delay in defence.

With three attackers who understand the importance of width and depth in attack, it is difficult for the single defender to pressure the ball player, who now has the time to both choose and execute the right passing or shooting option. As attacking play improves, progression to 3-v-2 , 4-v-3 or 3-v-3 games of increasing tactical and technical complexity becomes possible.

Attackers who outnumber defenders have several passing options and so should easily retain possession of the ball. Figure 9.2 in the soccer section, however, shows a game of 2-v-2 where passing options are very limited. Here both teams try to score by playing the ball through either of their two goals placed in the corners. This is a simple scenario, but one with the potential to help players develop valuable skill. Because the ball player has only one passing option, a teammate who will usually be closely guarded, he must develop both his dribbling and his ball-shielding skills while calculating if he can slide the ball past his defender for a score. This play practice also helps players understand how to break down defensive cover by the clever use of mobility.

At the highest level, play practices may be designed to give the defenders the numerical advantage in order to replicate the situation attackers are often faced with in the real game. For example, in top class soccer, attackers often receive the ball when they are outnumbered by defenders. They can learn how to overcome this disadvantage through well-structured play practices. In basketball if a team knows that their next opponents will probably employ aggressive full-court or half-court pressure defences, they can practice with five attackers facing seven defenders. In this way both the ball handler and the next logical receiver will be double teamed and there will still be no one else completely open! An hour or so of practice under those conditions should begin to prepare a team for any kind of pressure.

Altering the Size and Shape of the Playing Area

Altering the size of the playing area can shape play into specific forms. The basic rule is that whereas beginners need plenty of space to play effectively, good players must learn to play in limited space. This is a function of the equation

$$space = time =$$
$$skill\ (good\ decisions\ and\ good\ execution)$$

Stated simply, the more space there is between a player and defenders when the player receives the ball, the more time that the player has to control the ball, read the display, choose the best option in the context of the game and execute that option effectively. In soccer this could be striking at goal, making a pass of some kind, dribbling past an opponent or simply holding the ball up while teammates move into better positions.

The first game that absolute beginners in soccer play should have no boundaries at all so that space is almost unlimited. On the other hand, a game of five-a-side soccer played on a 20- by 30-yard (about 18- by 28-metre) pitch, where space is very limited, encourages players to value space, apply the principles of play in attack and defence, support the ball player intelligently and pass accurately.

Altering the shape of the playing area can also shape play. For example, five-a-side "long soccer", played on a pitch that is 100 yards long by 30 yards wide and with goals 20 yards wide, develops long passing and long shots for goal and, most importantly, forces players to lift their vision

Other small-sided games can take place in the corridors or squares of the teaching grid outlined on page 94. Naturally, the size of any playing area will depend on the players' age and ability. It may even be necessary to adjust it during a session to ensure a worthwhile practice. This is yet another reason that, after starting any practice, the instructor must watch carefully to see if it is working the way it is supposed to or if some adjustments are needed.

The Nature of the Goal

Though it is true that young players invariably prefer the real goal and the real rules, it is often necessary to adjust both of these. Since the goal in a sense defines the objective of the game, it clearly has a major impact on the way a game is played. The instructor must therefore use this as a powerful tool in shaping the nature of the play practice. The goal can be whatever the instructor specifies it to be. In simple terms, an easy goal encourages shooting whereas a difficult goal tends to encourage more passing. For example, a modified game of basketball in which the goal is the backboard would lead immediately to far more shots. It would also quickly force defenders to put pressure on the ball and stay far closer to opponents at all times; there would be no zone defences.

In the rugby codes the goal is the whole width of the pitch, but it is possible to use such a goal in practices for many other games. When developing one-on-one dribbling skills in soccer, hockey or basketball, the dribbler's goal can be to get the ball over the goal line at any point; this forces the defender to be honest and try hard to prevent the dribbler from going past, full stop. Obviously, this play practice could also help players improve their defensive skills.

Very large goals in soccer will encourage players to lift their vision and shoot from long distance, whereas very small goals will encourage them to interpass or dribble for a good close shot. Four-goal soccer encourages attackers to switch play from one side of the field to the other to counter defenders who use the principle of concentration to stop them. In lacrosse, attackers must learn how to play behind the goal. Irish lacrosse, outlined later in this chapter, encourages beginners to do just this.

Primary and Secondary Rules

The fundamental structure of every game is determined by its primary rules, rules which cannot be altered without the game becoming essentially a different game. The handball rule in soccer is perhaps the best example of a primary rule which cannot be changed without the nature of the game becoming fundamentally different. On the other hand, there are secondary rules which can be modified without the game changing its essential character. In soccer the "throw in" could easily be replaced by a kick in when the ball goes out of play at the sidelines, and the game would probably benefit.

In fact with beginners it is wise to start with as few rules as possible to allow play to flow. Sport educators must also be prepared to modify any rule where necessary to make a play practice simpler and more enjoyable for novice players. Since many children already know the "real" rules, it will often be necessary to explain the reason for the change. Naturally the real rule should be applied as soon as it is feasible to do so and at an appropriate time.

> **S**port educators must also be prepared to modify any rule where necessary to make a play practice simpler and more enjoyable for novice players.

Note that almost every rule change has repercussions, including some not contemplated at the time of the change. The offside law is especially interesting. In the rugby codes and in American football it is a *primary* rule, so any changes will fundamentally change the nature of the game, as occurred in the latter game at the turn of the last century. However, in soccer and field hockey, the offside rule is a *secondary* rule and so can be, and has been, changed several times without altering the fundamental nature of these games. However, each change has had a significant impact on the tactics of both games, sometimes in unanticipated ways.

Conditions Applied to the Game

Conditioning a game is a critical aspect of the Play Practice approach. The instructor can shape play in many ways, but especially by applying specific conditions that take on the power of rules for the duration of a specific play practice. Very often, an apparently simple condition has an immediate and obvious impact when first applied and continues to shape the development of both tactical and technical ability over time. The two-touch rule in a soccer practice is a good example. In the real world of sport, basketball coaches in the era of the Drake Shuffle offence required their players to make a set number of passes, up to seven in some cases, before they could take a shot. This condition ensured that every player handled the ball, and it was designed to develop teamwork and trust between players.

Irish lacrosse involves a simple modification in which the goals are turned to face away from the field of play. This condition forces players to play behind the goal if they want to score and so begins to help them learn how to exploit that valuable space in a real game. Such a modification is important because only in lacrosse, ice hockey and korfball does play continue behind the goal. Youngsters who have been playing other games may find it difficult to come to terms with this unless there is a condition which in effect forces them to play behind the goal.

In tennis and table tennis, allowing only forehand strokes in a play practice forces players to work much harder on their agility. It also begins to show them how to exploit the possibilities of "running round the forehand" to create better angles. Running round the forehand is a term commonly used in tennis as a shorthand way of saying that, instead of playing a ball in the backhand court with a backhand stroke, the player uses their agility to position themselves to hit the ball with their forehand. This enables them to hit with greater power and accuracy.

Using conditioned Play Practice games can improve performance at an elite level in many sports. If a 3-v-3 half-court game of basketball is conditioned so that the ball handler can go only one on one to score with no screens or give-and-go moves allowed, the player's ability to operate from the triple-threat position, combining outside shooting with fake and drive moves for the layup or the pull-up jumper, will improve rapidly. Under the direction of a knowledgeable coach, this condition can set the scene for a whole range of technical and tactical development. It can lead in an almost precise sequence to the improvement of one-on-one defensive skill, then defensive help, in-and-out cuts by receivers to get open, offensive spread and balance, penetrate-and-pitchout moves, defensive recovery by the helping defender, drive-and-dish moves and so on until players have explored and developed a whole range of skilled play in basketball. You will find many more examples of this approach in the practical sections in part II of this text.

Control and Development of the "Good" Players

Even with full games it is possible that the more experienced and capable players will take over and dominate play, squeezing out the less confident ones. This is even more likely with small-sided games, so it is essential that the coach makes sure teams are balanced and ensures that the better players are controlled by placing specific conditions on them. When handled properly, this will bring less-able players more into the game and actually help the stars improve their own play.

The coach can do this simply by restricting the better players' movements or options. The rules might specify that they can never move in

Most children want to participate in games and often dream of being the star player. These dreams can often become real as they play in informal pickup games with their friends.

front of the ball in attack or are not allowed to shoot at goal. Other ways to limit their individual impact and perhaps encourage a team view may include restricting the dribble in basketball or allowing only two touches in soccer or hockey. The most effective method, however, is to give them leadership roles such as playmaker, quarterback, or "schemer", as this role is often called in soccer, with the suggestion that they must try to play like a particular local or national hero known for a great ability to provide assists and lift his or her team. In some games they can be given a player/coach role with the task of improving the play of their team. This gives stars the recognition they might otherwise seek by dominating the game and gives them a chance to try on a real leadership role. Few youngsters can resist this opportunity, especially when the instructor is praising them for being "real team players."

This naturally leads to the possibility of assigning players to other roles such as coach, scorer, referee, feedbacker or even commentator.

Differential Scoring

Differential scoring systems can be a valuable tool in shaping play. Basketball introduced the three-point shot to help resolve some of the problems the professional game faced when defenders jammed the scoring lanes.

With beginners the problem is even worse because of their very low percentage shooting ability. In a simple one-on-one game only a very silly defender would try to stop an outside—two-point—shot that has virtually no chance of scoring if the child can simply drop back under the basket and prevent the layup. But if the rules allocate 10 points for an outside—15-foot—shot that hits the rim and 20 for a basket, players will quickly play honest defence, which in turn does open up other attacking options, such as a layup for 5 points.

In the sector games used to improve play in cricket, it is possible to allocate a negative score when a batsman's hit is caught. A large penalty will certainly encourage players to keep the ball on the ground. In baseball and softball, on the other hand, where a sacrifice fly is a tactical ploy, it may be necessary to work out a scoring system that rewards a long hit even if it is caught. This is yet another area of sport instruction that needs greater exploration.

Playing Time

Even a cursory glance at the contemporary sporting scene will show that there are critical periods, usually but not always at the end of the game, when time seems to stand still, seconds feel like hours and players commit everything as they strive for victory.

Despite this, using time as a variable seems to have attracted little interest from those who write about the teaching of games. This is surprising because it is clear that while most children love to play games, they will make a complete commitment only for as long as the game seems fair and the result stays in doubt. This, of course, is not unusual in adult play either, even among highly paid professional players. It is also fair to add that many youngsters have a limited attention span, even when they are playing a game.

Limiting the playing time of a mini game to between two and three minutes keeps the score close, captures the sense of urgency and purpose and enhances the quality of play; now every move counts and every score is important. In this way we can further heighten the games experience for children. In addition, with playing time limited, fatigue is less likely to contribute to poor performance or to lower motivation.

It is possible to extend this concept even further by playing random-time games. Here, games might last from 45 seconds up to three minutes, with the instructor choosing to end the playing time on a random basis. This ensures that playing intensity is high from the start, especially if every game is important. Implementing a "winners stay on" or "king of the court" system is particularly valuable when limited facilities mean that teams must rotate into play.

Manipulating time in this way brings another dimension to the game. It creates relevant and pressing problems that can be solved only by players who think for themselves, support each other when the going gets tough and understand the importance of never giving up. **A multitude of short games gives every player and team a chance to be reborn, to start with a clean slate, to use the lessons learned in an earlier defeat to their advantage in the next game.**

Tactical Time-Outs

Instructors can make good use of freeze replays to take advantage of teachable moments at any time during a game. With Play Practice, however, it is also possible to allow teams themselves the chance to call a limited number of tactical time-outs—of 30 seconds' duration only—to discuss what they are doing; to raise questions—for example, about the rules—and to make necessary adjustments to their play. When carefully handled, these situations can help youngsters better understand the nature of the game and of skilled play.

User-Friendly Balls and Equipment

Few people appreciate the revolution that has taken place in ball technology over the past 40 years. Moulded rubber balls are now available for virtually every game and are a huge improvement over the old balls with their inner rubber bladders and lace-up leather covers. They have many advantages for players but are invaluable for coaches, who no longer have to give up several thankless hours each week keeping balls in a usable shape. Because these new balls are also cheap, every enthusiastic child can have their own at home; even large groups at a school or club should be able to arrange for at least one ball for every two children.

Naturally, balls used in invasion games should be appropriate for the age, size and the gender of the players. Even the simple modification of using a volleyball in the early stages of teaching soccer will immediately encourage a more open game instead of the moving scrimmage that develops when beginners play with a regulation ball. The next revolution involves applying modern foam technology to the challenge of making balls even more user-friendly. We can now buy tough foam balls as well as soft-touch balls that reduce impact forces for young children in invasion games and in volleyball, and that in tennis can be combined with a high net to slow the game down and make it easier for players to track and hit the ball.

An excellent example of the new equipment's impact is in the teaching of American football, which has been made immeasurably easier by the development of a range of footballs. Some, like the Aerobie football, have fins to generate the spiral necessary for stable flight and let children with limited ability both throw and catch more easily.

Manipulating Variables to Shape Play Practices in Other Sports

The notion of shaping play by manipulating specific variables can readily apply to other sports. In racquet sports and volleyball, another divided-court game, it is possible to manipulate the size of the playing area, the height of the net, and the way points are scored as well as to use different balls to create appropriate play practices. For example, raising the net invariably slows the game down, giving beginners more time to move into position to play the ball. Changing the way points are scored can have an equally dramatic effect. In target tennis, points can never be lost; they can be won only if the target is hit. This immediately shapes and focusses play toward consistent stroke play and so helps to improve technique.

Performance in target games can be shaped by manipulating the size, location and nature of the target. In archery it is always tempting to give beginners a close, easy target, but this will only tend to encourage poor technique in terms of stance, draw and release. The solution is to use different targets positioned a long way from the archer, as suggested in chapter 13.

For many of these activities the process of shaping play is outlined in the relevant practical section.

A Framework for Play Practice

The Play Practice process is relatively simple, and any reasonably confident adult with sound communication skills and some knowledge of the activity can undertake it. We must emphasise here, however, that this will usually be possible only if the adult is helping small groups of motivated youngsters. Teaching larger groups of reluctant or resistant learners may require fully trained, experienced leaders with well-developed management and motivational skills.

Novice sport educators may find the following outline of value.

The Process for the First Session

1. Organise play practices that are as close to the real game as possible. In invasion games, form the smallest possible team size that still feels like the real game.

2. Stand back and carefully observe to determine the group's overall level of performance. This phase should last at least 10 minutes and could go much longer with more experienced players. Intervene during this phase only if major problems arise.

3. Identify the better players. Later, you may need to use these players as demonstrators or coaches. You may also need to control some of them by imposing conditions on their play to ensure that they make a positive contribution and do not dominate play at the expense of the less-experienced or less-talented children.

4. Decide what needs to be improved. Do this while the group continues to play. Experience, allied with the key concepts detailed in this book, will make this process easier; invariably, however, it comes down to determining priorities. Fortunately, with beginners it is possible to predict their needs even before they begin to play.

5. Set up practices that will help the group progress most quickly. Use play practices wherever possible (see practical examples). Where players must improve technique, use an efficient and stimulating practice situation (see chapter 7).

6. Let the group practise. Depending on the time available and the nature of the activity, these play practice periods should last from three to five minutes.

7. Stand back and carefully observe. This gives you time to really see what is happening, to reflect on how things are going in the session and to decide what feedback is needed.

8. Provide feedback to improve play. Use freeze replays where possible, but do not stop the flow of play too often. Youngsters find this very disruptive and frustrating.

9. Progress to the next practice/play practice or final game. Assess improvement.

10. Analyse the session. Did the players improve? Did they enjoy the session? Was there enough time given to playing?

11. Plan the next session. This must be based on the above analysis and should aim to review the previous session and take the players on to another level in terms of understanding and technical ability.

Clearly steps 2, 3 and 4 will become less important in the subsequent sessions, whereas increasingly more time will be allocated to steps 5 to 11. Again, one of the great advantages of Play Practice is that instructors can apply it in a completely ad hoc manner. They can incorporate any of the ideas outlined here into their usual instructional patterns on a one-off basis. Then, if they find that the idea has worked, they can try it again, adding another element. In this way it is possible to gradually build toward the Play Practice approach to teaching sport without throwing away methods that may have previously been effective.

The Ps of Perfect Pedagogy

Learning can only be done by the learner and not by some kind of transmission process from the teacher.
—Bugelski

● ● ● ● ●

As the previous chapter suggested, the Play Practice process is relatively simple and can be undertaken by any reasonably confident individual. At the highest level, however, the task of the sport educator becomes a complex craft as the science and art of instruction meld seamlessly. This requires wide-ranging knowledge, skills and competencies as well as many desirable personality traits, all leavened by experience.

A major objective of this text is to encourage sport educators to become reflective rather than intuitive practitioners. In his book *Educating the Reflective Practitioner,* Donald Schon (1987) makes a valuable distinction between intuitive individuals, whose "knowing is only in their actions" and "reflective practitioners", who know exactly why they are doing what they do. While both types can be highly effective, only reflective practitioners can continuously assess and react to new situations while at the same time monitoring and improving their own performance. Their understanding of the processes involved also enables them to communicate their expertise rationally and logically and so become mentors to other potential instructors.

> *A major objective of this text is to encourage sport educators to become reflective rather than intuitive practitioners.*

To become a reflective sport educator, it is necessary to have a clear model of the instructional process. To meet this need, I have developed a working model of instruction that complements the Play Practice approach to teaching sport. It is based on the precepts that people learn best when

- they know that a significant other really cares about their development;
- they really want to learn something;
- they feel safe;
- they have a clear understanding of what they are supposed to learn;
- they enjoy early and continuing success;
- they have many opportunities for purposeful, pertinent practice;

- they can see a clear relationship between practice and the real activity;

- they get usable feedback about their performance;

- they can quickly apply what they have learned to real situations;

- their significant others recognise their efforts, improvement and successes; and

- they can cooperate and play with peers, especially their friends.

These precepts are the distilled essence of years of empirical observation and practical experience on the part of teachers and coaches, supported and validated by a vast range of research into the learning/teaching process. They incorporate the key theoretical principles of academic learning time, maximum individual participation and alignment (also called transfer of training). They also underpin the Play Practice mantra, which states,

● ● ● ● ● ● ● ● ● ● ●

To become an effective performer, a learner needs plenty of perfect practice under conditions as similar as possible to the environment in which the new learning will subsequently be applied.

● ● ● ● ● ● ● ● ● ●

Though it provides a clear direction, this statement does not provide the specific action plans that sport educators need, especially at the beginning of their careers. I developed the Ps model, explained in this chapter, to provide a working model of instruction for novice sport educators. At first glance it may seem a facile approach to teaching; a deeper analysis, however, will confirm that it incorporates the key aspects of modern learning and teaching theory.

It simplifies the complex task of instruction into components that novice sport educators, for whom the global task of teaching may initially seem incomprehensible and overwhelming, can easily recall and apply. So although in practice the craft of instruction is a totally integrated process in which each element interacts with every other one, the discrete components of the Ps model make this complex craft more accessible.

The instructional process for Play Practice links the precepts detailed previously to the action plans of the Ps model of instruction. Though I developed it specifically to meet the needs of novice instructors, this model has the potential to be expanded as instructional competence improves. It can also be modified to cater to a range of direct and indirect teaching approaches.

Plan

Good planning manifests itself in many ways. It is demonstrated by the fact that sufficient equipment is available at the start of the session, the instructional area is marked out, no time is wasted starting activity, the instructor clearly knows what to expect from the session, and by a host of other details. Even the youngest learners, if only intuitively, appreciate these things and understand that someone cares about them and what they are doing.

Planning is a difficult process, however, because it is based on the answers to three questions:

1. What do children expect from a sport experience?

2. How do children best learn?

3. What competencies do children need to play a sport effectively?

Planning may involve preparing only the very next session or putting together a detailed program of training and practices extending over weeks or months. The depth of planning involved will depend on many factors, such as

- the nature of the activity;

- the skill level and experience of the players;

- the instructor's objectives, both long and short term; and

- the time available—especially if the instructor is preparing the group for a competition of some kind.

With limited time for practice the instructor must establish clear priorities and decide

- what *must* be covered in the formal sessions if any worthwhile improvement is to be made,

- what *should* be covered if good use is made of the time available, and
- what *could* be introduced if time permits.

The critical issue here—and one that is rarely addressed—is the amount of training or practice time necessary to achieve worthwhile improvement in specific components of effective play. Let us consider each component in turn.

Technique

While some of the techniques necessary for success in sport can be acquired relatively quickly, the advanced techniques good players employ in many sports require considerable practice to develop and refine. Many basketball players will take up to five hundred jump shots a day in practice merely to maintain their accuracy, golfers will hit just as many or more practice shots and world-class table tennis players practise up to eight hours a day. The idea of working models of technique helps to resolve this problem of time but does not eliminate it.

Agility

Athletes can improve their agility through specific training exercises, but again it takes dedicated practice to make significant improvements. This component is also strongly linked to genetic factors.

Fitness

The same applies to fitness, where it is accepted that a minimum of six weeks of committed training is necessary before worthwhile changes occur.

Understanding

Understanding of concepts, rules, tactics or strategy can occur instantaneously. So whereas it may take hundreds, or even thousands, of practice attempts to improve technical ability and several weeks to improve fitness and agility, understanding can come in milliseconds. Those who study sport pedagogy have rarely fully understood the importance of this fact. Even more significantly, the interrelationships between understanding and other aspects of effective play have rarely been spelled out or even fully appreciated, despite the fact that examples of this interaction occur in every game.

*U*nderstanding can come in milliseconds.

So though instructors must plan to balance all elements of effective play, they must also ensure that they fully exploit the contribution that a real understanding of rules, tactics and strategy makes to the development of the skilled performer.

The long-term objective should always be to improve every player's performance, as opposed to the short-term goal of winning the next match. It is a difficult choice, but one that is at the heart of a sound philosophy of sport education. One aspect of the reality of sport education, however, is that in the short term, instruction can release only what is already inside the learner. In certain sports it rapidly becomes obvious that some children—at least at

Reprinted, by special permission, of King Features Syndicate.

Early and continuing success is a critical element in the learning process.

that point in their lives—are not going to be able to master a specific physical task no matter how hard they try. For example, the extreme endomorph and the extreme ectomorph will find it difficult, if not impossible, to achieve any success in gymnastics and will be limited in many other activities.

Instruction can release only what is already inside the learner.

This reality will place considerable pressure on sport educators, who must do everything possible to give these young people a chance to fully participate. In many ways this is the most rewarding aspect of our work, especially so when over time, the fat melts away to reveal an athletic mesomorph, or the awkward beanpole almost overnight metamorphoses into a powerful—and very tall—basketball player.

Prepare a Protected Learning Environment

A protected learning environment is important because people learn best when they feel safe. Before any session begins, the instructor should ensure that all hazards are removed, that markings, goals and the like are in place and that equipment is ready. This will minimise wasted time, clearly show an instructor's con-

cern for the students and demonstrate a commitment to providing a worthwhile learning experience.

It is equally important that learners feel safe from embarrassment or even humiliation. One of the major factors limiting the involvement of many youngsters, especially adolescent girls, in sport is fear of failure and the derision this can bring. Yet for beginners facing the unknown challenges of a new experience, failure is both inevitable and natural. Without failure, often repeated failure, little or no progress takes place. Indeed, there can be no sport. One of the major tasks the sport educator faces is helping students understand that by their very nature, sports involve risk taking and errors. So to become truly effective, a sport educator must legitimate failure.

Accepting this notion will require a paradigm shift in thinking for many because it runs counter to much of the conventional wisdom in this field, especially in coaching at the elite level. Fortunately, these words by Teddy Roosevelt superbly capture, support and annunciate the philosophy of legitimating failure.

It is not the critic who counts, not the man who points out how the strong man stumbled, or where the doer of deeds could have done better. The credit belongs to the man who is actually in the arena; whose face is marred by the dust and sweat and blood; who strives valiantly; who errs and comes short again and again...who knows the great enthusiasms, the great devotions and spends himself in a worthy cause; who at the best knows in the end

Is this the only way he can learn?

the triumph of high achievement and who at the worst, if he fails at least fails while daring greatly so that his place shall never be with those cold and timid souls who know neither victory nor defeat. ("Citizenship in a Republic," Speech at the Sorbonne, Paris, April 23, 1910)

Perhaps the key here is to help youngsters understand that although success is more fun, failure is often the better teacher! In fact, some historians believe that the entire edifice of modern science derived from a small subculture of humanists—scientists, in modern terms—who legitimated failure and who were then free to experiment in myriad ways without risking the opprobrium that so often accompanies failure.

Prepare the Learner

Preparing the learner is important because people learn best when they really want to learn something. A strong set or desire to learn is crucial to rapid progress. Because most youngsters come to a sport experience with a positive approach, instructors must maximise this initial motivational set. With reluctant or even resistant learners it can become crucially important. First impressions do indeed count!

Often this kind of positive approach requires merely an enthusiastic instructor who dresses appropriately, gives a welcoming smile, calls each child by name and makes positive comments. There is little doubt, however, that beginning a session with a challenging pretest or some form of a game provides a major incentive for most youngsters to make a commitment.

Pretest

A pretest is important because learning will be optimised if youngsters enjoy early and continuing success. Though an acceptance of failure is a necessary part of the development process, the sport educator must structure a series of progressive learning experiences in which the student can be successful and therefore build both competence and confidence. To ensure early success, it is necessary for the instructor to first establish the group's entry level, that is, their competence in each of the key aspects of effective performance. This ensures that initial play practices and games are structured to produce early success and rapid improvement, because it is important to meet learners at their level of knowledge, competencies and attitudes.

The pretest can take many forms, ranging from simply eyeballing a game to arranging a series of objective challenges, or even to carrying out complex statistical analyses like those elite coaches use. It can accomplish more than merely providing the instructor with a starting point. For example, adolescent boys who have had some exposure to a game almost invariably believe that they are far better players than they actually are. A young men's basketball game will often become a riot of uncontrolled dribbling, one-on-one play, sloppy

Reprinted, with special permission, of King Features Syndicate.

Does Hagar have a clear understanding or model of what he has to master?

passing and reckless three-point attempts as each individual tries to show off. A simple pretest in which every individual must take three three-point attempts from each of five hot shooting spots, with a partner recording the results, will send the not-too-subtle message that while they can "talk the talk", they are not yet able to "walk the walk"!

The instructor can repeat this pretest in subsequent sessions to provide feedback on overall progress. As an additional advantage, such an approach provides a structured introduction to a session while still allowing students considerable freedom as they test themselves, independently or in pairs. It is an important strategy when working with difficult groups of adolescents, for it enables the instructor to define the situation from the outset and to develop a learning environment on the instructor's terms. It also gives the instructor a brief period in which to undertake some of the housekeeping tasks that need to be taken care of at the beginning of every session.

The pretest provides the basis for planning subsequent sessions and even the direction the whole unit will take. If the results are recorded or the initial games videotaped, the instructor will have a useful benchmark for judging the level of improvement during the unit.

Present the Task Efficiently

Present the task efficiently because learning will be enhanced when learners have a clear understanding or model of what they are to master.

The key to an effective presentation lies in showing rather than merely telling. So it is important to set up the learning situation and then clearly and succinctly present the following:

• A clear model or outline of the technique to be learned or the tactical problem to be solved. For example, in basketball this might involve placing players on the court, in position, to initiate the three-on-one fast-break game detailed in the basketball section in chapter 10. With the players in position, the instructor explains the notion of "running the lanes" to the attackers and outlines the defender's task. This means that the practice has real meaning and the explanation is no longer abstract. As a wise man once said, "A picture is worth a thousand words."

• How the practice task is to be carried out

• The objectives of the specific (play) practice

Any explanation should involve key phrases or cue words that give learners a specific focus when they practise. These cues are also the basis for subsequent feedback. Because poor instructors waste more time when presenting the task than in any other phase of instruction, novice instructors should practise key presentations beforehand, even preparing a script where necessary and rehearsing the scene just as an actor might.

Reprinted, with special permission, of King Features Syndicate.

How did he learn to do that?

Provide Plenty of Practice

Provide plenty of practice because learners need many opportunities for purposeful practice in a positive environment. Though failure must be legitimated, most people prefer to succeed at tasks. Success does indeed breed success, because the feelings of competence that successful performance generates can lead to confidence and a can-do attitude with regard to new challenges.

If one single indicator of effective instruction exists, it is a simple analysis of how much time learners actually practise. This means that instructors must undertake all their planning, presentation, organisational and management strategies with the primary intention of maximising ALT and MIP.

In practical terms,

- Each child should have his or her own ball when working to improve specific techniques such as shooting in basketball.
- Only two children should share a ball when practising kicking and stopping or throwing and catching.
- In play practices the instructor should use the smallest possible team size that will achieve the desired objectives.

As suggested earlier, however, ALT and MIP are relatively crude measures of teaching effectiveness and are unable to indicate either the pertinence of a practice task or the learners' level of commitment. Clearly, if only the learner can do the learning, it is vital that children practise persistently and purposefully if they are to make progress. A clear understanding of the learning task, early and continuing success as well as enjoyable challenges will all contribute to this. It may be necessary to help children learn to take responsibility for their own learning and in a sense help them learn how to learn. At the very least, children must be able to listen carefully, follow instructions and watch demonstrations.

The methods instructors can use to facilitate persistent and pertinent technical practice are detailed in chapter 8. In essence, the challenge is to create a series of progressive learning experiences that lead the learners toward mastery.

Initially these challenges should be well within the capacity of the students but should gradually increase in complexity.

Pertinent Practice

Ensure that the practice is pertinent, because young people will practise more purposefully when they can see a clear relationship between the practice and the real activity and when the practice is appropriate to their ability level.

One of the major advantages of the Play Practice approach is that almost all practice takes place in the context of the real game, thus enhancing the possibility of transfer. Here the concept of alignment, introduced in chapter 3, is of critical importance. It is also vital that any practice task be appropriate for the ability of the group or individuals involved. This is not an easy assignment for novice instructors, especially when the ability or experience of the players varies widely. For this reason, pretesting to establish the group's entry level is a vital first step in the instructional process.

Provide Feedback

Provide feedback because learning is also enhanced when learners get usable feedback about the quality of their performance.

Feedback is a critical factor in the learning and teaching process. No matter how effectively the instructor presents the model or task, beginners' initial attempts will rarely be perfect. The instructor's task is to provide feedback that will help the students bring their performance more closely into line with the required model. This is because practice does not make perfect—it only makes permanent! Practising the wrong thing will only help learners become good at doing the wrong thing. So practice all by itself makes permanent; only plenty of perfect, pertinent practice will make perfect.

Practice alone makes permanent; only plenty of perfect, pertinent practice will make perfect.

It is important to provide useable and meaningful feedback.

Feedback is built in naturally to many sporting tasks. In golf, for example, a shot's flight path, direction and distance all provide the player with immediate feedback about the effectiveness of his or her stroke. This built-in feedback is generally termed knowledge of results and is an important aspect of effective learning. To maximise the effects of this simple form of feedback, instructors should first try to help learners understand the relationship between their performance and its result, in a sense helping them become reflective golfers.

Second, they should try to structure situations that provide learners with immediate knowledge of the results of their efforts. This means employing distance markers, targets and goals of all kinds. The sports-specific sections in part II of this book provide examples of this.

Although knowledge of the result of a specific performance is valuable, it does not provide the reasons that a player fluffed a shot or hooked the ball viciously out of bounds. Even more importantly, it does not tell beginners what to do in the future to avoid these problems. Feedback that helps explain why a particular result occurred and suggests remedies is termed augmented feedback.

Providing useful augmented feedback is difficult. It is a higher-order instructional skill because it involves many competencies, some of which can be developed only through experience. To begin the process, the instructor needs a theoretical concept of a perfect model and a clear visual picture of it in the mind's eye. This picture may be a composite of the visual images of a vast number of performers. It is in a sense a distillation of all those images into a single clear picture of the best practice in the activity.

A clear verbal model of the activity is also important. This verbal model should include a large number of key phrases or cues that can convey to the performer a more precise meaning of what is required. The best verbal cues convey an effort or rhythm quality as well as define the spatial elements of a specific movement pattern. Most experienced sport educators have a fund of such cues, so the enthusiastic novice instructor should make a special effort to borrow them.

Ideally, an instructor needs a kinesthetic or feeling picture of the event that can come only

Presenting the task is an important aspect of instruction.

from having performed at a good level him- or herself. The instructor who lacks this feeling picture can compensate by developing special verbal abilities and mastering the key progressive training drills and practices.

Next, the instructor must be able to see what the performer is doing. Seeing in this sense implies being positioned in the right place and knowing what to look for. However, being able to observe several different body parts simultaneously when each is moving at high speed is difficult. Instructors can easily verify the complexity of this task by comparing a live performance with a slow-motion video replay of the same performance.

Then the instructors must

- compare what they see with their model of ideal performance,
- identify the differences between the model and the performance,
- determine whether the differences are significant,
- decide on the causes of the differences,
- determine teaching and feedback priorities, and
- ensure transfer of the modified technique into the real situation.

Occasionally, it may be necessary to repeat the initial presentation for the whole group when it is clear that a majority are having problems. More often, it is necessary to help an individual or small group who have not grasped what is required. The instructor can do this by

- restating the cues,
- trying different cues that contain the same message,
- demonstrating the task again—perhaps from a different angle, or
- providing intermediate progressions.

While feedback is a crucial aspect of effective instruction, prompts are equally valuable. Dave Eldridge, Australia's leading high school volleyball coach, makes extensive use of prompts that remind players of what they should be focussing on in their play; he calls this "feed forward".

To facilitate communication he has developed a series of cue words that every player, and that means virtually every student in the school, must learn. Using this system Dave is able to instantly remind or prompt players and so focus them on key elements of performance.

Dave's Feed Forward Cue Words

General

Anticipate—never be taken by surprise; expect every ball to come to you.

Feet—beat the ball to the spot; stay on your feet as long as possible.

Ready—be balanced to move in any direction.

Talk—make a call before and after contacting the ball.

Passing

Platform—arms away from your body, arms angled to the target.

Track—follow the ball from the server's toss to your arms.

Line up—line your body up with the ball; make the easy pass.

Setting

Face—knees, hips and shoulders must face the target.

Forehead—ball set from the forehead.

Extend—follow through to the target; fly like Superman.

Hitting

Wait—wait till the ball is set, how high, where?

Accelerate—the approach should build in speed: slow, slow, quick, quick.

Reach—contact the ball high and in front of you.

Blocking

Front—position your body in front of the spiker's arm.

Penetrate—hands over the net; block the ball on their side of the net.

Hands—hard hands, spread fingers.

Clamp—surround tight sets.

Defence

Stop—feet must be stopped and wide on hitter's contact.

Low—contact the ball from a low position; come up to meet the ball.

Arms—soft part of arms up; two hands if possible.

Serving

Think—decide your serving target, then execute the technique.

Toss—toss the ball in front of the hitting shoulder.

Tough—we serve harder than any other team, so do it.

Ensure Good Positioning and Perception

Good positioning and perception enable the instructor to really see what is happening and therefore to

- provide feedback,
- assess performance and progress,
- modify practices or games where needed,
- provide reinforcement and praise,
- better manage a group and keep them on task,
- decide when progression is needed, and
- ensure good pacing.

Clearly, these are vital competencies for any instructor but especially for those using the Play Practice approach. This is because Play Practice requires an interactive teaching method in which instructors base their planning and progression on their perception of student needs.

Although it is relatively easy to make good positioning second nature, perception—that is, being able to really see what is happening—is a much more difficult task, especially with regard to observing team games. While the concept of a continuous, progressive and revolving diagnosis, outlined in chapter 16, Bench Coaching, may be of help, ultimately this important element of instruction can be developed only through reflective experience.

Playful Practice

Practice should be playful because people learn best when they know they are preparing for real situations. This is the great strength of Play Practice.

Praise Performance

Praising performance is important because youngsters will practise more purposefully when significant others recognise their efforts, improvement and successes. In the literature this is termed providing positive reinforcement.

Sport educators can take the praise process one step further by holding presentation ceremonies at the end of a season or unit of work. These can range from very informal occasions involving just the group to carefully planned and structured functions to which parents, friends and dignitaries may be invited.

What is important is that every child get an award, even if it is a humorous one, that recognises his or her participation. Good-quality certificates that recognise attendance, achievement, teamwork or being a good sport are easy to produce, but instructors can supplement these with items that are even more concrete. These can include things such as a "golden" bat, ball, bowling pin, arrow, boot, track shoe or basketball net—gold paint is both cheap and easy to apply. Just as attractive to youngsters are small wooden cutout awards, which any competent carpenter can produce. The vital thing is for the awards to commemorate some specific performance or incident that everyone remembers or can identify with.

With established groups, not all awards need signify praise. The South Australian pole vault squad has its "Soft as Melted Butter" award, presented annually to the athlete who fails to clear a height in an important competition. Naturally, this presentation has to be handled sensitively, but when it is pointed out that the first recipient went on to win a Commonwealth Games gold medal and competed in two Olympics, the athletes put the award in perspective. In addition, this group awards permanent trophies in memory of two young athletes who died while they were members of the group, one in a car smash and the other from leukemia.

Naturally, the instructor should present small trophies of the golden ball type to the winners of any competitions held during play practice, but I have discovered that jelly bean sweets issued on an individual basis to recognise special performances or improvement have been as effective as any gold medal could be. Another approach to providing praise that has a profound effect on performance is encouraging the development of commentators in a group. Invite these individuals to act just like television commentators, naturally geared to noting the positives, even down to the awarding of "plays of the day".

Finally, whereas elite performers are ready to accept critical feedback, beginners are often already anxious because they are attempting something new and therefore need constant positive reinforcement. It is important that an instructor who needs to make a critical comment precede it with some kind of empathetic or moderating statement: "That was a really good try. . .now see if you can. . . ." Or, "This is a difficult task. . .try again, but this time try to. . . ."

Progressive Practice

Practice should be progressive because the challenge and complexity of what the group is practising should continually and gradually in-

Reprinted, with special permission, of King Features Syndicate.

Perhaps Lucky Eddie needed feed forward, not feedback!

crease. This requires well-developed observation skills on the part of the instructor, but most people can recognise the more obvious signs that youngsters are ready to move on. An increase in chatter, a general restlessness, pointed looks at the instructor and sometimes inappropriate behavior all signal a need for progression.

Though it is important to progress, it is also important to revisit and review previous levels of performance, to take learners back to a point where they feel comfortable. This can happen early in a session or at any time that the group reaches a sticking point at the next level. This is very important in activities such as skiing, where fear is always lurking around the corner. Practice of previously acquired skill is always reassuring and can produce the positive mind-set the learner needs to attack new challenges.

Paced Practice

Practice should be paced in a way that ensures that the quality of the practice does not deteriorate because of fatigue or boredom. As suggested earlier, this means that the instructor must always be reading the group to pick up on the often subtle signs that they are not fully committed to the specific task, perhaps because they have already mastered it, or because they have found that it is too difficult.

Personalised Practice

Practice should be personalised to the extent that it is possible and necessary; instructors must always attempt to consider differences between individuals and be prepared to modify the practices to ensure that they meet the needs of those individuals. This is a higher-order instructional skill that is difficult to achieve except in activities such as weight training, where the very nature of the activity requires structuring workouts to individual athletes' capabilities.

The instructor must carry out all of these components of effective instruction with poise, patience and empathy, qualities that tend to make learners feel comfortable and thus encourage positive participation in the future. This is not always easy because sport educators themselves often live complex lives, full of stress and occasional trauma. This means that they do not always arrive at a session in a positive, cheerful frame of mind.

"Know yourself" has always been good advice, and if this type of situation arises it is better to tell the youngsters that you are a little out of sorts and let them play freely with as little intervention as possible. Just perhaps, their energy and commitment will revitalise you and bring a sense of perspective to your day.

Direct Versus Indirect Teaching Methods

Like all good working models, the Ps model has the potential to be developed into an advanced model, employing indirect teaching methods such as problem solving or guided discovery. For many years vigorous debate has taken place,

Modify practices to ensure they meet the needs of individuals.

especially in the United States, about teacher-directed versus indirect methods of instruction such as problem solving or guided discovery. In his seminal work *Teaching Physical Education: From Command to Discovery,* Muska Mosston (1966) implied that indirect methods were educationally more valuable than direct methods. Though this may indeed be true, sport educators should take a pragmatic rather than ideological view of this issue and select the most appropriate method for each situation.

When there is one clearly accepted best way to do something, as is the case with many techniques in sport, an instructor should use direct teaching methods to ensure efficient use of time. Here the instructor explains where and when the technique is used, provides a demonstration with clear teaching cues, sets up the practice task, observes the players' performance and then provides feedback before moving on to the next progression.

Where danger or discomfort may be involved, such as in heading a soccer ball, or when the activity is too complex to be mastered as a whole, as in diving, direct teaching methods allied to a progressive part approach should certainly be employed. The progressive part approach is commonly used in the teaching of activities such as Olympic gymnastics. The instructor introduces a small part of a complex activity and the gymnasts practise this part until they have mastered it. Now the next part is added and practised and the process continues until the whole activity has been mastered.

When it is important for youngsters to learn the principles underlying a technique, however, an indirect teaching method may be more effective. For example, in teaching ball control in soccer, guided discovery may help youngsters

identify the critical principles they must employ to be able to "catch" a ball with any part of the body. This gives them ownership of the knowledge gained so that they are more likely to remember and apply it. This has the additional advantage of presenting ball control as a dynamic flexible activity rather than a series of static trapping techniques. The guided discovery method, especially when used along with freeze replays, is the most effective way of helping players understand tactical or strategic principles and appreciate the logic of rules when they are introduced.

Be sure to study some of the specific references provided in the bibliography at the end of the book. The sources listed detail these important areas more thoroughly. In particular, Darryl Siedentop's text *Developing Teaching Skills in Physical Education* is an excellent resource.

Culminating Activities

Elite sport is characterised by a wide range of culminating activities that provide a focus for training and preparation. While the Olympic games and world championships in a vast range of sports are probably the most significant, a host of other culminating activities exist, including national, regional and state championships. In American sports, many teams view just making it to the playoffs as a major goal.

With this in mind, consider planning and organising culminating activities for children. This can involve a community or school Olympics, in-house tournaments, round-robin competitions, or visits to neighbouring communities or schools.

Play
Practice
Applied

CHAPTER

8

Play Practice in Action: An Introduction to the Practical Examples

The most powerful drive in the ascent of man is his pleasure in his own skill. He loves to do what he does well and, having done it well he loves to do it better.
—Jacob Bronowski

● ● ● ● ●

It is not possible for this book to deal with every one of the vast range of sports played around the world, simply because with many of them, coaches and sport educators have not yet tried the Play Practice approach. It is clear, however, that although some activities are ideally suited to this approach, others can benefit only from specific aspects of Play Practice, and some may gain nothing at all. Only when more sport educators try to develop play practices for their specific sports will we be able to determine what will or will not work.

The intent of the following sections is not to show how all the activities outlined should be taught or coached. They merely illustrate examples of the way sport educators can apply

Play Practice to make the teaching or coaching process more interesting and enjoyable. In fact, Play Practice will achieve its full potential only when sport educators develop their own ideas; as E.M. Forster caustically observed, "Spoon feeding in the long run teaches us nothing but the shape of the spoon."

Developing Play Practices

Sport educators can begin to use play practices in several ways:

- They can simply use ideas generated by others.
- They can directly transfer ideas that others have applied successfully in a similar sport.

- They can take ideas others have generated and modify them slightly.
- They can follow the process of reflective tinkering, which has proven so effective in the evolution of Play Practice.
- They can develop their ideas from scratch using the principles outlined in chapter 5.

The following examples illustrate the way in which each of these alternatives has led to worthwhile play practices.

We have already discussed the important role soccer has played in the evolution of the ideas and methods that underpin Play Practice. With its long tradition of teaching through small-sided conditioned games, soccer not only helped to lead the way to Play Practice but also provided many practical examples that can apply to the teaching and coaching of other sports.

Field hockey, which is conceptually identical to soccer, has already benefitted from this transfer of ideas. The differences between the two games, however, are such that coaches cannot transfer practices carelessly. To clarify this idea and to suggest the kinds of modifications that might be necessary in transferring practices from one activity to another, a vastly experienced Australian field hockey coach, Trevor Cibich, trialled all of the soccer play practices with elite field hockey players.

The best example of ideas borrowed and slightly modified are the sector games for cricket, softball and baseball. These games evolved from a Games for Understanding approach to teaching cricket originally developed by the Loughborough group. Though the games can still be used in this way, in Play Practice the emphasis has changed slightly, from understanding to simply striking and fielding. Any enthusiastic sport educator working with youngsters in any of these sports could quickly combine these different elements of skilled play to create even more satisfying play practices.

The Play Practice approaches to racquet sports, target sports, track and field and skiing have all evolved through a process of reflective tinkering, sometimes extending over many years. This gradualist approach carries few risks in that coaches can make small changes without significantly altering their normal instructional pattern. The most important advantage, however, is that it gives ownership of the inno- vation to the individuals concerned and proves to them that they can initiate worthwhile improvements in their own work.

The table tennis unit is especially significant because it introduces the notion of target games. Even more important, the original idea was developed by a second-year (sophomore) student teacher at the University of South Australia, Lorraine Cronshaw, as she struggled to find ways of inducing 12-year-old students to practise purposefully in a laboratory school setting.

The Play Practice approaches to both touch and American football were developed entirely from the principles outlined in this book, for a simple reason. This was necessary because no suitable resources existed for student teachers assigned to teach these games during major teaching blocks. Nothing could be found to suggest how they could introduce the complex game of American football to beginners, and all of the available materials on touch were based on a complete misunderstanding of the game's fundamental nature. Only by returning to the three questions

1. What do young people want from a sports experience?

2. Under what conditions do young people best learn?

3. What competencies do players need to play effectively?

were we able to develop a suitable sequence of practices for touch.

With American football the task was slightly more difficult because it was clearly impossible to deal with all aspects of this complex game in a limited time. The answer to the question "What would learners like to do in this sport experience?" provided the solution because in football, all participants want central roles involving throwing, catching or running with the ball!

The games in the volleyball section are important because although they use many of the principles of Play Practice, they were developed independently by Dave Eldridge. This confirms the statement in this book's preface that many experienced teachers and coaches would quickly identify similarities between Play Practice and their own methods. As soon as Eldridge,

Australia's leading high school volleyball teacher and coach, learned about the concept of Play Practice, he saw that his methods closely matched the Play Practice model. In fact, he immediately began to see ways he could improve his methods by applying the simple principle of "advantage defender" to improve his players' ability to deal with the double block.

Though this part provides many examples of Play Practice in action, the greatest rewards will come when sport educators try out their own ideas within the suggested overall framework because whole new worlds of possibilities are waiting to be discovered. It is clear, however, that some sports are not amenable to the Play Practice method. Tenpin bowling falls into this category simply because the game itself is a play practice and there is no point in modifying the rules or trying to simplify the demands of the activity. The only area where Play Practice might help beginners is in the introduction of a working model of bowling technique, because the advanced model requires special equipment, specific physical strength as well as hours of practice for mastery.

Emphasis on Games Sense and Technical Ability

The primary focus of this text is to suggest how sport educators can devise play practices to develop games sense and technical ability. In addition, many of these practices can also be used to improve agility, fitness and communication skills. The key issue is how much time is available because improving fitness, as with the development of advanced technical models, is very time intensive. Because of this, sport educators must carefully analyse the nature of the activity and the level of their players before deciding what to emphasise. Remember that the relative importance of each element of skilled play will change as players develop, especially if they are determined to move to elite levels of performance.

In the pole vault, for example, an initial emphasis on mastering a working technical model of the event will be replaced by a gradually increasing regimen of conditioning and drills as the young athlete moves toward championship level over a period of several years. Finally, once the physical parameters are established and the athlete's technique is sound, the keys to improved performance may lie in psychological skills training designed to improve the athlete's ability to cope with both intense training and the pressure of high-level competition. This process, which could last eight years or more, would see a young athlete move from one training session a week during the athletics season to a year-round commitment of over 20 sessions a week.

The major objective of this text, however, is to help sport educators better understand how to use play practices to help youngsters improve their technical ability and develop games sense. The following sections suggest ways instructors can develop these elements within the context of Play Practice.

Development of Technical Ability

The analysis in chapter 4 confirmed that skill in sport is a complex phenomenon and that technical ability, that is, the ability to control and direct a ball, shuttle or implement, is important in most activities and crucial in some. Achieving technical mastery is very time intensive, however, and often requires years of dedicated practice and training. Even maintaining high performance levels is time-consuming; top-class golfers will hit thousands of practice shots every week merely to retain their consistency, while elite table tennis players often practise for eight hours a day.

Because the formal sessions will rarely provide sufficient time to master complex techniques, it is vital to encourage youngsters to practise as much as possible on their own time. The instructor's role is to introduce players to a suitable technical model and provide enough practice for them to develop at least a cognitive understanding of it so they can practise intelligently on their own time.

The use of target games to teach table tennis is a good illustration of the way in which instructors can employ play practices to develop technical ability. In some activities, however, it may not be possible to use games to develop technical ability to the level necessary.

For example, the batting strokes in cricket involve specific techniques that children must master at least to the level of a working model

• • • • • • • • •

It is important to note the importance of providing many opportunities for informal play. At least two recent studies have confirmed that informal play and practice are important elements in the development of elite players, and little doubt exists that informal pickup games have been critical in the development of many great players.

Any community that wishes to make sport a core activity need only provide the facilities, equipment and basic leadership. Enthusiastic parents, even those with no background in a sport, can grow into many roles; they can certainly organise low-key competitions. All sports should be competition driven, so there should be a vast expansion in low-level leagues and tournaments with an atmosphere similar to that of pickup games. In fact, one attractive idea is to have all the youngsters who want to play turn up at a set time and organise a tournament for them based on limited-time games. Every child plays every other in a round-robin format. With team games, sides are randomly chosen and youngsters take turns in the various central roles and as officials. Consider using the fantasy game approach detailed in chapter 15 to add even more interest to the play experience.

• • • • • • • • • •

before they can play sector games. In this case the instructor must create the most efficient learning situations possible.

The volume and quality of technique practice for all sports can be improved in the structured sessions when the following factors are in place:

• Organisational and management strategies ensure that individual practice opportunities are maximised. As indicated in chapter 7, this is one of the most important aspects of effective instruction.

• There is enough equipment. This means a ball for each child in a basketball dribbling practice and a ball for every two for kicking and stopping practices in soccer. For invasion games, this implies the need for the smallest possible team sizes that are compatible with achieving the objectives of a play practice.

• Players clearly understand why a specific technique is important and how it fits into the overall pattern of the sport. Little doubt exists that if players understand the relevance of new learning to the game, they are more likely to practise purposefully.

• The practice is turned into a challenge. With novices this must be handled carefully so continual failure is avoided. For example, to ask children how many baskets they can score out of 10 attempts creates a situation where a few may fail to score even one. On the other hand, asking them to see how many shots it takes them to score 5 or 10 baskets gives everyone a chance to succeed. It is far easier to find extension tasks for the better players than to reassure a child who feels that they have failed. Above all, it is important to avoid comparisons between children and to emphasise individual performances and improvement.

• Learners can clearly see the results of their performance. Again, in some activities such as basketball shooting, knowledge of results is built in, but in others it may be necessary to create specific equipment or develop a suitable learning environment. The section on target games suggests how to do this.

• Performances are recorded. This demonstrates the importance attached to the learners' efforts and provides a datum against which to assess subsequent improvements. Sometimes it is valuable evidence that certain players are not as good as they think they are! The recording process was crucial in the evolution of the Play Practice approaches to cross-country running and track and field. It is important, however, to ensure that mere recording of performances does not obscure the importance of the augmented feedback essential for technical improvement.

• The amount of practice is clearly defined in terms of time or number of attempts. It is vital that practice does not just drift along for an indefinite period. Specify the practice time or number of attempts at the beginning and then "count down" the time or the number of attempts left. This is a strategy that aerobics instructors employ to great effect to maintain effort and intensity.

The use of what are termed buildups can be very valuable in any repetitive practice situation. For example, when practising digging a volleyball, instead of encouraging children to try to make as many consecutive attempts as possible from the beginning, ask them to try for two consecutive digs, then three, then four, and so on. When the sequence breaks down, they go back to two and build up again. This ensures more stable progression and a practice situation that rewards consistency.

Rapid improvement is more likely if the following statements are true:

- The practice is enjoyable, with an element of fun where possible.
- The practice involves a lot of variation around a specific technical theme.
- The practice follows an obvious progression.

The suggestions for teaching dribbling in chapter 10 provide examples of how to achieve all three of the goals stated here.

Where it is difficult to maintain high levels of motivation and commitment using the suggestions just outlined, it is important that learners know they will be playing a game and applying their new expertise within a clearly defined time frame. To do this a "parallel" approach to instruction is recommended. Instead of using long blocks of repetitive practice, the instructor simply switches from practising key techniques into a game and back again throughout a session. The combination of technical practice with mittball games in the teaching of lacrosse is a good example of this strategy.

Clearly, good pacing is important to ensure that the session has a good balance between active involvement and instruction. The instructor will need to use all of his or her skills in proximity, positioning and praise as well as the provision of feedback to ensure that learners stay positively involved in the practice task.

Working Models of Technique

The techniques elite players use are often advanced technical models. These exploit biomechanical principles; usually require special physical qualities such as strength, flexibility, excellent body control or superb hand-eye coordination and often depend on the use of specialised and expensive equipment. As suggested earlier, mastery often requires years of high-quality practice and training.

The concept of "working models of technique" evolved in parallel with the Play Practice approach. The major advantage of working models is that they enable young players to take part in the real activity much earlier than if they had to wait for mastery of more advanced techniques. They also make it possible to delay the introduction of advanced techniques until novices are better able to cope with their complexity and thus are less likely to fail or to develop bad habits. This is a very important consideration because once a youngster has overlearned a technique, it is very difficult to make changes, especially subtle ones, if the technique needs to be improved later.

> *T*he major advantage of working models is that they enable young players to take part in the real activity much earlier than if they have to wait for mastery of more advanced techniques.

As a sage once observed in relation to human progress, "Nothing fails like success." Success can often block the search for better ways of doing things, thus hindering further progress. It often leaves people trapped in a psychological safety net that they cannot escape and that makes further development impossible. Failure, on the other hand, often acts as a spur to improvement.

Developing Games Sense

At its simplest level, games sense means merely that players can get into the best possible position at the right time and make sensible decisions about what to do next. Many players appear to have been born with games sense and seem to know intuitively what to do in a game. **Intuition, however, is simply the ability to instantly access the distilled essence of past experiences to solve immediate problems.** It is a kind of preprogramming that ensures rapid, effective autonomous responses to the challenges players continually face, especially in ball games. This appears to be confirmed by Martin Peters, a former England soccer great, who said, after scoring a dramatic goal in a match against Germany,

With me it is instinct. I just try to work out where the ball will land and try to reach the spot at the same time. The thing is to come in behind, to bend the run if necessary so as to keep out of the range of vision of the defenders who are watching the ball. This is one case where it doesn't pay to advertise. So I don't shout for the ball or make a big fuss about moving. I try to look as though I am just loping about without any real purpose—although I know exactly where I am hoping to be at the end of a run. (Jones and Welton 1978, p. 135)

This statement is interesting because although he initially says that his ability to get into great scoring positions is instinctive, he then proceeds to explain in exact detail how he did it! It is a wonderful example of games sense in action.

It is highly likely that this apparently intuitive ability comes from playing in endless pickup games from an early age, and the opportunity to play and practise with more experienced players may be a key factor in this informal learning process. The postscript at the end of this book provides examples of studies that suggest this has been the case in the development of many elite performers, especially those growing up in small towns where competitions are more likely to include multiple age groups.

Intuitive or not, games sense is merely common sense applied to sport; so although it varies from one individual to another, young people can acquire games sense in the same way that they develop other human attributes. For example, in invasion games, some players have an almost uncanny ability to lose their defenders, if only for an instant, at critical moments. As Martin Peters suggested previously, they do this by exploiting the tendency of defenders to watch the ball and lose sight of the player they are guarding.

At the junior level, ball watching by defenders is a major reason that attackers score in all invasion games. The give-and-go or wall pass work well at this level because inevitably, defenders turn to watch the ball when it is played behind them or to the side; this allows attackers to easily cut past them on the blind side to receive the ball for an open shot. Even experienced players sometimes fall into the ball-watching trap. This occurs because defenders must always know where the ball is, even when they are closely covering their direct opponent.

Clever attackers exploit this by carefully watching their marker's head and eyes; the instant they see a hint that their opponent's vision is shifting toward the ball, they drift quietly in the opposite direction. In this way they make it even more difficult for the defender to watch both the attacker and the ball at the same time. Martin Peters would call this "making a curved run", but the same principle is employed in basketball when players make a move that many coaches' playbooks label—interestingly— "Blind Pig". In each case, the instant the attacker knows that they can no longer be seen, they cut behind the defender to receive the ball.

This is simply one example of how it is possible to analyse the complex and apparently intuitive behavior that good players demonstrate, in order to tease out simple principles that any willing youngster can learn. And it is easy to find others. Though the primary issue here is the link between intuition and games sense, at least the possibility exists that similar factors also influence other aspects of skilled play, including technique. It appears that great players in many sports have an as-yet unexplained capacity to pick up cues that enable them to predict the speed and direction of a ball—even before it is thrown or struck!

So it may be that the ability of the great players to be in the right place at the right time and to do the right thing when they get there derives from a combination of games sense and target prediction. The former enables them to predict their opponent's most likely response, whereas the latter enables them to compute the probable trajectory of the potential target, be it ball or shuttle, before it is delivered.

Though it is clear that athletes can develop complex behavior of this kind through simply playing and practising from an early age, it can also be developed through a well-structured instructional process. In fact, the real significance of games sense to sport educators is that understanding, which underpins games sense, can come in an instant. So while it may take months or even years to improve agility, fitness or technical ability, it is possible to become a better player almost instantaneously by learning how to exploit a rule, learning a new tactic or grasping a key element of strategy.

● ● ● ● ● ● ● ● ● ●

It is possible to become a better player almost instantly.

● ● ● ● ● ● ● ● ● ●

For example, in many American cities, almost every youngster can dribble a basketball, and many can drive to the basket to shoot a layup or dribble behind the back with either hand. But how many of them, if any, would know how to use the dribble draw tactic shown in figure 8.1, or know how to create a better passing angle by using a dribble as shown in figure 8.2? Yet a simple explanation or demonstration of these tactics can ensure that young players immediately grasp a simple idea that could make them more effective throughout their playing careers. This confirms that a sport educator who knows how to present the concepts that underpin games sense and who can then create learning situations that develop this important aspect of skilled play can have a powerful and lasting impact on young players.

Figure 8.1 Player O2 drives right drawing their defender, then reverses the ball to Player O1 who now has more space to work his defender. O1's defender will have sagged toward O2 and the ball.

Figure 8.2 Player O4 cannot pass in to Player O5 because Player X5 is overplaying high. Player O4 drives to the baseline to create a passing angle in to Player O5 who is rolling to the basket after pinning Player X5 high.

Teaching Games Sense

The fact that games sense is underpinned by an understanding of the rules, tactics and strategy provides a simple starting point. Play Practice provides an ideal vehicle to both introduce these concepts and help players translate understanding into action. With its emphasis on beginners playing the real game as early as possible and continuing to play in every session, Play Practice is arguably the most effective approach to teaching games yet devised. The early play experience gives youngsters a chance to appreciate the fundamental nature of an activity from the outset so it is easy for them to understand the relevance and importance of rules, tactics, strategy and techniques when these are introduced.

Since knowing the rules is critical to successful play, the instructor must emphasise the rules early on. Some primary rules, such as the handball rule in soccer and rules affecting player safety, need to be introduced before children begin to play a game. Most rules, however, are best introduced as suitable opportunities occur in the game and it becomes clear that a particular one is needed to ensure fair play or to allow the game to develop. The simplest way to introduce many rules is to let children play until an incident occurs that might lead to a dispute or even a confrontation, and then to stop play and discuss a possible solution to the problem.

The "held ball" situation in lead-up games to basketball or netball is a good example of this. The instructor simply freezes play and opens up a discussion about what has occurred, leading players to devise an appropriate rule. When a rule is introduced in the context of the game in this way, everyone involved is more likely to understand why it is necessary and to know how it is enforced. Involving the players in the process also means that perhaps they will be more likely to abide by the rule than if a higher authority simply imposes it on them.

The importance of introducing and clarifying key rules early on was also impressed on the author as a graduate assistant teaching an activity class of table tennis. Four weeks into the class, a student quietly and very seriously asked when the techniques of volleying would be introduced! A simple question, but one which exposed the fact that I had not made it clear at the beginning of the unit that—unlike in tennis—volleying the ball is not allowed in table tennis!

Many games have unwritten rules that players need to observe if play is to be fair and rewarding for everyone. These rules are part of the tradition of a game and in some sporting cultures are often more powerful than the ones that are written down. Since they are usually ethically driven and may run counter to a win-at-all-costs philosophy, they will often engender serious discussion among young players.

Many players and coaches alike regard tactics as a highly complicated aspect of games, important only at the elite level. This is not the case. In invasion games the aim is to take an opponent's goal. The best way to do this is to get the ball to an unmarked player who has the space and the time to shoot accurately. Tactics is simply the term that describes the way in which attackers combine with teammates to get open to receive the ball, *and* the way defenders move to prevent this from happening.

In many sports, tactics have been broken down into a series of rules, as in basketball, or into a coherent package of principles, as in soc-

cer. As young players begin to learn these rules or principles and to apply them intelligently, they are acquiring games sense. So the tactical education of novice defenders in invasion games starts simply with them learning how to mark an opponent and guard important space. At the same time, on offence they will be learning how to get open to receive a pass and beginning to master the more difficult task of choosing the best possible receiver.

Young players begin acquiring games sense as they apply the rules and principles of play intelligently.

In racquet sports, tactics are based on using intelligent positioning to defend one's own territory and the use of placement, high speed or spin to invade an opponent's. In badminton, for example, the player uses the clear, the smash and the drop shot in combination to force opponents into mistakes as they try to deal with the long/short tactics that the effective use of these techniques permit.

While good tactics will help players win many of the skirmishes in a game, a sound strategy will give both teams and players in individual sports a better opportunity to win a match and perhaps be successful throughout a season. Effective strategy has two components. The first is that strategy is based on the strengths of an individual or a team, and the second is that a strategy tries to exploit the specific weaknesses of a particular opponent when it is translated into a game plan.

Although strategy might seem the sole province of coaches, it adds another layer of complexity to games, thus making them even more interesting for all participants. So while it is not as important initially as the ability to understand and apply tactics, an appreciation of strategy can gradually grow, especially if youngsters begin to play in formal competitions. Another advantage of such an approach is that it brings an intellectual component to a sport experience that makes sport more interesting and challenging and at the very least will help youngsters become more perceptive spectators.

It is important to remember, however, that games sense is understanding in action. Youngsters will develop it only as they play in actual games and apply their knowledge to solve the problems they meet. At the same time, as they apply their understanding of rules and tactics, they will begin to develop other important aspects of games sense, such as the ability to assess their own strengths and weaknesses compared to their opponents. In team games, they will also learn the importance of factoring into their decisions a clear appreciation of their teammates' capabilities.

●●●●●●●●●●●

Games sense is understanding in action.

●●●●●●●●●●●

By its very nature, Play Practice ensures that players have the opportunity to develop games sense while giving sport educators an ideal vehicle to foster it. One of the major advantages of Play Practice is that it makes it possible to create a wide range of realistic, gamelike situations through which young players can enhance their understanding and develop their games sense. The structure this approach provides, along with the processes of shaping, focussing and enhancing play (detailed in chapter 6), enables an instructor to fast-forward a learning process that might otherwise take years of informal play to develop.

The key to the development of games sense lies in giving youngsters the chance to play in realistic scenarios that gradually increase in complexity. But it is not enough to allow play to continue without intervention. Instructors must teach for understanding, ideally through the use of freeze replays combined with a guided discovery approach or through more structured methods if necessary. This is because although a few individuals will grasp critical concepts unaided, most will do so only with guidance, and a few may need a clear demonstration and explanation of key points.

●●●●●●●●●●

Instructors must teach for understanding.

●●●●●●●●●●

The fact that games sense can be taught in this way has several advantages. It enables intelligent but less physically gifted youngsters to use their heads to compensate for lack of agility. They now have a template that enables them to read the game, anticipate what is likely to happen and begin to move into position early. Gaining possession of a loose ball in soccer is not simply a footrace in which the fastest player gets to it first; the thinker also has a chance. In racquet sports it means that players can be in position early with more time to select and execute a stroke. This allows a more diverse group of young people to participate successfully in sport.

Important though it may be in many sports, games sense must not be overvalued. It is vital that sport educators realise that understanding is the critical factor only in games such as chess. In ball games, skilled performance involves the melding of understanding and games sense with other elements of effective play such as agility, fitness and technical ability as well as intangible qualities such as courage and determination.

Even between ball games, marked differences exist. For example, compare an invasion game such as soccer with table tennis. In soccer, a player has to play without the ball for the majority of the game. This means that understanding the tactical principles of good play and applying them appropriately—using games sense—is at least as important as the ability to control and direct the ball. On the other hand, in table tennis the light ball and small playing surface mean that mastering the techniques required to control the ball with topspin or backspin are essential if a player wants to even keep the ball on the table. Thus, while tactics become very important later on, technical ability is the key to early success in table tennis.

The recognition of this simple fact is the key to the success of the Play Practice approach to teaching sport. It accepts that skilled performance in sport is a very complex phenomenon that varies from one activity to the next. Sport educators have the task of identifying and prioritising the crucial elements that may be limiting the development of their athletes in a particular sport. If lack of understanding or games sense is holding back development, they must improve these through a clearly defined sequence of play practices. If technical ability is the limiting factor, they must highlight it through specific games and challenges and give it priority over understanding, as the table tennis example suggests.

Games sense is not a mystical key to success in sport but is merely one element, albeit an important one, among many that may contribute to skilled performance in sports. At higher levels of performance, the limiting factors may be poor agility or fitness, low motivation or an inability to stay focussed or even to cope with winning. In some sports, lack of power or flexibility may have a crucial impact on performance. Sport educators working with athletes at this level must quickly identify the crucial weaknesses and develop training programs to eliminate them.

Of equal significance for sport educators is the fact that the relative importance of all the elements of effective play, including technical ability and decision making, may change from one age group or performance level to the next.

Field Invasion Games

Soccer is a game for gentlemen played by hooligans, rugby is a game for hooligans played by gentlemen, American football is a game for hooligans played by chess pieces, Australian rules football is a game for hooligans played by hooligans.
—Anonymous

● ● ● ● ●

The field invasion games of soccer, Rugby Union and Rugby League and American football (gridiron) all evolved from a common ancestor that was played in Britain in the early 19th century. This ancestor was itself a composite of many other versions of football that had been played there since the Middle Ages and was probably very similar to Gaelic football, a sport still played on a highly competitive basis in Ireland.

Although field hockey and lacrosse initially seem unrelated to these games, they are in fact conceptually and tactically very similar to soccer. That one appears to have evolved on the Indian subcontinent and the other in North America is a testament to the great popularity of games of this kind.

Soccer

Like all of the great games of the world, association football, or soccer as it is more gener-

ally known, is simple in concept but complex in practice. Though the aim of the game is simply to place the ball in a goal positioned deep in "enemy" territory, players at the highest level must be agile and fit and possess high levels of technical ability. Above all, they must have well-developed games sense. This is because soccer is a game of fluid, almost continuous movement and frequent unexpected changes of possession. Except in dead-ball situations such as corner kicks and free kicks, play can rarely be structured or controlled by the coach, so every player must be capable of reading the play and making sound decisions. This is well illustrated by the analysis of what is required to play soccer. Good soccer players

- know the rules and understand the way they structure the game and how they influence strategy and tactics,
- understand the basic concepts of strategy

91

and how to apply them to develop a game plan against a specific opponent,

- understand and can instantly apply tactical principles so that they are always moving into the best possible positions to help their team,
- can "read the game" and anticipate developments well ahead of the action,
- are agile enough to get to the ball ahead of opponents and get into good positions at exactly the right moment,
- are fit enough to keep on moving into good positions while maintaining a high level of concentration and technical expertise for the entire game,
- are technically competent so that they can control and direct the ball quickly and accurately,
- can make good strategic decisions,
- can make good tactical decisions,
- can make and execute good technical decisions,
- are always ready to play and determined to give their best at all times,
- are mentally and morally resilient and will never give up, and
- understand the true nature of sport and respect opponents.

In attack these players can

- create space for themselves by moving into good positions at the right time,
- create time because the opponent must take time to close the distance,
- use this space and time to be skillful,
- indicate where they want the ball delivered,
- scan the play as they receive the ball,
- decide what move to make—shoot, pass or run,
- select the best possible receiver,
- deliver the ball to the right spot at the right speed for the receiver, and
- create space and time for their teammates, who in turn can be more skillful.

In defence the players use their knowledge of tactics to

- respond instantly to a change of possession,

- ensure there is always pressure on the ball,
- cover the defender who is putting pressure on the ball,
- closely mark opponents who move into dangerous positions, and
- deny important space to attackers.

In addition to all of this, these good players remain controlled and calm yet aggressive.

*S*port educators working with other games may find that carrying out this kind of task analysis to develop a "job description" for players is a valuable exercise in clarifying both the nature of the game and the demands it makes on players.

While agility and fitness are clearly important elements in skilled play and cannot be ignored, sport educators working with young players should focus on the development of games sense and technical ability. In Play Practice these two elements are developed in parallel. Youngsters move from a game to technical practice and then quickly back into conditioned mini games so that they always apply their newly acquired techniques in "real" situations. This helps them understand the importance of improving their technical ability while clarifying the nexus between technique and tactics.

In soccer the tactical component of games sense is based on the principles of play developed by English soccer coaches. These principles begin with attackers trying to play behind defenders, thus penetrating the defence to score, while defenders naturally try to stop them. To understand how these principles apply in a game situation, consider a moment when a change of possession occurs.

As shown in figure 9.1, O1, who has just gained possession of the ball, must immediately try to penetrate the defence by passing or carrying the ball forward. Since this moment of transition provides attackers with a good chance to outnumber defenders and to score, it is important for players to learn how to exploit it. So other attackers move into position to support the ball player and provide a range of passing options to ensure possession of the ball and to break down the defence. O2 and O3 move close to offer easy options, O4 and O5 use the principle of width to outflank the defence, and O6, O7 and O8 use mobility to run forward to penetrate the defence or create space for teammates by pulling defenders away from critical areas.

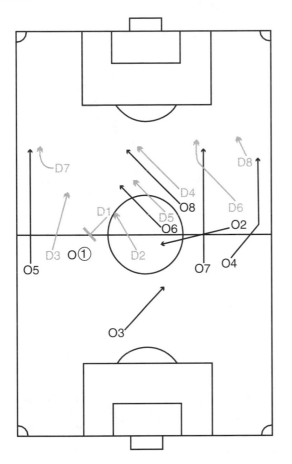

Figure 9.1 The principles of play in the moments after transition.

When faced with a well-organised defence, attackers may need to do something unexpected, to improvise, in order to wrong foot defenders and thus create the time and space for a strike at goal.

Figure 9.1 also shows how the defence tries to counter these moves and stop any penetration. The nearest defender, D1, instantly tries to delay, channel and pressure the ball so that it cannot be rapidly pushed forward. The time bought in this fashion allows teammates D2 and D3 to move goal side of the ball to provide depth

in defence, while D4, D5 and D6 ensure concentration to guard important space and prevent easy penetration. Simultaneously, D7 and D8 move to balance the defence so that it cannot be outflanked. All simultaneously pick up, follow and cover potential receivers. Because they are often under pressure, defenders must always play with control and restraint to avoid careless mistakes near the goal.

Paradoxically, despite its complexity, soccer is a very easy game to introduce to beginners if the instructor follows the sequence outlined here and especially if the "teaching grid" is used effectively. Originally devised by English coaches to complement their understanding approach to teaching soccer, the teaching grid is one of the most useful devices in sport education and can apply to a range of games, including rugby, American football, lacrosse and Aussie rules.

The basic pattern is a 20-yard by 30-yard rectangle subdivided into six 10- by 10-yard squares as shown in figure 9.2. Note that these dimensions are not sacrosanct; you can modify them to suit the specific abilities of any group.

Using cones, however, you can easily convert the basic pattern into

 a. Basic 20 x 30 playing area (5-v-5 game)

 b. 6 x 10 x 10 squares

 c. 3 x 20 x 10 corridors (for dribbling games)

 d. 30 x 20 field (continuous 3-v-1 or 3-v-2 games)

 e. 3 x 10 x 10 squares

 f. 30 x 20 field for continuous 4-v-3 go-for-goal games

Clubs and schools would be well advised to mark out as many of these grids as possible, preferably on dead ground that is not normally used for match play. This will save an immense amount of time in formal sessions while also providing areas for informal play. Children always like to play with goals, even mini goals, so any enthusiastic sport educator should try to make small soccer goals available.

A Possible Teaching Sequence

The following sequence of practices will be effective in helping youngsters learn the primary rules, develop technical ability and begin to understand the principles of effective tactical play.

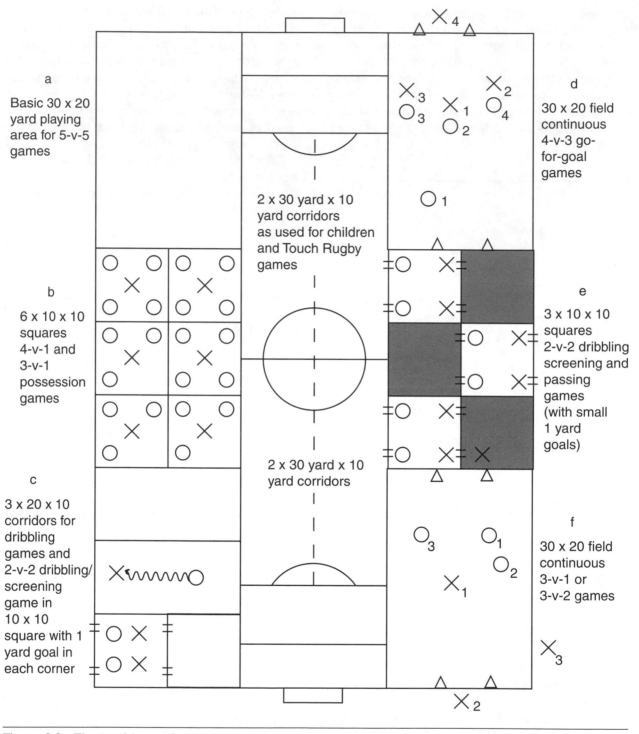

Figure 9.2 The teaching grid.

1. After outlining the basic rules relating to handballs, kicking or tripping opponents, gridiron-style tackling and so forth, begin with small-sided games—5 to 7 a side—on a pitch 50 yards long. Set up crude 8-yard-wide goals using cones or even sport bags, but dispense with sidelines or goal lines. In this way play can continue unchecked by any boundary and even continue behind the goal. This eliminates the need to introduce the rules for goal kicks, corner kicks and throw-ins and also ensures a free-flowing game.

This simple game gives the instructor a

chance to assess the players and determine teaching priorities. It can be played with or without goalkeepers; if goalkeepers are used, they should play as "rush goalies", that is, they play as field players but are allowed to use their hands to stop direct shots at goal. To ensure that the youngsters do not force the least-competent players to stay in goal, make a rule that says a new player must become goalie after every score. Note that in this game, and in every other play practice, it is essential that players use balls of a size and weight appropriate to their age and ability. If in doubt, always use smaller, lighter balls with beginners; volleyballs are ideal for very young beginners.

2. In pairs standing 10 to 15 yards apart, players kick and stop the ball using the inside of the foot and the instep. Use cones to create 2-yard "goals" as targets. Improving kicking ability is an ongoing priority in this game; instructors will find that giving youngsters the opportunity to shoot at goals—especially a real goal—will always produce more purposeful practice.

3. Play 4-v-1 possession games in 10-yard squares using the teaching grid (figure 9.2b). This game introduces the need to control the ball quickly, read the defender's position, decide which teammate is best positioned to receive the ball and then play the ball to that teammate. This practice introduces reading the play, decision making and accurate execution under pressure from a defender. All subsequent play practices contain these elements, which gradually increase in complexity.

The aim of this game is to make five consecutive passes, and then a new player becomes the defender. A defender who manages to touch the ball during play switches places with the last player to touch the ball.

4. Play 3-v-1 possession games in 10-yard squares (see figure 9.2b).

This play practice incorporates all of the elements of the game outlined in step 3 but also requires players to move intelligently to make an angle for the pass and therefore begin to learn the principle of support in attack. Most importantly, it also introduces the concept of playing in triangles. The same rules apply as in the preceding game.

5. Play 5-v-2 possession games with unlimited space. Now the ball player must deal with the

pressure from the nearest or first defender *and* lift his or her vision from the ball to see the second defender before deciding where to pass the ball. Vision, or the ability to read the display, is a critical aspect of good play in soccer, as in any invasion game, and must continually be emphasised. The instructor must continually focus play by emphasising the need to support the ball player and to create passing triangles. Though a simple concept, the passing triangle is important because it is the smallest attacking unit that can ensure both width and depth in attack.

This is a crucial progression because it illustrates the importance of really understanding the nature of skill in sport. The logical progression from 4-v-1 would seem to be a 4-v-2 in the 10- by 10-yard square. But this simply would not work with inexperienced players. In a 4-v-1 situation the ball player just needs to play the ball past the first—and only—defender, and the pass will be successful. They can watch the ball and at the same time know where the defender is, even if they can see only their feet. This means they can keep their head down as they receive and pass the ball.

With two defenders, however, the situation changes completely. The novice ball player must now deal with the pressure from the first defender *and* look up to see where the second defender is. This is a far more difficult task for beginners, and play will break down repeatedly. The 5-v-2 practice outlined here is played with no boundaries and gives youngsters more time and space as well as another passing option so that they are far more likely to be successful.

6. Play continuous 3-v-1 "go-for-goal" games. This game is one of the most popular play practices in basketball, where coaches use it primarily to teach the principles of the fast break. It can be modified and applied in many different ways to many invasion games.

The format is simple and is shown in figure 9.2d. Three attackers (O) are confronted by one defender (X) as they go for goal. After a score or a change of possession, the lone defender is joined by two teammates, who have been waiting behind the goal, and they begin to counterattack against a single player of the opposing team, whose teammates drop out of play until their side regains the ball and they can again join in as attackers.

The game flows continuously as each player

in turn takes on the role of defender, who must learn to delay and channel the ball. Once again, the emphasis in attack must be on width to ensure ball possession and to outflank the defender. In defence, stress the principle of delaying the ball player and containing the attack for as long as possible.

To alter the balance between attack and defence and thus create an even more pertinent practice, you can vary the size of the goal. A large goal makes it easy for attackers to score from long range with minimal passing, whereas a smaller goal forces them to pass more often to set up a scoring shot. In this way it is possible to use the goal as a "defender", so a 3-v-1 game becomes a 3-v-1 1/2 game.

7. Play continuous 3-v-2 go-for-goal games (see figure 9.2d). Now the first defender can pressure the ball while the second defender covers the goal and looks for interceptions; this means that attackers must pass skillfully, use the principle of support to retain possession and the principles of width and mobility to pull defenders out of position and create space for a shot at goal.

8. Play continuous 4-v-3 go-for-goal games with a "schemer" (see figure 9.2f). This is similar to the previous game, but the third defender makes outflanking moves difficult by balancing the defence as well as providing more cover. With cover behind them, the first defender can put even more pressure on the ball player. Attackers must therefore be patient and counter this pressure by playing the ball back to a supporting player, the schemer, to retain possession and change the point of attack. With three defenders to beat, attackers must now begin to understand how clever movement can be used to create space and perhaps a shooting chance for a teammate.

The function of the schemer is similar to that of the point guard in basketball—that is, to bring other players into the game. This is often a good way to use better players, particularly if the instructor enforces a condition that the schemer can never move in front of the ball in attack or can have only two touches. One of the schemer's major roles is to switch play from side to side to outflank defenders and continually use the principle of mobility to create gaps in the defence as they go for goal. As players develop, it is important to give all youngsters an opportunity to take on this role, perhaps in tandem with a more experienced player who can coach them during play.

9. Play 5-v-5 mini games on a 50- by 30-yard pitch with no goalkeepers. This gives young players the opportunity to apply all they have learned about passing in a more competitive situation but with plenty of space and therefore time to work with it. By conditioning the game and varying the size of the goal, the instructor can create very specific and pertinent play practices that can emphasise any aspect of technique or skill.

In all of these games, the emphasis is on keeping the ball on the ground with low passes. This makes it easier for the ball player and emphasises the need for receivers to move into good positions. **Be sure to remember that you should continually revisit all of the games outlined here, especially the go-for-goal games, to emphasise various elements of effective play.** In the 4-v-3 game, for example, attackers will find that it is difficult to break down the defence without improvising, and this will force them to find that delicate balance between retaining possession of the ball and risking it in an attempt to break through. Defenders, on the other hand, will learn the importance of good positioning, patience, not selling themselves in foolish attempts to get the ball and remaining cool under pressure. This is the time to point out that in soccer, more goals are scored because of mistakes by defenders than through great moves by attackers.

While the emphasis of this chapter so far has been on introducing the game to young players, Play Practice can be used at all levels to develop both technical ability and understanding. The following games are examples of pertinent play practices conditioned to develop specific aspects of the skill of passing.

10. With young players, play 5-v-5 games of "long soccer" on an 80- by 30-yard pitch with 20-yard goals. With experienced players it is possible to simply divide the normal pitch down the middle to create two 100- by 40-yard pitches. The long, narrow pitch with big goals encourages players to make longer passes and to shoot from farther away. To do this they must lift their vision to scan play 30 or even 40 yards away, a crucial aspect of passing in the full game. Even though the essential theme is passing, other aspects of play will become important. For example, longer passes will mean the ball is in the air much more of the time, creating many more opportunities for players to control high balls.

At this point the instructor can introduce the techniques needed to control high balls. In the Play Practice method, players learn the principles of "catching" a ball with the body—obviously without using the hands. These principles can be either directly taught or drawn from the players using a guided discovery method. In brief, they are as follows:

- Move quickly toward the flight path of the ball.
- Choose a body surface to control the ball—the bigger and softer, the better.
- Let the body give to "catch" the ball.

Because this approach encourages movement and the flexible use of any body part to control the ball, it is far better than the old, static trapping approach used in traditional methods. The instructor can introduce the throw-in at this time and use it to deliver the high balls needed for players to practise this technique.

11. Two-touch soccer is a conditioned game in which players are allowed only two touches of the ball at any one time. This eliminates dribbling, encourages good ball control and forces youngsters to become aware of potential receivers even before they get the ball. It encourages all attacking players to support the ball player intelligently and to use good, clear calling to tell the player how much space and time they have to control and direct the ball. This game, as well as the progression to one-touch soccer, prepares players to pass accurately and quickly in the limited space and time near their opponent's goal.

12. Four-goal soccer in figure 9.3 can teach players the importance of using cross-field passes to switch play away from heavily defended areas. With a large goal in each corner of the pitch, attackers facing a strong defence on one side can switch play to the other side for a more open shot at goal.

The preceding examples demonstrate the complexity of teaching passing, a skill that has traditionally been viewed as fairly simple. Each of these play practices is structured to ensure pertinent and progressive practice. In all of them, the coach can manipulate the conditions, the space/time variables or both to shape learning situations that are even more pertinent to the full game and that are also appropriate to the players' ability.

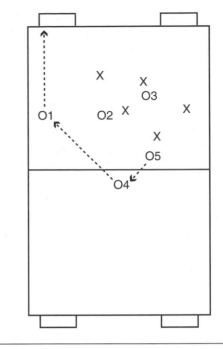

Figure 9.3 Four-goal soccer—switching play to outflank the defence.

Varying the size of the playing area can give players either more or less time to be skillful, that is, to assess the situation and make decisions. In the same way, changing only one condition can shape many other aspects of play. For example, with the condition that goals can be scored only with the head, players will quickly work out that this is far easier when the ball is crossed in the air from the flanks. This in turn will encourage the use of width in attack and lead to more attempts by ball players to dribble past defenders so that they can create the space and time to make a good cross. The instructor can then focus play on any of these elements—for example, working on near- and far-post positioning for the header or continually stressing the importance of taking on and dribbling past defenders on the wings.

Players can develop both heading and dribbling though simple games. Because of the possibility of injury if a ball is incorrectly headed, instructors should use a direct teaching approach in which they carefully monitor each progression. It is possible, however, to quickly move to a "throw, head, catch" game. With 5 to 7 players on a 20- by 30-yard pitch, the goal is the entire 20-yard goal line, across which players must head the ball for a score.

The game is simple, but it always takes beginners a few minutes to grasp. After a jump ball to start play, the player with the ball tosses it in the air for a teammate to head forward for another teammate to catch. The players repeat this process until a goal is scored. The opposition can gain possession only if a player on their side manages to get a head to the ball at any time and the header is caught by a teammate.

Dribbling is a word that describes two different phenomena in soccer. On the one hand, it means merely running with the ball close to the feet, but on the other it means trying to beat an opponent. Though you can introduce the basic principles of running with the ball in the very first session, you should introduce dribbling past opponents much later, after players have become competent team players through well-developed passing skill.

Dribbling past a defender involves a combination of ball control and agility, that is, a change of direction, a change of pace or a combination of both. These can evolve from simple ball-control practices in which children learn to change direction and speed while retaining possession of the ball.

At this point the children can play simple 1-v-1 games in a grid. Here the attacker tries to get past an opponent to reach the goal on the other side of the grid. After a score or a change of possession, players switch roles and repeat, playing until one of the two scores three goals. This is tiring play, and the necessary breaks give an instructor the chance to once again draw out the key principles.

By continually changing opponents, players can make a considerable amount of progress. Following this with 5-v-5 games played on 30- by 20-yard pitches where players can score a goal only by dribbling the ball over the goal line will help players begin to develop a contextual feeling for this aspect of play. This game will also teach players to value space and apply all of the principles of play. If you divide this pitch into thirds, youngsters can begin to understand that they should try to dribble past opponents only in the attacking third, where losing the ball is not going to cause major problems for their team.

The following game illustrates the Play Practice approach at a higher level. To improve ball control, dribbling and especially shielding the ball, organise a 2-v-2 game in a 10- by 10-yard square. With each pair able to score in either of two small goals, this game shapes and focusses play very powerfully (figure 9.2c).

The ball player now has only one potential receiver, who is likely to be closely marked, so passing will be difficult. Pressured by their own marker, they must learn to shield the ball while looking to pass the ball, shoot for a goal or dribble past their opponent to put the ball in. This is a tough game even for experienced players, but it will gradually improve the player's ability to protect the ball under pressure and force them to lift their vision while doing so.

It is important that players learn the purpose and place of dribbling in soccer—in other words, how to apply games sense to dribbling. When a player tries to dribble the ball past an opponent, there is always the chance of losing possession. This is a risk worth taking near the opposition goal because if the dribbler is successful, a score may result; however, it can never be justified near one's own goal because a loss of possession there may result in an easy goal conceded.

The preceding examples provide some indication of how to apply the principles of Play Practice to soccer. The possibilities are limited only by the sport educator's commitment and imagination.

Field Hockey

As an invasion game, field hockey is conceptually similar to other games of this kind such as basketball, lacrosse and especially soccer. In fact, recent changes to the offside and obstruction rules have brought it even closer tactically to these games. Because of this similarity, instructors can use many of the play practices outlined in the soccer section in the teaching and coaching of hockey.

Before attempting to transfer play practices between similar games, however, be sure to consider the differences between them. This is in itself a valuable exercise for sport educators because it forces them to carefully analyse both games, a process that may in turn lead to the development of important new insights about the fundamental nature of the game they are most involved with.

The first and most obvious difference between soccer and hockey is the potential danger that exists when a careless individual with a stick whacks a small, hard ball in close proximity to others. For this reason it may be advisable to begin instruction with a soft ball and immediately condition all play practices so that the ball stays below knee height. It is vitally important to find or develop more user-friendly equipment when introducing field hockey to beginners. With very young children, consider using small foam balls and plastic ice hockey sticks, and allow them to play the ball with both sides of the stick.

The second difference between these two games, which is far more subtle than the first, is that the space/time equation is much less favorable to attackers in hockey than it is in soccer. As we have seen earlier,

$$space = time =$$
$$skill\ (good\ decisions\ and\ good\ execution)$$

A hockey pitch is smaller than a soccer pitch, especially in the key dimension of width. Most importantly, the shooting/scoring zone is restricted by the rules and is much smaller than in soccer.

The key issues are as follows:

- Whereas soccer is a game played in three dimensions, hockey is essentially played in only two—especially in the scoring zone. This is because lofting the ball is difficult in hockey, so it is much harder to play the ball into the space behind defenders.

- Hockey's much narrower pitch means that it is easier for defenders to prevent penetration by balls played along the ground.

- The small goal and restricted shooting area mean that attackers must take the ball much closer to the goal for a shot than in soccer.

All of these factors make it easier for the defenders to deny space and closely mark attackers, especially in the scoring zone. With space limited, time is limited, and it is thus more difficult to be skillful.

When you factor in the problem of controlling and directing a small ball with a long lever, it is clear that attacking play is much more demanding in hockey than in soccer, especially for beginners. This problem is further exacerbated by another significant difference between the two games, which even hockey coaches rarely address. A soccer ball can be controlled and directed by any part of the body, with the exception of the hands, whereas in hockey, players can use only one side of the stick. This means that players must pre-position the whole body as they prepare to control and direct the ball. As a result, in hockey it is not enough for players to support the ball player at the right distance and angle; they must also be thinking ahead about how they will take the ball and considering passing options before they do so.

The one area where attackers have an advantage compared to soccer is in the rules that make any defensive infringement in the circle potentially very costly. Because of this, many goals in hockey come from short corners that occur as the result of defensive errors, both forced and unforced.

The implications of all of this are as follows:

- The fast break is as important in field hockey as in any invasion game—getting there "fustest with the mostest" is a high priority.

- Technical ability must be given a high priority in both passing and dribbling.

- Players must exploit tactical width to provide new angles of attack and to pull gaps in the defence. The ability to disguise the direction of a pass until the last instant is very important.

- Attackers must counter defensive pressure on the ball by maintaining depth in attack. This also helps the attackers retain possession and gives the schemer the chance to continually change the point of the attack.

- As often as possible, the ball must be played or taken into the circle by a dribbler.

So although sport educators can use many of the play practices recommended for soccer in hockey as well, they must sometimes modify them or use them to emphasise different elements of play. For example, the 4-v-1 and 3-v-1 games played in the coaching grid must emphasise good body position when preparing to receive the ball. With experienced players they can introduce or develop the ability to disguise the direction of a pass until the very last instant.

While experienced players will be able to use the go-for-goal play practices detailed in the soccer section with little modification, with beginners the attackers should be given an extra advantage in the early stages. For example, a 3-v-2 continuous go-for-goal game becomes 4-v-2, and 4-v-3 becomes 5-v-3. In each case the extra player is a schemer, a position that you can initially assign to the best player but then rotate as other youngsters improve. The schemer, who is not allowed to go forward of the ball, is crucial because they ensure depth in attack, even when enthusiastic teammates run forward, leaving the ball player under pressure. From their deep position they must be prepared to switch play from side to side and be ready to make penetrating passes if defenders leave gaps in the centre of the defence.

You can use many but not all of the other play practices detailed in the soccer section to develop games sense and technical ability in hockey. In addition, all of the dribbling practices detailed in the basketball section are appropriate for beginners. However, using the principles of Play Practice, hockey coaches should be prepared to develop games specifically for their sport. An example is illustrated in figure 9.4, which shows a slight modification to the usual go-for-goal games. In this variation, attackers score goals by dribbling the ball into one of three small circles marked inside the shooting area. This play practice encourages attackers to use the dribble wisely and to redirect the ball if it becomes clear that they cannot penetrate further because of good defensive play.

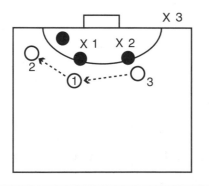

Figure 9.4   3-v-2 play practice for hockey with referee. Three attackers, O1, O2, and O3, interpass the ball against two defenders, X1 and X2, and try to get open to dribble the ball into the three-foot diameter circles positioned as shown. Player X3 can be a referee. Each team has 5 to 10 attempts on offence.

This is an important concept because, as with soccer, players must learn where and when to take on opponents in a dribble. Though the concept of the attacking third is useful, it is even more vital that attackers understand the importance of using the dribble to take on defenders in the circle. Often this will force a defensive error, which in turn leads to a short corner and thus a good shot at goal. In this context players with the ball can learn the importance of exploiting the obstruction rule to create fouls.

As youngsters improve, they can move to 5-v-5 games played on a half pitch. If possible, use real goals, but, as with all play practices for hockey, do not have a goalkeeper. The goalkeeper in hockey is a very specialised and potentially dangerous position, and those who play it must be carefully prepared and equipped for the role. Again, this is different than in soccer, where rush goalies can be used from the outset.

Once again, it is important for instructors to determine a suitable entry level for their players. Always bear in mind that you can revisit even the simplest play practice to achieve specific outcomes.

Lacrosse

Since lacrosse is conceptually very similar to soccer, once again instructors can employ the basic Play Practice approach to that game. Obviously, the technical demands are different, but this is easy to deal with.

Because catching and throwing a ball with a lacrosse stick presents a difficult challenge for beginners, youngsters need considerable practice before they can play a proper game using this equipment. Play Practice uses mittball and gripball, games created especially to solve this problem. Use mittball at the beginning of the first session and at appropriate times through a unit. Instead of handing children a lacrosse stick, give them a softball mitt to wear instead. Catching with the glove and throwing with the free hand, youngsters can immediately begin to play a keep-away game in which teams of four or five players try to retain possession of the ball for a set number of passes, for example, 5 or 10, while their opponents try to intercept the ball and start their own passing sequence. Gripball is essentially the same game, except players use special balls and Velcro-covered "grippers" instead of gloves.

With some groups it may be better to play a mittball or gripball version of the full game of lacrosse immediately. This introduces beginners to the fundamental nature of lacrosse and especially to the primary rules of no contact and a four-second carry. The children therefore learn the principles of attack and defence before attempting the difficult task of controlling and directing the ball with the crosse. In this way, early in the unit they experience the joy of playing. They are then more likely to be motivated to practise lacrosse techniques purposefully so that they can quickly move on to play the challenging and interesting real game of lacrosse.

Mittball can also be used whenever an instructor wishes to return to the simple joy of playing a game or to emphasise a particular tactical principle, such as attacking from behind the goal. For example, if the students use mitts to play Irish lacrosse, in which the goals are turned to face outward instead of inward, play is shaped to force attackers to play behind the goal, something that playing other invasion games may not have prepared them for.

Clearly, the instructor cannot neglect technique if children are to move from mittball to the real game of lacrosse. You can build practices to develop the techniques of scooping, catching, carrying and throwing the ball into any session to ensure development of at least a working technique. One simple motivational practice to use with beginners is shown in figure 9.5. Here, player 1 runs forward, carrying the ball to a "shooting mark" approximately 10 yards from an open goal, that is, one with no net so that the ball passes through. It is collected by player 2, who scoops it up and delivers a long pass out to player 3. Player 3 repeats the process by running at the goal and shooting. Players maintain continuity by following their pass or shot. This is a good practice for up to six players sharing the three active slots.

Using the parallel method, instructors can switch from technique practices of this kind to any of the mini games detailed in the soccer section. Once again, the 3-v-1, 3-v-2 or 4-v-3 continuous go-for-goal games described in the soccer section (numbers 6, 7 and 8 in the teaching

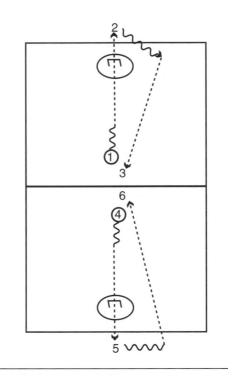

Figure 9.5 Lacrosse drill.

sequence) will prove especially valuable. With some groups it may be necessary to have an extra attacker, as suggested for these games in field hockey.

The format for a continuous 3-v-1 go-for-goal game is identical to that for soccer and shown in figure 9.2d. Three attackers (O) are confronted by one defender (X) as they go for goal. After a score or a change of possession, the single defender is joined by two teammates, X1 and X2, who have been waiting behind the goal, and they begin to counterattack against a single player of the opposing team. The game flows continuously, with each player in turn taking on the role of defender, who must learn to delay and channel the ball. Once again, the emphasis in attack is the use of the triangle to ensure ball possession and wide attacking opportunities. In defence, stress the principle of delaying the ball player and containing the attack for as long as possible.

In continuous 3-v-2 go-for-goal the first defender can pressure the ball while the second defender covers and looks for interceptions; this means that attackers must pass skillfully, use the principle of "support to retain possession" and the principles of "width" and "mobility" to pull defenders out of position to create space for shot at goal.

A continuous 4-v-3 go-for-goal with a schemer as shown in figure 9.2f is similar to the previous game but with a third defender providing more cover and making outflanking moves difficult by balancing the defense. With good cover, the first defender can now put even more pressure on the ball player. Attackers must therefore be patient and counter this pressure by playing the ball back to a supporting player, often the schemer, to retain possession and change the point of attack. With three defenders to beat, attackers must now begin to understand how clever movement by one player can be used to create space and perhaps a shooting chance for a teammate.

The function of the schemer is similar to that of the point guard in basketball, that is to bring other players into the game. This often is a good way to use better players, particularly when there is a "condition" that the schemer can never go forward of the ball in attack or that they can only have two touches at any one time. The attackers must now try to switch play from side to side to outflank defenders and continually use the principle of "mobility" to create gaps in the defense as they go for goal.

Here it must be stressed that the go-for-goal games can be continually revisited to emphasise various elements of effective play. In the 4-v-3 games for example, attackers will find that it is difficult to break down the defense without improvising, and will be forced to find that delicate balance between retaining possession of the ball and risking it in an attempt to break through. Defenders on the other hand will learn the importance of good positioning, of patience and not selling themselves in foolish attempts to get the ball and remaining cool under pressure.

The Play Practice approach to introducing lacrosse therefore involves the following:

- Mittball so children learn the principles of play through playing

- Technique practice so children learn how to control and direct the ball with the crosse

- Small-sided games so children learn how to apply the techniques skillfully in a real situation as well as gain a working knowledge of the rules

- Intelligent intervention by the instructor to focus and enhance play

American Football (Gridiron)

American football, or gridiron as it is called in some countries, is arguably the most tactically complex ball game played. It is sometimes difficult to appreciate that it developed from the same roots as games as diverse as soccer, Rugby Union, Australian rules football and Gaelic football.

Because of its complexity, the potential for injury and the cost of the protective equipment required, American football is rarely if ever played informally. Flag football was developed in an attempt to retain the game's crucial elements while reducing both the injuries and the need for expensive equipment. Flag football enables ordinary people, even those who are unfit and possess very limited skill, to play informally in pickup games and formally through intramural competitions. It is likely that more players take part in flag football each year in the United States than play the real game.

Perhaps because American football is so deeply embedded in North American culture, most people there grow up with a basic understanding of how to play it. Interestingly, though it is **coached** very intensely from junior high school on, it is rarely **taught** in schools. It is probable that many flag football players played gridiron to a certain level and then, as is common in the American sport system, were not good enough to play at the next and therefore moved "down" to flag.

Even in countries where it is not a part of the normal sporting culture, American football still sparks keen interest. The question is, how can sport educators best introduce this very complex activity to youngsters who may have only seen it played on television and who have little real understanding of the fundamental nature of the sport?

The best way is to focus on the flag football version and return to the three key questions that underpin Play Practice.

1. What do children expect from a sport experience?
2. How do children best learn?
3. What competencies do children need to play a sport effectively?

In this case the first question is the key, because it is clear that children prefer to be actively involved with the ball. As always, then, the Play Practice approach is based on small-sided mini games in which every child has the opportunity to take one of the key roles in attack—

- the quarterback, who delivers the ball,
- the receiver, who catches the ball, or
- the running back, who carries the ball

—as well as be directly involved in a defensive role, covering a potential receiver or stopping a ball carrier.

Although many youngsters who have grown up with American football can throw a perfect spiral with a regulation ball, others, especially those from different cultures, find this a difficult task. Fortunately, tough foam balls are now available that look like a regular ball except they are smaller, have grooves to indicate how the ball should be held and, most importantly, have tail fins that ensure a good spiral. These balls not only make it easier for more children to throw the ball properly, but they are easier to catch as well. Equally important, children can throw them farther, which opens up a wider range of tactical possibilities.

Throwing and catching practice begins with the youngsters facing each other approximately 10 yards apart. For younger children who have not yet developed a throwing arm, this may in fact be their maximum range, but encourage the pairs to see how far apart they can move while still delivering the ball accurately and with a

spiral. Turn this practice into a challenge by putting out distance markers or tape measures. The distance recorded is the distance thrown minus the distance the ball lands from the tape, a method that factors in accuracy as well.

After this introduction, as quickly as possible introduce the group to the hook pattern shown in figure 9.6a. The potential receiver snaps the ball back to the quarterback and runs downfield 10 to15 yards before suddenly checking and breaking back toward the quarterback, who delivers a pass at the chest. This is the easiest pattern for a passer to complete, because the receiver is moving back toward the ball. With absolute beginners it can help to use ropes or permanent markings to indicate the exact pattern they should run. Once again, the corridors of the teaching grid will prove invaluable.

Each player gets from three to five attempts in each role. At this point introduce the concept of the line of scrimmage, along with the notion of the quarterback signal cadence. Players change partners for another sequence of passes.

The other basic pass patterns shown in figure 9.6 can be introduced in the sequence

- down and out (b);
- down and in (c);
- post pattern (d);
- flag pattern (e);
- down, out and up (f); and
- slant pattern (g).

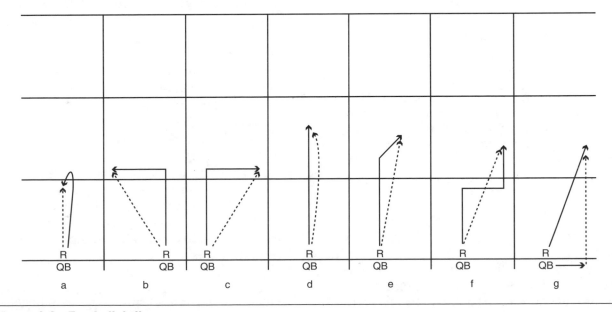

Figure 9.6   Football drill passes.

As you introduce each pattern, it is important to explain when and why each is used. In addition, encourage the youngsters to understand the way these different pass patterns interact with each other. At some point, allow the quarterback to move behind the line of scrimmage to improve the passing angle.

With Play Practice, however, it is important to create a game, and this can occur after the players have learned only two of these options. Now the quarterback and two potential receivers face a single defender who attempts to intercept the pass (see figure 9.7). Clearly the odds are weighted in favor of the offence, but this is necessary in the beginning with novice players. During this practice you can introduce the flags to wear and the rules associated with them, along with the rules about interference.

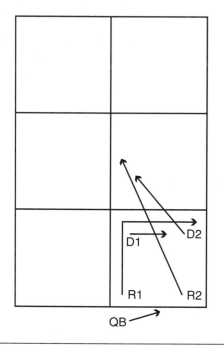

Figure 9.7 Football play card. Player R1 goes down and out to pick up 8 yards. Player R2 uses a slant pattern crossing in front of R1 looking for a touchdown pass. QB can move behind the line of scrimmage.

This is a "game" in name only because receivers are not allowed to run on with the ball after making a catch; the game is simply to beat the defender to the ball. To introduce greater interest, treat the second square in the teaching grid as the end zone so that any catches made there

become touchdowns. Naturally, players rotate positions on a regular basis to ensure that everyone takes on each role.

The next play practice is a 2-v-1 game with the single receiver breaking downfield to receive the ball while the defender tries to intercept. Now, both the quarterback and the receiver are under far more pressure. The fourth member of the group can take on an official's role to determine where the catch was made. Once again, the receiver stops after making the reception but can again "score a touchdown" by receiving the ball in the end zone. As before, players rotate through each position, including that of the official.

As soon as it is clear that players can cope with a more realistic situation, have them play a 3-v-2 game. Now two receivers face two defenders, and the quarterback is allowed only five seconds from the snap to release the ball; the quarterback can, however, move along the line of scrimmage to improve a passing angle.

Here, you can introduce play cards (figure 9.7), to save time and unending arguments. They can be based on the patterns shown in figure 9.6. A range of up to 10 cards randomly drawn from a box can introduce an element of chance into the game without disrupting its essential purpose. You can make these cards from cardboard and laminate them so that they can be reused many times. Making these cards can be another project for parents or friends of children. While it is possible to call the receivers simply R1, R2, and so on, using the names of football's great receivers will please young players. Photographs of these players will make the cards even more attractive and interesting, as will brief histories of the players' records or descriptions of the great catches they made during their careers.

Now it is possible to move to a 3-v-3 game played in a 20-yard wide by 30-yard long corridor with the object being to score a touchdown—that is, move the ball 30 yards—in four plays. The quarterback still has only five seconds to throw the ball but for the first time is allowed to run with it. In addition, receivers can run with the ball after making a catch. If a defender makes a two-hand touch or takes the ball carrier's flag, that position becomes the next line of scrimmage. It is also at this point that the mini game becomes a real game.

Each team of three rotates through the quarterback position for the first three plays. If they do not score a touchdown, the farthest point they reach is marked, and their opponents begin their offence from that field position. Ties are resolved with each team running one extra play, and the team that gains the most ground is awarded the match.

The play cards can be used in this game for the first three plays of a sequence. The offensive team should determine the fourth play to suit the situation.

By introducing the essential principles of American football in this way, instructors can decide for themselves whether to proceed to the full seven-a-side version of flag football. Clearly, the size of the playing area will be important, and more complex play cards will be needed. Apart from that, it may be necessary to add running plays and introduce the elements of blocking.

Touch (Rugby)

The invasion game of touch has grown rapidly in popularity in Australia since it evolved as a training game for both rugby codes, and it has now been accepted as a major game in its own right. It can serve as a valuable lead-up game for Rugby League and Rugby Union, especially the popular "sevens" version of Rugby Union.

Touch is a simple and safe game that can be played by both sexes, separately or together. It is easy to organise and requires little equipment or playing space. Because it is essentially a running game, touch can contribute to participants' cardiovascular fitness without placing them under extreme physical stress.

The approach to teaching touch detailed in this section was developed by Wendy Piltz and myself in South Australia by applying the principles of Play Practice, after it became clear that traditional methods of teaching the game were unsatisfactory. The objective in touch is to gain ground, get behind the defenders and score a try. Because the ball cannot be thrown forward or kicked, players can gain ground and score a try only when the ball is carried forward, so touch is fundamentally a running game, not a passing game.

Effective play in touch is based on the following:

- Agility, especially running in all its forms— forward, backward, diagonally, accelerating and stopping suddenly, varying speed and changing direction.

- Ball handling, although this is clearly much less important than traditional approaches to teaching touch have assumed.

- Above all, games sense, which in turn is based on a clear understanding of the rules and the way they determine the structure of the game. In touch more than in any other ball game, the rules determine the tactics of the game.

One of the most important things for a beginner to learn is that it is often better for the ball handler *not* to try to pass the ball. This is because a forward pass or a dropped pass turns the ball over to the opposition, and an intercepted pass often leads to an easy score by the opposition. On the other hand, the ball carrier who initiates a touch and quickly plays the ball can gain 10 yards immediately by catching defenders offside.

Players must therefore not only learn how to pass the ball but also develop the ability to decide if or when they should pass it. Games sense is therefore a critical element of effective play in touch. More than any other invasion game, touch illustrates the vast gulf that exists between mastering the simple techniques of throwing and catching the ball and developing the games sense needed to pass the ball effectively. The instructor must therefore teach passing in the context of game situations that lead simultaneously to the development of all the important elements of play rather than through isolated throwing and catching practices or unrelated minor games.

Because touch is new to many sport educators, it may be worthwhile here to clearly detail the advantages of the Play Practice approach when teaching this game:

- Using small-sided games means that all players can be positively involved, thus enhancing the rate of learning.

- With small-sided games, it is easy to group children by ability if necessary and maintain a flexible approach to progression. In the same way, it is easy to organise mini tournaments between balanced teams to further encourage purposeful play.

- The progressions gradually introduce players to the idea of a contact sport. This is particularly important for many girls whose past experiences with contact games may have been limited.

• Children grasp the principles of successful play more rapidly than with traditional methods because all the practice takes place in a game context, making the relationships between techniques, rules and key concepts easier to understand.

• It is easy to point out the similarities and differences between touch and other invasion games, therefore minimising the problems of negative transfer from these games. For example, in the mini game approach it is easy to show the importance of taking or effecting the touch to hold ground already gained instead of running backward away from the tackler as children may have learned to do in other invasion games. Players will quickly learn the importance of carrying the ball forward and delivering a pass only when they are certain it will go safely to a teammate. They will also learn to retreat quickly in defence to avoid penalties.

• The Play Practice method gives all players the chance to take an officiating role. This not only clarifies their understanding of the rules but also helps them appreciate the importance of the official in ensuring a fair and enjoyable game. A skillful and sensitive teacher can then find many opportunities to deal with the moral and ethical issues associated with fair play.

• The Play Practice method lends itself readily to a teaching for understanding approach.

With Play Practice it is usual to reduce the technical demands of a sport in the early stages so that novice players can begin to understand the fundamental nature of the game. The game of mittball used to introduce lacrosse is an excellent example of this.

In touch, however, the technical demands are already relatively low, so in the early stages of this game it is necessary to modify the rules instead. This is important because rules of touch heavily penalise errors in both attack and defence, making it difficult for novices to develop coherent patterns of play. For example, offsides by a defender can cost a side 10 yards, while a dropped ball by an attacker gives the ball to the other team. This means that crucial

modifications must be made for the early play practices. They are as follows:

1. Eliminate the offside penalty against defenders by ensuring that the ball cannot be played at the mark until the defenders have retreated the required 5 metres.
2. Reduce the penalty for a dropped pass from the loss of the ball to the loss of two possessions of the six allowed.

These modifications penalise an offence but still allow the game to flow without continual turnovers caused by simple but inevitable errors. Naturally, as players become more competent, you can phase in the official rules and their penalties. This will occur as players progress through the 3-v-2 and 4-v-3 mini games. You can also introduce secondary rules when a teachable moment arises.

The Play Practice approach to teaching touch begins with the simple running game shown in figure 9.8. It is played in a 10- by 30-yard corridor of the teaching grid shown on page 94. Note that although the dimensions of a touch field and the rules of touch are based on metric measurements, it may often be more convenient for teachers to use the coaching grids they have already prepared for games like soccer or lacrosse and which have been measured in yards rather than metres. It is even possible to use yards instead of metres in those measurements which are important in the rules of touch, as in offside, for instance. However, this is not a crucial issue until youngsters begin to play proper competitive games and it can be left to the discretion of the instructor.

In this first game, the ball carrier, O, runs forward and tries to dodge the

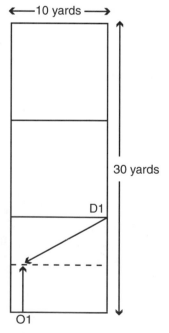

Figure 9.8   Running game in touch.

defender, D, to get to the scoreline, which is essentially the same as running into the end zone in American football. If D touches O, the spot is marked with a bib (pinny) or flag.

- The new ball carrier, D, tries to make more ground than O.
- These two opponents have three attempts each to beat each other, and then each player partners with a new opponent.

In this simple game players learn

- that touch is a game in which the attacker gains ground only by carrying the ball forward,
- that in defence a touch stops the attacker's forward run,
- how to carry the ball safely, and
- how to use change of pace and direction to dodge the defender.

The next game, which is identical to the first except that after a touch is made, the defender moves back 5 metres.

- The attacker starts from the point at which the touch was made and tries to beat the defender and get to the scoreline in five more attempts.
- Players change roles, and D tries to score a try or at least proceed farther than O in six attempts.

This game restates much of what players learned in the first game, but they also learn the concepts associated with the mark, scoreline and touchdown. In addition, they learn that in attack you have six attempts—possessions—to carry the ball forward before the ball automatically turns over to the other team.

Figures 9.9a and 9.9b illustrate the next game in the series, which is also played in a 30- by 10-yard corridor.

- O1 picks the ball up from the ground and passes it to O2, who runs it forward to try to beat defender D1 and score.
- If the defender touches O2, the ball is marked at that spot, and after the defender has retired 5 metres, O1 and O2 switch roles as passer and receiver and repeat the pick up, pass and run sequence until they have had six possessions or until they score. D2 acts as the referee and determines where the

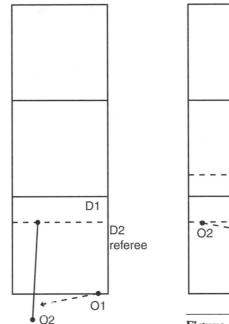

Figure 9.9a Second stage of touch played in a 30- by 10-yard corridor.

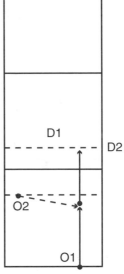

Figure 9.9b Part 2 of the second stage of touch.

touch was made and how far the defender must retreat.

When this game is completed, the two teams switch roles, with D1 and D2 becoming the attackers and O1 and O2 taking up the defending and the refereeing positions.

The game is given the following conditions:

1. The ball must be placed on the ground at the mark after each touch. Players cannot pick it up and run it over the mark.
2. The ball cannot be played in attack until the defender has retired 5 metres in line with the referee. This helps all participants learn to judge this crucial distance.
3. A dropped or forward pass is penalised by the loss of two possessions, not the loss of the ball as in the real game. This will ensure greater continuity in the game.

While superficially very similar to the preceding games, this game can help youngsters understand the following key concepts:

- The gain line is an imaginary line drawn across the field through the mark where the ball is played (see figure 9.10).

- The ball cannot be passed forward, that is, in front of the gain line.

- The receiver must initially set up well behind the gain line to be able to accelerate forward and take the ball at speed while still behind the gain line. This helps ensure that the receiver does in fact gain ground after getting the ball.

The crucial concept here is that although the ball cannot be thrown forward, it should not be thrown backward—behind the gain line—any more than is necessary.

- The principle of supporting the ball player. Once O1 has passed the ball to O2, O1 must immediately follow O2 and get into a position so that when a touch is made on O2 and the ball is marked, O1 is in position and ready to make a forward run to receive a pass. This sequence of pass and support repeats each time and is crucial to the development of skilled play in touch.

In attack players will learn that in the real game a bad pass is heavily penalised by the loss of possession, even though in this modified game they lose only two possessions.

- In defence players will learn that if they do not retire the required 5 metres, immediately they will be penalised 10 metres, even though in this game they are given ample time to retire.

The next game is 3-v-2 in a 30- by 20-yard corridor. Because it requires some specific techniques and several new concepts, however, instructors need to set up a simple practice situation before starting the game. Carry out this practice in a 30- by 10-yard corridor as shown in figure 9.11.

O1 executes a roll ball to O2, who is the "acting half".

O2 then makes a short pass to O3, who has set up diagonally behind the teammates and now bursts forward close to O2 to take the pass while still accelerating.

O3 makes an imaginary touch and prepares to execute a roll ball to O1, who has been trailing O3.

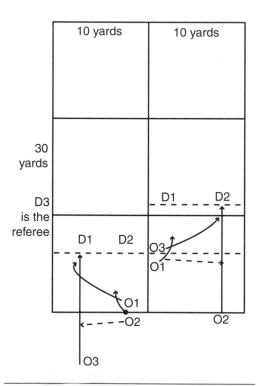

Figure 9.11 Player O1 runs the ball to O2; O2 passes the ball to O3 who takes the pass just behind the gain line and runs forward to make as much ground as possible. Meanwhile, O1 trails O3 and as soon as the latter is stopped, takes the roll ball and passes to O2 as they run forward. The sequence continues until the attackers have had six attempts.

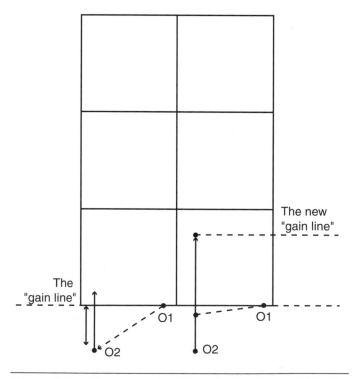

Figure 9.10 The concept of the gain line is crucial in the rugby codes. The ball must be passed backward but with the least distance possible.

O1 now passes to O2, who has been moving into a support position.

O2 accelerates forward, takes another short pass and runs forward to an imaginary touch.

In each case the player who rolls the ball follows to become the acting half.

Players will quickly establish an automatic pattern of run, initiate the touch, roll the ball and pass and will gradually speed up the process. This is important because if they become efficient, they will be able to catch defenders offside—meaning that the defenders have not retired the required 5 metres before the roll ball occurs. This is an ideal time to introduce both the offside law and the penalty for its infringement because this provides a clear rationale for using the important tactic of "rucking the ball" or "running the ball up". In this tactic, the first attacker to receive the ball drives up field as far as possible without risking the ball by attempting to pass. The object is to advance the ball out of the danger zone without making a turnover.

Rucking the ball makes it possible to advance the ball quickly and safely away from a dangerous position near the opponent's scoreline.

Only one short pass is made on each play, and if the attackers are quick, they can easily catch their opponents offside and gain 10 metres without risking the ball at all. It is also a tactic that can be used to settle play after a change of possession. (Note that the term "rucking the ball" has a completely different meaning in Rugby Union.)

In the 3-v-2 game shown in figure 9.12, the referee now becomes increasingly important, especially in deciding the point at which the touch is made and if the defence has retreated the correct distance. As before, the attacking team has six attempts to score a touchdown before turning the ball over to their opponents for their attempt to score.

In this play practice players will learn

- to ruck the ball efficiently so as to catch defenders offside,
- the offside rule and the penalty,
- the importance of not overrunning the mark because this wastes time coming back to the mark, and
- rolling the ball quickly.

Players will also have many opportunities to practise previously learned techniques.

Figure 9.13 shows a 4-v-3 game played on a pitch 30 yards wide by 20 yards long. It follows the same pattern as the 3-v-2 game, but the extra player provides more opportunities for teamwork in the attack, and the extra width makes scoring easier. Again, the referee plays an increasingly important role.

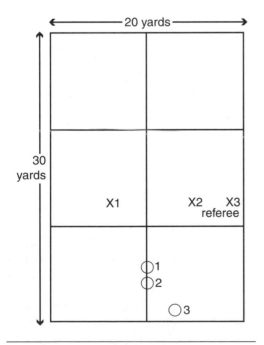

Figure 9.12 3-v-2 with referee. Each team has six attempts to score or to carry the ball as far as possible.

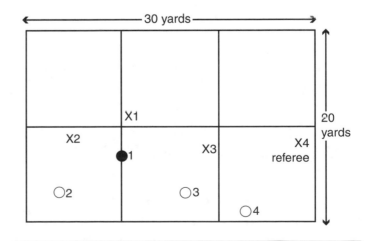

Figure 9.13 4-v-3 game.

O1 has the ball and begins play with a tap. The object is to score a try by advancing the ball to the scoreline 20 metres away.

With the real rules now enforced, the attackers must ensure that they do not turn the ball over carelessly. If they do, their opponents will take over at the point the ball is lost. On the other hand, defenders must move back quickly to avoid being caught offside, thus giving up easy ground on penalties.

If the O team scores, their opponents begin their offence from the scoreline. But if the Os turn the ball over at any time or fail to score in their six possessions, the D team begin their offence at the mark of the turnover or the sixth touch. The attackers therefore employ the rucking tactic with short passes for their first three possessions to advance the ball safely away from the danger zone. After that, they use their extra player to overload the defence and create scoring opportunities with good running and intelligent passing.

To set up an overload, attackers must quickly move to either outflank the defence or cut through gaps as defenders respond to the outside threat.

In this game players will learn the following:

- An intercepted pass usually results in an opposition score.
- A dropped or missed pass results in a loss of possession.
- Overrunning the mark results in a loss of possession.
- An illegal roll ball results in a turnover.
- A pass after the touch results in a turnover.
- If the acting half is caught with the ball, it is a turnover.
- Defenders who do not retire quickly will be caught offside, and their team is penalised 10 metres.

This makes it clear to the players that understanding the rules is a critical part of effective play in touch. Gradually introduce all of the primary and secondary rules at appropriate moments during play.

The players will also have the chance to

- improve their all-round agility;
- improve their passing skill—especially moving into good support positions;
- learn how to draw a defender before passing;
- learn how to fake a pass and continue running;
- learn how to take defensive positions and respond to attacking moves; and
- improve the positioning, timing and acceleration of their runs to take a pass.

The final play practice can be games of 4-v-4, 5-v-5 or 6-v-6—in essence, the full game. The issues to consider here are the number of players in the group, their level of ability and the importance of maximum individual participation (MIP).

While the six-a-side game should be played on the full 40- by 50-metre pitch, the small-sided games can be played on pitches 30 metres wide by 40 to 50 metres long. This ensures enough width to make a range of attacking moves productive if properly executed. It also means that attackers will have to be very positive if they are to move the ball 40 metres in six possessions, especially if they must use the rucking tactic for the first three attempts.

In these games, attackers without the advantage of an extra player must learn to use tactics such as the overlap or wrap, the switch, the reverse and the double overload to create—if only for an instant—a situation where the defender faces two attackers.

This Play Practice approach to teaching has proved highly successful in Australia, and sport educators should consider it when introducing either of the rugby codes.

Australian Rules Football

Aussie rules, as the game is commonly known, is, along with Gaelic football, which is still played in Ireland, an almost direct descendant of the football games played in Britain in the early 19th century. It is therefore related to virtually all the football codes now played around the world, including, remarkably enough, gridiron.

Played on large fields up to 200 yards long and 100 yards wide with 18 players a side, Aussie rules is a very vigorous and physically demanding game with heavy body contact and frequent injuries. Clearly, these elements must be avoided with beginners.

Players advance the ball by handballing—a technique unique to this game in which the ball is punched with the free hand rather than thrown—and by kicking it. They score goals by kicking the ball between two uprights of unlimited height.

Aussie rules is ideally suited to the parallel approach used in Play Practice to develop both understanding and technical ability. For example, to develop the important technique of kicking, use a challenge approach in which youngsters must kick for goal from predetermined distances and angles, and record their performances. Carry out this testing in every session to encourage a purposeful approach to improving both technique and performance.

Meanwhile, you can introduce the basic concept of Aussie rules through a game like lineball, a lead-up game introduced in the basketball section of chapter 10, but with the ball handballed, not thrown. No tackling is allowed, so the only way defenders can get the ball is through interceptions. With teams of five to seven per side, these handball games can be played in the 20- by 30-yard teaching grid. This will ensure a high-scoring game while reducing the amount of running required.

Players can bring kicking and handballing together through a simple conditioned game. Teams of five to seven per side play on grounds 50 to 70 yards long; because the play is controlled by the position of the goals, the width of the field is not especially important.

The condition is that once a team has made five consecutive handballs, the final receiver is allowed a completely free kick for goal—which, of course, can be of any size the instructor feels is suitable. Though this is an artificial condition, it does in fact match the reality of the real game, in which five handballs would almost inevitably see a player bearing down on goal for an open shot—although it would be a running shot.

Coaching Aussie Rules

Aussie rules at the elite level would benefit from the application of the principles of Play Practice because of the need to create realistic practice situations that carry a minimal risk of injury. In the real game, pressure comes from aggressive defenders who are prepared to throw their bodies into the play to get the ball and who are often ready to tackle the ball carrier no

matter what the cost. This inevitably leads to many injuries that, while perhaps acceptable in the real game, cannot be justified in training. The challenge for coaches is to manipulate the variables described in chapter 6 to create suitable play practices. Because defensive pressure reduces the time available for a player to be skillful, it is obviously important to focus on the way you can reduce space to create play practices that begin to reflect the pressures of the real game without giving players the chance to build up the momentum (mass times velocity) that leads to injuries.

An Example

One of Australia's leading coaches, David Parkin of Carlton Football Club in Melbourne, has been applying the principles of Play Practice for several years. Among a range of games he has developed is the centre clearance game, which incorporates the principles of Play Practice outlined previously.

This game focusses practice on one of the critical areas of successful team play in this vigorous game—rapidly moving the ball forward after gaining possession at the centre bounce. The centre bounce is equivalent to the old centre jump in basketball that took place after every score. The difference is that when an oval-shaped ball is bounced, it is difficult to predict its subsequent height or direction, so neither side can be guaranteed possession. It is a perfect example of a moment of transition, and both teams must be ready for instant attack or instant defence. In fact, in the initial fight for the ball, several turnovers may occur in a few seconds, so any player who does get the ball must instantly try to move it forward before being tackled. This involves instantaneous decision making and great execution under intense pressure, the fundamental challenge for players of all great games.

The centre clearance game tries to replicate this situation—without the continual risk of injury. In the game, two "ruck men", with some body protection, run in and compete—as do centers in basketball—to knock the high-bouncing ball down to the four members of the attacking team. An equal number of defenders, protected with padding, try to harass and pressure them as they try to bring the ball clear of the centre area and attempt to deliver it with a kick to whichever of the two forwards is open.

The attackers score 3, 2 or 1 point depending on the zone in which they receive the ball.

Although defenders cannot tackle the ball player, they must make it as difficult as possible for the attacking team to advance the ball by blocking or bumping opponents. Because play is initially in a confined space, it is difficult for defenders to generate the momentum that can lead to very serious injuries. After the attackers have had 6 to 10 attempts, teams change roles, and the new attacking team tries to score more points than their opponents did. Clearly, the instructor can manipulate the ratio of attackers to defenders to get the game precisely focussed.

At Carlton up to six teams rotate into this game, which can take up to half of each training session in the preseason period. Naturally, the players can occupy themselves with many other games and drills during a training session until it is their turn to play in the centre clearance game.

10

Court Invasion Games

If you select the most vulnerable spot in the enemy's anatomy, isolate that particular element—you will have achieved tactical superiority over him at that moment in time, even though he may have an overall strategic advantage.
—Anton Myrer

● ● ● ● ●

Unlike the field invasion games which seem to have evolved from a common ancestral "football" game played in England during the Middle Ages, the court invasion games were all invented. They were made possible by the Industrial Revolution during the 19th century, when it became possible to build large indoor playing areas cheaply and to provide the electric light necessary for them to be used in the evenings. For the first time, it became possible for people to play after working hours, and many indoor games were devised to cater to their needs. Along with table tennis, the games in this section were all devised at this time.

Basketball

Basketball was created in 1891 by a talented sport educator, Thomas Naismith, at Springfield College in the United States. Naismith used a play practice approach to develop an indoor game that did not involve the almost brutal play

that football at that time embodied. A major feature of this new game was the goal, a peach basket suspended from a balcony, which ensured that a score could be achieved only through skill and not brute force.

Sport educators can introduce the basic concepts of basketball through lead-up games such as lineball, benchball and matball, which are very similar to Naismith's original game. These games are virtually identical to each other but, as the names imply, the goal in each case is slightly different. The value of these games will depend on the place basketball holds in a specific sporting culture. In some areas they may be useful for youngsters age 6 to 12, and in others for the 10 to 14 age group. The size and nature of the ball should match the group's ability level, although in a basketball culture the children will inevitably want to play with a "real" ball.

All three games can be played with teams of five or six per side on a court 21 to 27 metres (70–90 feet) in length. In all three, the basic rules state that the ball can only be thrown, not kicked or punched, and there is no dribbling. The ball cannot be taken away from the player in possession.

In lineball, the attacking team tries to advance the ball by interpassing as in basketball and then to pass it in to a teammate—the "goalie"—positioned behind the end line. To make scoring easier, the goalie can run anywhere behind the goal line to receive a pass, just like a receiver in American football. The passer who "scores" the goal changes places with the goalie. After a goal is scored, the ball is given to the other team.

Play is similar in benchball, but the goalie stands on a gym bench behind the goal line. In matball, the goalie is positioned on a gym mat. Each progression makes scoring just a little more difficult so passing must become more sophisticated. Skittleball is another variation on these games, but experience suggests that the chaos that results when attackers try to force the ball past packed defenders to hit the skittle, or large plastic cone, and score makes this an unsuitable game.

In all of these games, the instructor can introduce rules dealing with out of bounds, held ball and restarts as and when needed. This approach makes the rules relevant, so children are more likely to both remember and abide by them.

With the youngest beginning players, these games can introduce the idea of attacking and defending a goal (i.e., directional play), the concepts of teamwork and supporting the ball player and simple tactics such as passing and moving for a return pass. You can introduce different passing techniques and gradually deal with the notions of the fast break and covering attackers.

Use the next series of games in parallel with the lead-up games just outlined. Most importantly, these games introduce the idea that passing is a team activity involving skill on the part of both the passer and the receiver.

Teaching Passing

1. 2-v-1 in free space: A defender tries to prevent an attacker from receiving a pass from a 'free player' who is not allowed to move. The attacking team wins if the receiver catches two consecutive passes. Players change roles after a win or after four attempts.

In this simple game attackers can learn

- how to cut late and fast to get open,
- how to use a hand to indicate where they want the ball thrown,
- how to fake a cut and change direction, and
- different passing techniques.

Make sure this game does not become a pointless version of "piggy in the middle"!

2. 3-v-3 in open space: This game is played in the same way as the preceding game, but now the ball handler must select the best possible receiver while under pressure from a defender. Again, stress the same basic elements of passing along with the technique of pivoting to protect the ball. Three or five successful receptions by one team wins the game. Play best of three, or change opponents.

Teaching Shooting

1. Shooting the ball through the basket is one of the great attractions of basketball. Begin by introducing the technique for set shooting. The children stand 1.5 metres (5 feet) from the basket on the layup diagonal to begin an individual shooting game. They move back one full step every time they score until they have three consecutive misses, and then they must begin again from 1.5 metres, at a different angle to the basket.

2. Follow this with a team shooting competition. Assign five players to each basket at a range of 4.5 metres (15 feet). On a signal, free shooting begins; the first team to score 11 or 21 baskets wins. Teams must call out each successful shot, for example, "Twelve! Thirteen! Fourteen!" When teams reach 11 or 21, they must sit down with the ball above their head.

3. Now have players use this shooting technique in a game of goalball, which is played like lineball except the ball is returned to the successful passer for a set shot from the free throw line. An alternative game is 3-v-3 half-court. Here, the team that makes five consecutive passes is entitled to a set shot from the point of the last reception or the free throw line, whichever is the easiest.

4. In a basketball culture the layup shot is taken for granted, but youngsters who are not immersed in the game find it difficult to master.

The problem is that if the instructor introduces the layup too early, beginners cannot control the ball in a dribble while simultaneously organising their footwork to produce the necessary right-foot, left-foot takeoff (for right-handers), nor can they take advantage of the two-step rule when they catch the ball in the air. The bounce-one-two layup eliminates the need for dribbling and makes it easy for youngsters to grasp the notion of taking the ball in the air and using the two steps with the ball in hand to sight the basket and put the ball up onto the hot spot on the backboard.

Teaching the layup using a progressive part approach still presents the problem of incorporating the dribble and the two-count step. Once youngsters have mastered a working model, encouraged them to test themselves with the buildup challenges. This means that after they have scored one basket, they then try for two in succession, then three and so on. Any time they miss, they drop back to their previous successful score, repeat it and try again. This system provides a simple challenge that ensures a lot of practice. You can follow this with a team challenge in which teams of four to six players try to build up to the highest number of consecutive baskets or play best of 11 baskets.

5. Organise the 3-v-1 half-court game as shown in figure 10.1. Attackers try to score using only set shots or layups, which will give each child plenty of opportunities to be involved. This is a good time to introduce rules about personal fouls. In addition, you can introduce the basic concepts of positioning in the form of spread and balance—once again, the triangle is used. Players cannot receive the ball in the key.

6. Players set up a 1-v-1 game at a range of about 4.5 metres (15–16 feet). The attacker can shoot from outside to score 20 points for a basket or 10 for hitting the ring, or the attacker can fake the shot and drive to the basket for a 5-point score. This differential scoring encourages defenders to play honest defence and not drop back to stop the layup. Change partners frequently. A game can be based on any number of points the instructor believes suitable for a group or even for specific pairs of players.

7. 3-v-2 half-court game: Organise as for the 3-v-1 game, but have two defenders to make life more difficult. Players still score only through the set shot or layup.

Teaching Dribbling

Dribbling a basketball is automatic for children who have grown up with one, but it is another technique that takes time for novices to master. The following sequence illustrates the Play Practice approach to the teaching and development of an essential technique in sport. With clever use of variety, progression and pacing instructors can keep youngsters involved and practising purposefully for long periods. The important thing is that players must be able to dribble competently with both hands while keeping their heads up and watching play.

1. Have the children kneel with the ball close by and begin bouncing the ball. Tell them to "treat the ball like a friend" and move their hands with the ball and not against it, using the fingertips. Gradually they move the ball around the body and farther out. Change to the nonpreferred hand. Close eyes and repeat while trying to keep the ball bouncing throughout this and succeeding practices.

Children repeat the sequence standing.

Children repeat the sequence moving slowly, using the free arm to feel the way when their eyes are closed.

Children run freely and fast, eyes open, in open space.

Gradually compress the space from open space to full court, to half-court, to one-quarter, to the keyway only.

2. In pairs moving freely, one child follows and copies the partner, who continually changes hand, height and speed of bounce and direction of movement. Pairs continually interchange roles and/or partners.

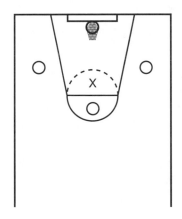

Figure 10.1 3-v-1 game. Individual attackers can only score with a set shot or a layup. As soon as players are ready, move to 3-v-2 game.

In pairs facing each other, one child mirrors the partner, who varies the movement and speed as much as possible. As before, pairs switch roles and partners.

3. Players set up in threes or fives as shown in figure 10.2. Every child has a ball, which must be continually bounced—dribbled—throughout the exercise. Player 1 dribbles toward player 3, who, while still bouncing the ball with their

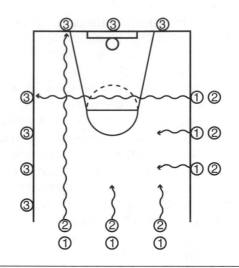

Figure 10.3 Players are crossing paths and must be aware of other bodies to avoid collisions.

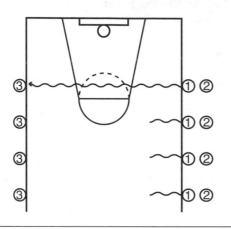

Figure 10.2 Players 1 dribble toward Players 3 who use their free hand to indicate number of fingers. As soon as Player 1 calls a number Player 3 changes. A "turn" and "stop" can be added soon.

nonpreferred hand, holds up the other hand and indicates a number of fingers. Player 1 immediately calls out the number of fingers shown; player 3 then continues to change the number every time player 1 is correct. When player 1 reaches player 3, the latter sets off dribbling their ball toward player 2, who holds up fingers—and so it continues. When players have improved, a stop signal can be added. Now the dribbler must stay in place until another signal to move is given. After that, signals can be added that indicate the dribbler must turn, change hands, go faster or slower, back up, or dribble behind the back or through the legs, and so on.

This simple system is a fun way of encouraging players to keep their heads up and not watch the ball as they move.

The formation can then change to that shown in figure 10.3 so that players must be aware of players coming at right angles. Their "guides" deliberately try to cause collisions with other players. Using their peripheral vision, the ball player must avoid any contact.

Now return to the bounce-one-two layup; progress to bounce-bounce-one-two and then on to the half-court dribble and layup, maintaining the rhythm and two-count gather and shoot.

Move to a full-court dribble with little pressure, teaching defenders how to defend the dribbler using the head, the feet and no hands.

Move to a full-court dribble against defensive pressure.

Move to a half-court dribble—the attacker must practise two rear turns and then is free to try to beat the defender and go for the layup.

Set up a 1-v-1 practice as before but from 6 metres (20 feet).

At appropriate times

- the dribble can be incorporated into the classic fast-break game,
- you can show players how to use the dribble to make a better passing angle,
- players can learn how to draw defenders away before passing in the opposite direction, and
- players can learn how to use the dribble in penetrate-and-pitch-out and drive-and-dump moves.

Teaching Combination Play

At any point, the instructor can also use simple games such as dribble freeze tag. In this game the group is divided into two teams, and each player has a ball. Any player touched by an opponent must freeze to the spot while keeping the ball bouncing, until released by a teammate.

The sequence of games continues with 3-v-3 half-court. Along with the fast-break game outlined later, this is the fundamental play practice for basketball. This game, or one played 4-v-4 depending on the numbers in a group, can introduce virtually all the tactical concepts of the half-court game, including screens on and off the ball, clearouts and the basic principles of rebounding. At the same time it ensures maximum individual participation (MIP) of all the key technical elements of basketball. At this stage you can use drills to refine some of the important techniques and develop simple tactical moves such as the give-and-go.

Introduce the fast break through the classic fast-break drill converted into a game. Begin with 3-v-1, then progress to 3-v-2 and finally 3-v-3 as shown in figure 10.4. The best way to introduce

new defenders and make the situation even more gamelike is to specify that the second defender can join in after two passes are made and the third can join in after three. If only three teams of three are involved, this play practice will challenge players' fitness; with youngsters, it may be necessary to organise four, or a maximum of five, teams to give them sufficient time to recover. If enough courts are available, keep the number of teams to a maximum of five. If there are too many children for this arrangement, the instructor may have to balance MIP against alignment and settle for half-court games.

The ideal situation is to place a portable double backboard on the half-court line to create two mini courts. Not only does this reduce the distances children have to run and ensure more action around the basket, but it also makes the game seem more real to the children.

Do not use the full 5-v-5 game until the children have made a commitment to the game or unless enough courts and instructors are available to ensure the children have help coming to terms with the much-increased complexity. 5-v-5 is an infinitely more complex game than 3-v-3 or even 4-v-4, so the instructor must very carefully plan its introduction.

Netball

Netball is a major game in many of the Commonwealth nations; these include Australia, Canada, England, Northern Ireland, Scotland and Wales, New Zealand and some of the West Indian nations. While some male competitions exist, netball is usually played by females.

Netball provides many advantages as a game for young people because it is very simple in concept, evolving very easily from the team passing games outlined previously as lead-ups to basketball. Because of its simplicity, players do not need to spend hours developing technical ability as in basketball or learning large numbers of tactical moves. In addition, because players are restricted to certain areas of the court, netball does not require the fitness level of basketball.

With no dribbling and only two shooters allowed for each team, the keys to successful play are agility, especially quickness over 2 to 5 metres, and passing skills. Because players are not allowed to travel with the ball, passing is

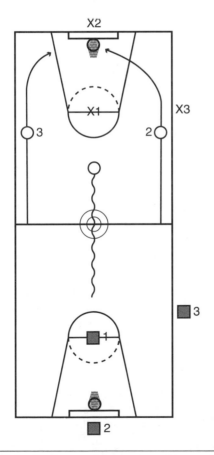

Figure 10.4 3-v-1 game. As soon as Xs get the ball they break down court to attack. Game is continuous. As players improve a second defender is added and then a third—perhaps after attackers have three passes.

the only way to advance it. The problem here is that potential receivers are, or should be, tightly guarded. In addition, the rule that restricts the time a ball handler can hold the ball ensures that players have very little time to select their target and deliver the ball. This means that the passer is always under pressure. Because of this, all players must quickly improve their ability to cut late and fast—perhaps after a fake cut—show where they want the ball and be reading the play as they receive it.

The Play Practice approach to netball is geared to maximising individual participation through small-sided, realistic games. As indicated previously, netball evolves quite naturally from the lead-up games of lineball, benchball and matball. In addition, the 2-v-1 and 3-v-3 passing games outlined in the basketball section are very valuable play practices for netball. Two other games have been found to be very effective as well. The first involves dividing the court right down the middle and having a four-a-side game on each side of the divide. The problem that occurs occasionally when both sides are attacking the same goal is easily resolved. Once the group gets used to the idea, it is possible to play best of three or five goals and then rotate to meet other opposition.

The second game is based around the shooting circle. Inside the circle, two attackers play against two defenders who try to stop the ball being fed in by a third attacker positioned outside the circle (see figure 10.5). Another player—a teammate of the defenders—can act as an official in this game to ensure that the players adhere to noncontact rules. This game can have a condition that the ball must pass through the hands of the outside feeder two, three, or even four times before a shot can be taken, or that all three attackers must touch the ball twice before a shot. This ensures that the shooters must work very hard to

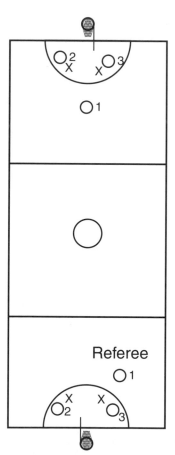

Figure 10.5 3-v-3 game. One unguarded "feeder" tries to get the ball in to two shooters in the circle for a shot at goal. Each team has 5 to 10 attempts before changing over and rotating roles. Player X3 acts as the umpire.

get open, show where they want the ball and begin to work as a team. Another advantage of this game is that it puts every player into a central role at some point, and the fact that it usually leads to a shot at goal ensures a high level of commitment from both sets of players.

Clearly, it is very easy to turn this game into a straight 3-v-3 mini game, again with rotation to different opponents as appropriate. In both games, as with all play practices, be sure to allot time for tactical time-outs and discussion among the players on ways to improve their performance. Once again, these small-sided games are ideal for Play Practice scenarios.

Korfball

Korfball is a game played by two teams on a grass pitch approximately 90 metres (98 yards) long by 40 metres (44 yards) wide. Each team has 12 players—six men and six women—who are positioned within three zones on the pitch. The object of the game is to score goals by shooting a round ball, similar to a soccer ball, into a basket 3.5 metres (4 yards) above the ground, placed inside each end zone. It is essentially a team passing game that does not allow physical contact but that does allow tight marking.

Although it is mainly played outdoors in Europe, korfball can be played indoors. Because of this and because it has greater similarities with the other games in this section than with field invasion games, I include it here. Korfball is a unique game with many advantages as a team game for young people, but it rarely receives the recognition it deserves. It is especially popular in Holland, where massive korfball festivals take place, but it survives elsewhere only in tiny pockets driven by enthusiasts. It should be especially attractive to sport educators for the following reasons:

- The rules of the game actually incorporate and reward good sporting behaviour.

- Players must progressively change from attacking to defensive roles after every two baskets.

- The baskets are freestanding without a backboard, so play can continue behind them. This ensures that games sense and agility are more valuable than height and eliminates the continual physical contests under the basket that are so much a part of basketball.

- Because of its great similarity to basketball, instructors can use many of the play practices from that game in the teaching of korfball. Players from all of the other court invasion games will find it easy to make the transition to korfball because of the many similarities between them.

Team Handball

Team handball is one of the world's fastest games and is an Olympic sport very popular in central Europe. It is played by two teams, each with seven players, on a court that resembles a small soccer pitch. The object is to score goals by passing or dribbling the round ball until a scoring opportunity is created and the ball is thrown past the goalkeeper for a score. Players may use hands, fists, arms, heads, bodies, thighs or knees to move the ball.

Like korfball, it has much to offer and is easy for players of other games to pick up. As played by beginners, its open, free-flowing manner makes it an ideal recreational sport. As playing standards improve, however, zone defences markedly change the nature of the game. Snappy passing around the zone leads to highly athletic jumping and diving movements as attackers try to elude defenders and create space for a strike at goal. Once again, the play practices for basketball, especially the go-for-goal games, make introducing this game to beginners relatively easy.

11

Court-Divided Games

In America you are conditioned to regard everything as a contest. You have to make the Ten Best Dressed List, win this, win that—it drives me nuts sometimes. Who cares…?
—Arthur Ashe

● ● ● ● ●

As we have already seen, skill in games is a complex phenomenon in which many different elements interact. Though all of the elements outlined in chapter 4 are important, the initial key to success in court-divided games is technical ability, that is, the ability to keep the ball or shuttle in play. With beginners this is crucial, because it defines the basic level of competence essential if they are to continue playing. At the elite level, technical ability impacts both strategy and tactics. Put simply, a tennis player cannot rely on serve and volley tactics without a good serve and volley! Perhaps this is why many tennis players base their games on simply keeping the ball in play and avoiding unforced errors. Though these tactics are unlikely to bring a Wimbledon title, for many players on the professional circuit they are good enough to ensure a steady income!

If merely keeping the ball in play can bring rewards for professional players, it must surely be an appropriate tactic for beginners. But this is no easy task! In all court-divided games, chil-

dren must learn how to track a fast-moving object, predict its flight path, move into position to intercept it and then strike it so precisely that it will return to the other side of the net. In racquet sports all this must be performed by beginners using an unfamiliar implement.

Racquet Sports

Each of the three major racquet sports presents its own unique problems to beginners. In tennis, the relatively large playing area places a premium on agility just to get into position to strike the ball. In table tennis, the speed of the very light ball and the small playing surface mean that simply tracking it and finding the time to prepare for the stroke is difficult. **In fact, the game is so fast that a pressing need exists to develop a larger and slower ball, at least for beginners.** Finally, badminton brings the special problem of a target that, unlike a ball, decelerates rapidly and drops suddenly in a way that beginners find very difficult to predict. In

Professional tennis player Venus Williams overcame obstacles from her economically depressed and often violence-riddled neighborhood in Compton, California to make it to the top. Her father Richard Williams taught himself to play tennis through films and books, then taught Venus and her sister Serena on public courts in their tough neighborhood. Although they showed a lot of promise, Richard Williams kept his daughters out of the junior-circuit play to protect them from pressure and to allow them to focus on their schoolbooks as much as on the tennis ball. Although many people in the tennis establishment frowned upon this move, it worked for the Williamses. Both Venus and Serena are now top tennis players.

the early stages some youngsters may be able to hit a shuttle only if it is stationary, perhaps suspended by a string.

Developing Technical Ability

In all of these games, developing effective technique, even in the form of a working model, requires a great deal of carefully controlled practice. To give beginners the time necessary for

them to concentrate on correctly executing a specific technique, it is necessary to make tracking and prediction easier and to reduce or even eliminate the agility demands of the task. One way to accomplish this is to use ball-feeding machines in tennis and table tennis; these can be programmed to serve the exact ball required in terms of line, length, trajectory, angle and spin for both tennis and table tennis. Coaches who are good players can also provide the kind of consistent service or ball feed necessary for a beginner to improve, but usually this occurs on a one-to-one basis.

Because ball machines are rarely available and one-to-one coaching is expensive, it may be necessary to rely on youngsters to provide accurate feeds for each other. With children who are prepared to cooperate this can be effective, particularly if the instructor creates a game in which players can earn points for providing a good feed, that is, a ball that is thrown or hit to exactly the right place so that the novice player can concentrate on the basic elements of technique.

Sport educators can also use the more experienced players in a group as assistant coaches. Their primary task is to put the ball exactly where a partner needs it to play a particular stroke, but they can also provide reinforcement and even some augmented feedback. This arrangement challenges these "coaches" to perfect their own ball control or improve some aspect of their own technique while helping a beginner. Use this strategy only sparingly, however, because the best players in a group like opportunities to play and practise with partners at their own level.

The fundamental problem is that children are not always motivated to strive for perfection, especially when the task is merely to feed the ball so that another player can hit it past them. They intuitively understand the essential concept that Timothy Gallwey presented in *The Inner Game of Tennis* (1974), which is that the role of players in any game is to create problems for their opponent.

Even when a task is supposed to be cooperative, it often quickly degenerates into a game in which the feeders try to make it as difficult as possible for their partner. This is particularly likely to happen in a practice when both players are supposed to be hitting the ball consistently to each other.

Inevitably, as youngsters begin to compete rather than practise cooperatively, they try to make it as difficult as possible for their partner to even reach the ball, far less hit it. At worst, the practice breaks down into very short and sporadic rallies, while at best, players adopt survival methods to keep the ball in play. Players will make few attempts to produce the repetitive series of thoughtful, well-controlled strokes necessary for the development of good technique. Instead, to survive against their partner, novices will often adopt a dead-end technique to keep the ball in play. One method commonly used in table tennis is to use an exaggerated backhand grip and simply block the ball back, whereas in tennis, beginners will shorten their grip or choke up on the racquet.

Both of these dead-end techniques enable the player to survive at a beginning level but will usually prevent them from improving beyond that. Because beginners are far more likely to be motivated by short-term success than by the prospects of long-term improvement, the instructor may find it very difficult to help them improve, especially if they have overlearned the wrong technique in the first place.

Change the Game and Change the Focus

In the Play Practice approach to table tennis, place a small target on each side of the table as shown in figure 11.1. The challenge of the game is to hit this target to score a point, using a designated technique or stroke. Points can be won only by hitting the target, and they cannot be lost, even if the ball is hit off the table or into the net.

This modification naturally changes the whole character of the game. Players now have no reason to create problems for their partner by constantly changing the angle, direction or even spin of the shot.

Players can win a game, of perhaps three or five points, *only* by hitting the target more frequently than their partner. As both opponents strive to score points by hitting their target, the line and length of shots will inevitably become more and more consistent. This in turn reduces the perceptual and movement demands of the task and gives both players more time to position themselves and then prepare for the specified stroke.

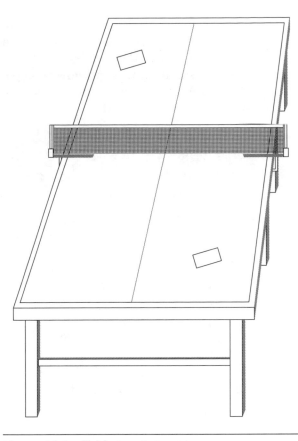

Figure 11.1   Table tennis targets.

Another major benefit is that young players will not only watch the ball but will begin to learn to watch their opponent as well. This is a crucial but often underestimated aspect of skilled play in racquet sports. Only by watching the preparation of the racquet, the angle of the racquet as it makes contact with the ball, as well as the effort qualities of the whole swing as the opponent strikes the ball or shuttle is it possible for a player to begin to anticipate the target's speed and flight path. In fact, **the success of the great players in many games, especially in racquet and the striking/fielding sports, is due more to their ability to anticipate the speed, spin and direction of a ball (or shuttle) before an opponent hits or delivers it than it is to their superior reflexes.** Although this ability, like games sense, could simply be labeled intuitive, it is likely that the athlete is simply better able to register important cues, even if subconsciously, that provide important information before the ball is on its way. This being the case, target games of the kind outlined here are likely to be even more valuable than ball machines for developing critical aspects of skilled performance in racquet sports. It would certainly suggest that **coaches should encourage players to watch their opponent's preparation for a stroke as much as they presently exhort them to watch the ball.**

In table tennis, the importance of watching the opponent's bat is critical because it is possible to have a high-spin rubber on one side of it and anti-spin rubber on the other. To help players cope with this problem, the rules state that the two faces of the bat must be of different colors. So in addition to watching their opponent's stroke very carefully, players must also note which side of the bat the opponent used to hit the ball and then work out the likely degree of spin.

In a sense, the target game described previously creates the ideal Gallwey game, in which both players contribute to the improvement of the other. In target table tennis, true competition does indeed become true cooperation, because as players strive to win a point, they in fact make it easier for their opponents to do the same thing.

A target the size of a videocassette (15 by 10 centimetres, or 6 by 4 inches) is suitable for beginners, but even novices will soon find this too easy, so quickly progress to an audiocassette-sized target (7.5 by 5 centimetres, or 3 by 2 inches). Targets can take many forms, and teachers should encourage students to make or bring their own for a session. You can make the targets even more interesting by pasting photographs of sports stars or popular entertainers on them.

Perhaps the most successful targets used so far by teachers in South Australia, although admittedly with upper elementary school children, have been toy plastic cowboys and Indians on horseback! Whatever targets you use, it is easy to arrange a handicapping system in

which better players must aim at a smaller target than their opponents.

Shaping Play

Practising attacking strokes may necessitate a further modification to slow play down and give beginners the time they need to prepare for and execute the lifting, brushing motion necessary to produce topspin. All that is needed is a higher net, as shown in figure 11.2. This prevents players from hitting fast, flat shots—which are risky—and forces them to lift the ball high over the net. This not only makes them execute the correct technique but also ensures that their partner has plenty of time to deal with a slow, looping ball. Though this innovation takes a little time and thought to set up, it is well worth it in terms of the pertinent and purposeful practice it provides.

Instructors can develop play practices in racquet sports by conditioning games in spe-

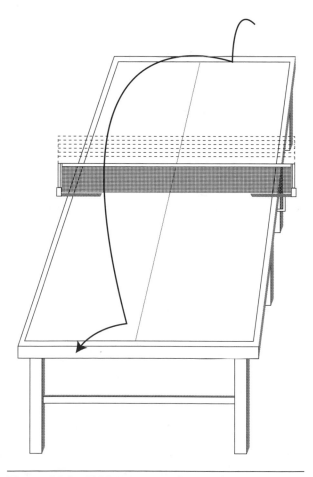

Figure 11.2   Table tennis with raised net.

cific ways. For example, a game played only in the backhand court in which players must hit alternate forehand and backhand shots forces players to concentrate on footwork and positioning. Because a large proportion of kills in table tennis are made with the forehand, often with players standing outside the line of the table, this practice is likely to transfer tactical understanding as well as good footwork. Though it is not as critical in tennis, running round the forehand is still an important element of tactical play in that game because it opens up a wide range of angles.

Teachers and coaches have used these modifications successfully across a wide range of age groups, and they almost invariably lead to more purposeful play practice. In tennis, you can employ a whole range of horizontal targets; even a game played in the tram lines, that is, the lines that differentiate the singles from the doubles court, will quickly improve the line of shots and thus reduce the need for lateral movement to the ball, which young players especially find difficult.

It is possible to combine the development of technique using target games with the Games for Understanding approach. Using the ideas of Rod Thorpe and his coworkers, you can slow down the game of tennis by raising the net, using a slower ball and modifying the racquets so players have more time to focus on the tactical, "understanding" elements of play. Thus, the first session might use the Loughborough approach to focus on the essential nature of the game and its tactical elements, whereas subsequent sessions might balance out both tactical and technical development, using target games to improve technique with the real equipment. In this way both elements are drawn together, and players begin to combine intelligent movement and

positioning with good technique as they progress toward the full game.

Another way to give beginners more time in tennis is to use the modification that wheelchair players use, namely, two-bounce tennis. This modification allows youngsters to play the game early on in their tennis experience. And there is little doubt that technology will eventually produce better "slow" balls that will give players more time to move into position and play the stroke.

Target games may be only one of many possible solutions to the problems that arise in the teaching of racquet sports, but instructors will find that the target games described in this chapter will lead to the purposeful practice that is essential if beginners are to develop the technical ability they need to play racquet sports. When integrated into an understanding approach, these games will help teachers create the challenging and enjoyable learning experiences that may lead children to a lifelong commitment to sport and an active lifestyle.

In racquet games the concept of a working technique is especially valuable. In table tennis the advanced techniques of elite players are based on the high-friction/high-spin bats they use and the fact that when playing attacking shots, they take the ball early, before it reaches the top of its bounce (figure 11.3). They can therefore hit the ball with a flat stroke, with the racquet angled down as shown in figure 11.4. This advanced technical model becomes a fast, flat sweep through the top quarter of the ball. It is impossible for beginners to use such a technique because they cannot take the ball early and rarely have the necessary equipment.

Beginners use low-spin bats and must invariably take the ball late, often after the top of the

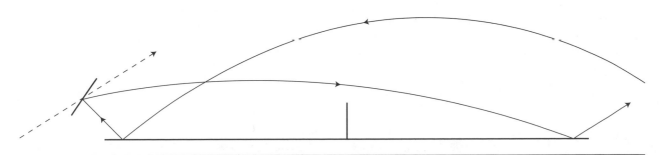

Figure 11.3 The expert can take the ball early before the top of the bounce.

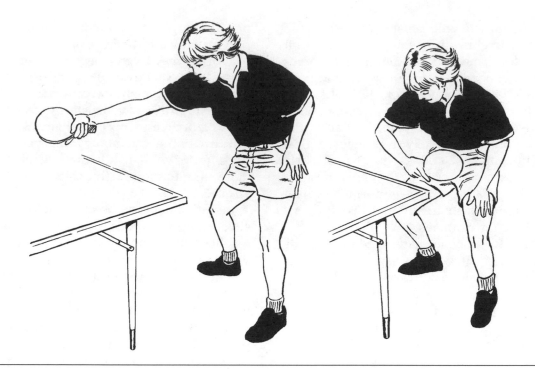

Figure 11.4   An expert uses a fast flat stroke with the racquet angled forward.

bounce, because they need extra time to track it and compute its flight path. These two factors mean that they must play with an open bat face and a much more vertical swing, as shown in figure 11.5. This working model of technique is a simple lifting swing up through the bottom quarter of the ball as shown in figure 11.6.

In tennis, a slightly different situation exists. Here the working model could be a double-handed backhand combined with an exaggerated forehand (Western) grip. This allows young players to control the racquet without having to modify their grip as they prepare for a stroke. The enormous advantages of this model are that

it largely eliminates the problems caused by beginners' often weak arms and wrists, and it enables them to play the game much earlier than they otherwise could.

A Play Practice approach to use with good players is mimicry. If a player needs to make technical improvements, instead of giving feedback in the form of cues, encourage the player to play the stroke like a particular well-known player does. Elite professional players know every other player's game, so they should be able to visualise and then mimic specific elements of their play. However, videotape of every player who has played at a high level in the

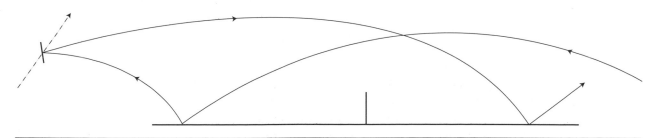

Figure 11.5   The beginner needs more time to track the ball and therefore hits it late with an open racquet face.

Figure 11.6 Table tennis working model of technique showing a long lifting swing with the bat face angled back.

past 30 years is readily available and can provide good student players with a model of the specific technique needed. This approach has possibilities that are crying out to be exploited. Developing it will require a lot of creative experimentation.

As mentioned earlier, badminton presents unique problems for beginners. Because the shuttle must be volleyed, the learner has to make a very early prediction of its flight path. This is difficult because the shuttle decelerates rapidly compared to a ball and often drops vertically at the end of its flight.

A number of play practices can help novices in several ways. First, play a game with balloons instead of shuttles. These are far easier to hit than the shuttle, especially with an overhead stroke, so youngsters can keep them in play much longer. Since balloons also decelerate rapidly, there is some feel of the real game. Note that equipment manufacturers are already beginning to develop alternatives to the regulation shuttle that are larger and easier to track. An even slower "bird" is needed, however, to re-

ally give children a chance to get into position and execute effective techniques.

The tactical keys to badminton are the overhead clear and smash along with the drop shot. Unfortunately, most novices find the overhead shots difficult. To ensure plenty of perfect, pertinent practice with the real shuttle, have the students play a game over a net that is 2.75 metres (9 feet) high initially, rising to 3.75 metres (12 feet). This net can be merely a line of elastic shock cord tied to vertical uprights that are in turn attached to the usual net posts. Track and field equipment such as pole vault poles and bars or high jump bars are very effective, but any long rod will do.

Initially, award points for any hit over the net, but gradually adjust this to scoring as in the real game—with the exception that only hits over the net count. Bringing the play practice net down to 30 to 45 centimetres (12 to 18 inches) above the real net means that students can play a drop shot game. This device also shapes good low serves.

To introduce youngsters to the real game of tennis, consider using the short tennis game Rod Thorpe developed in England or the mini tennis game used in Sweden. In both games youngsters play on a badminton court with the net lowered to 80 to 90 centimetres (32 to 36 inches). With both of these games the instructor can implement a scoring system that rewards consistency and keeping the ball in play rather than going for winners all the time. A range of different racquets and balls can be used. Paddle ball racquets or, better still, short-handled tennis racquets combined with soft tennis balls or foam balls produce the best results.

While players use ordinary tennis racquets, the ball should be a soft foam "slow" ball that gives players more time to track and play it. Many types of these balls are now available, although my experience shows that the ball sold as a "soft" softball is better than the "soft" tennis ball. It is easier to see, travels more slowly and is a bigger target to hit. Most importantly, the players must hit these balls with a full swing of the racquet if their stroke is to be effective, unlike the real ball, which can often be returned with a tentative poke. You can also buy "elephant skin" softball-sized balls that have a strong plastic cover. These balls last longer, especially with children who tend to pick holes in the ordinary foam versions unless watched carefully! Even good players will find it interesting and enjoyable to play a game with these balls, on a full court with a net, perhaps a volleyball net, that is about 2 metres (6 to 7 feet) high.

As suggested earlier, coaches in many sports have been employing the principles of Play Practice for some time. A talented Australian tennis coach, Chris Deptula, a graduate of the University of South Australia, uses a series of conditioned games to shape focus and enhance specific elements of technical and tactical play.

The first of these games is the serve volley game, which, as its name implies, is designed to develop these aspects of play. The server must volley the ball on both the first and second serves to win the point, while the receiver can win points only by returning the ball to marked sections of the court.

The second turns the traditional butterfly drill into a game. After a cooperative feed, one player must hit every stroke cross-court to win a point while the opponent can win only down the line.

The third of many possibilities that Chris uses is a game with a tactical emphasis. Players rally cross-court for as long as they wish before one of them chooses to hit down the line to start the real game. Points can be won only with a shot down the line or with a cross-court winner.

Other games involve restricting the playing area in which points can be scored to create variations on target tennis. Of these, one of the most interesting variations, and one that is potentially quite beneficial to players' development, is a game where points can be won only if the ball lands in the service area. This very quickly leads players into making tightly angled shots with increasing use of topspin.

Volleyball

When William Morgan created minonette, the immediate forerunner of volleyball, he was trying to develop a simple game that ordinary people could play—a true recreational game. The fact that he used a balloon instead of a ball carries two messages. First, he wanted a game where players were rarely under great pressure

so that the ball stayed in play for long periods. Second, the nature of the ball is a crucial element, especially with beginners.

Inevitably, the game Morgan created evolved in a different direction to become "power volleyball", a tactically complex game in which power and athleticism are as highly valued as in basketball. But what might be termed "real volleyball" is still suitable for the target audience Morgan was aiming at, and when taught correctly, it can still lead players toward the power game. The proviso "when taught correctly" is important because it is very easy to allow the game to become virtually a catch-and-throw game rather than one in which the volley is the defining feature. A dead-end game is created that is not particularly satisfying for players and will lead them nowhere.

Sport educators must decide which version of the game is suitable for their group given the talent and the time available. It is not worthwhile introducing the power game if the children are not ready for it or if there is insufficient time. This is because, in contrast with other team games, the techniques of volleyball are sequentially dependent. In other words, the spike is possible only if the ball has been passed—set—to the right spot at the right height; in turn, the set usually depends on the quality of the dig or bump that has been used to receive the opponent's service. Finally, the dig is possible only if the server can actually get the ball over the net, and this is not easy for many youngsters. Players must therefore master three relatively difficult techniques—the serve, the bump and the face pass—before they can use the spike to smash the ball down into the opponent's court.

This inevitably means that if beginners are put into a full game with regulation equipment and rules too soon, they will make many unforced errors and rallies will be rare. It will be a stop/start game with only a few children actually involved. This is frustrating for both the players and the instructor because, unlike soccer, which can remain enjoyable even when played very badly, the joy of volleyball unfolds only when players keep the ball in play through rallies, where the tension builds as the ball is continually retrieved and returned.

If there is one simple concept that underpins volleyball, it is to keep the ball in play at all costs. It may therefore be better to concentrate initially on the control and passing of the ball rather than worry about introducing the spike and block. In a sense, you should teach the equivalent of a ground stroke game in tennis that relies on consistency to win points rather than trying for winners at the net. But children really enjoy spiking the ball, so clearly instructors must develop this technique as soon as general ball control is good enough. To motivate some groups of reluctant youngsters, it may be worthwhile to use a low net and allow overhead hits—spiking—at the very beginning. In this way the children may appreciate that volleyball is an athletic and challenging game but that if they want to spike the ball consistently, they must first master the techniques necessary to control the ball. The fact that it is possible to use two apparently conflicting approaches to teaching this game is a testament to the complexity of games teaching and the complex decisions instructors must make.

Although volleyball is a team game, games sense, as it is defined in this book, is not as critical a factor in effective play as it is in free-flowing invasion games such as soccer and basketball. This is because each team gets only three touches at any time, so that even with beginners, play is virtually preprogrammed. Indeed, at the elite level, once the ball has been successfully controlled on the first touch, the second and third touches often involve set plays that are directed by the setter. Note that at the elite level, the options a team chooses are often in response to a virtual real-time computer analysis of the opposing team's tactics.

Because play is very predictable, drills are far more valuable in the teaching and coaching of volleyball than in any other team game, except perhaps American football. On the first two touches, players can concentrate completely on controlling and directing the ball without any distraction from defenders; only when attacking does a player have to read the defence and decide where to hit or dump the ball. It is therefore relatively simple to ensure a high degree of alignment between drills and the real game and thus to improve the players' agility and technical ability.

Despite this, play practices are still of vital importance in both teaching and coaching. They always bring a higher level of commitment and effort, especially if the players see the competition as meaningful. This becomes a critical issue with elite players, who must endure long, demanding training sessions over months or years. Play practices also give defenders a chance to read the play and therefore anticipate attacking moves; as with racquet sports, this gives them a better chance to move early to play the ball.

Once beginners understand the basic concepts of attack and defence within the context of three touches, the initial focus should be on the development of the technical ability players need to control and direct the ball. The approach to teaching this game has more in common with table tennis than with soccer. In the teaching of volleyball, all initial play practices are therefore based around individual and group challenges and cooperative games to develop ball control.

As suggested earlier, the nature of the ball is very important, and a wise instructor will take advantage of the wide range of user-friendly balls that are now available. It is possible to begin playing with a ball only slightly faster than Morgan's original balloon; in fact, this ball is a balloon covered with cotton cloth. This creates a larger ball that floats longer and is therefore easy for novices to track, control and direct, and it virtually eliminates the sting factor. As players improve, the group can move to a volley trainer ball, which is 25 percent larger and 40 percent lighter than the regulation ball; then to a regulation-size ball that is 25 percent lighter; and finally to a high-quality "soft-touch" regulation ball. This gradation of balls allows beginners to gradually develop the technical ability they need in the real game.

In the preface I stated that many sport educators are already employing the principles of Play Practice, albeit intuitively. One example is David Eldridge, the coordinator of volleyball at Heathfield High School, the Australian Schools Volleyball Champion every year from 1993 to 1999.

When the basic principles of Play Practice were outlined to him, David reviewed his methods and realised that he had unwittingly been applying many of these principles in his teaching and coaching for several years. With his own ideas brought into sharper focus by the insights Play Practice provided, he was immediately able to improve his methods. In his coaching, for example, he saw that by assigning each team an additional player when defending, he could ensure that there were always four blockers at the net so that every spiker always faced a double block.

In his developmental program David uses Play Practice principles to shape both games and drills by modifying the size of the playing area, varying the number of players controlling the height of the net and conditioning the game. He then focusses play through the use of differential scoring and enhances it through continual challenges.

One of the most significant aspects of his approach, however, is the way in which he uses specific combinations of regular services and what are termed free balls to keep the scores close and motivation high. This strategy, one commonly used throughout volleyball coaching, is detailed later in this section.

Above all, David is always conscious of the need for MIP, even when the nature of a play practice or limited playing areas mean that players have to take turns. For example, he eliminates the usual stop/start nature of the game as played by beginners by using strategies designed to keep the ball in play as much as possible. He rightly believes that the fun of the game lies in keeping the ball in the air for as long as possible through long rallies. This builds excitement and commitment from the players and is a major factor in inducing them to learn the tactics and techniques of volleyball.

He therefore introduces the game to beginners through short-court volleyball with a reduced playing area and a net height that initially prevents spiking. Team sizes can vary from four to six players or even more in some circumstances. He has found that youngsters always like being randomly drafted into teams. This can be accomplished in several ways, but he has an ongoing system where players' names are written on small cards and kept in a box, and the teams are subsequently drawn during the warm-up activity.

The objectives of short-court volleyball are very simple.

1. Keep the ball in play as long as possible. This is achieved by eliminating the formal serve and by having the player who recovers the ball after it hits the ground immediately throw it back over the net to restart the game.

2. Keep the ball off the ground and in the air at any cost. This is an absolute imperative, so the scoring system rewards and continually reinforces retrieving the ball. Special sacrifice efforts, where players totally commit themselves to keeping the ball off the floor, are highly rewarded, even if they are unsuccessful!

3. Get the ball over the net to put pressure on the opposition; force them to retrieve.

Because of the soft serve and the high player density, most of the time players meet the ball head height, and they are simply encouraged to push it back into the air without much concern for technique. In fact, with six players on a side in this short-court game, the ball is more likely to hit a player on the head by accident than it is to hit the floor! Although the ball is almost always traveling slowly in this game, with some groups you may still find it worthwhile to use foam or "gatorskin" balls in the early stages instead of the regulation volleyball. At the very beginning even the three-touch rule is waived, but introduce it as soon as ball control is good enough.

Dave uses a system of continuous informal competition to keep players motivated. He begins with the simple system of court rotation. Here "China" stays at home throughout while the remaining teams rotate clockwise every five minutes. This system, which keeps children "playing new faces in new places," enhances performance in almost every sport at all levels. He then changes the rotation so that the winning team moves toward court 1 while the losing team moves in the opposite direction. This eventually brings teams of even ability together to face each other in that session. His next move to ensure balanced competition is to gradually allocate the most talented teams more space to defend.

Rarely have coaches and sport educators given enough emphasis to ensuring balanced competition among young players, despite the fact that even hardened professional players often lack commitment in a one-sided game. The ideas of random team selection, playing for a limited time, bringing more talented teams to play against each other and the use of conditioning where necessary all ensure more balanced competition. This in turn ensures more enjoyment for all players and a greater commitment from them. Gradually, the number of players on all teams is reduced to four. In coaching situations or with talented classes, the number can drop even further, to three and then two, and court size increases progressively.

Finally, the instructor's attitude is crucial. Dave shows little interest in the results of the initial mini games, but he does look for and reward good movement skills and, as noted earlier, especially rewards players' sacrificial attempts to keep the ball in play. In this way he communicates his priorities quite clearly, and it is little wonder that his school has been so successful over many years.

Once youngsters have been introduced to and are enthusiastic about these games, you can introduce and refine key techniques. Even with more relaxed rules, ball control is still the key to this game and certainly no understanding of tactics can compensate for points lost through simple technical errors. Because of this and because volleyball is tactically far more predictable than other team games, drills have traditionally played a much larger role in the teaching and coaching of volleyball than in other team games.

David therefore uses the parallel approach detailed earlier in this text in which technical practice and small-sided game play are continually interwoven. This ensures high motivation and leads to persistent and purposeful practice. As players learn how to control the ball and begin to spike, he sets a net height that is essentially the group's average stretch height.

A key aspect of technical practice is that it usually involves three players, not two. This is simply because volleyball is a game of angles and redirection, and an instructor should introduce these elements as early as possible. This is not to say that individual practice or work in pairs is not permissible at the very beginning, but triangle work will better prepare players for the realities of the game; in essence, alignment is closer.

In fact, in their first practice, Dave does have the players work in pairs for a "set-and-set" game. It begins with the players warming up by setting the ball to each other over the net. They then move to setting the ball to themselves before playing it over the net to their partner, who repeats the process. This warm-up gives play-

ers a chance to develop or improve this important technique before beginning a game in which each pair competes against every other pair to keep the ball off the ground the longest. As players improve, this becomes a "set and dump" game. Both the set and the dump are likely to be crude versions of the real technique at this point, but performing a high volume of purposeful practice ensures that players will improve rapidly.

With motivation and intensity high, the instructor is free to focus on any players who need help with technique and to constantly reemphasise the importance of keeping the ball off the ground. After a suitable time, the short-court volleyball game resumes, with an emphasis on cleaner contact with the ball.

The next step is to introduce the dig or bump technique players use to receive difficult services. Because even a thrown ball can impact painfully on players' wrists, make sure foam or gatorskin balls are available to any youngsters who prefer to use them.

After initial practice in which the instructor constantly emphasises the critical elements of the dig/bump technique, every player gets 10 attempts in each position and the total number of successful catches is recorded, both to compete with other teams and to indicate ongoing improvement. Though this is initially a teaching practice, it can serve as a warm-up drill for experienced players, who can gradually make the initial overhead serve increasingly difficult for the receiver.

Use shaping to introduce another of the key elements in skilled play: communication between players. With beginners, inevitably everyone tries to play the ball, or everyone leaves it. In most practices players are spaced far enough apart that it is clear who the ball is going to, so they do not need to call to each other. Bringing three or four players virtually shoulder to shoulder, however, and asking them to keep the ball in play for as long as possible vertically above the group forces them to begin calling early and clearly to ensure that everyone knows who has the ball. Naturally, players need to transfer this into the game, but experience suggests that once youngsters develop confidence in their own judgment, they are willing not only to call their play but also to take on the important responsibility of calling balls in or out.

Play Practice and Volleyball Coaching

As suggested previously, one way to keep scores even is to use the notion of the free ball, a ball that is thrown over the net to the defending team rather than served. The rationale is simple. Even the underhand service that beginners use can be traveling hard and fast when it arrives, while the overhand service that more capable players employ can sometimes be unplayable. Clearly, this gives the serving team an immense initial advantage. Replacing the service with a free ball removes this advantage, and manipulating the ratio of real serves to free balls can create a finely balanced system of handicapping. This can keep the score between teams balanced and therefore maintain the players' sense of determination needed for really high-quality play.

Although a ratio of two or three free balls to one service is often sufficient, you can set it at any figure. For example, when the U.S. men's volleyball team were preparing for the 1996 Olympic Games by playing intersquad games, the second squad were at times given 12 free balls for every service they faced. Since they were allowed to serve normally throughout the game, the second squad had the huge advantage in being able to set up attacks. This naturally forced the first team to play exceptionally well if they wanted to stay in the competition.

Because of the tactical and technical simplicity of volleyball, the threshold between teaching and coaching is small. Thus, once players have mastered the technical elements to a working level, the instructor can use the same drills and games in both teaching and coaching with little modification.

Most importantly, it is possible to convert a drill into a play practice by basing scoring around what is termed a "wash system". This rather strange term simply means that to score a point, a team must win both its service rally as well as the rally that begins when their opponents are serving. If this does not happen, that is, if both teams win a rally, then the score is "washed out". Naturally, it becomes much harder to win a point under these circumstances, so the games, which can be played up to any number of points, become very hard fought. When the free ball system is then added to handicap one side or the other, the competition can become even tougher. The advantaged team wants to prove it does not need the help, whereas the handicapped team wants to prove it is the better team by overcoming the handicap. In both cases players have a heightened desire to keep the ball in play, thus ensuring purposeful practice.

Naturally, you can condition all of these games in some way. For example, the "deep hit game", usually played three on three, is conditioned so that rallies can only be won by a hit made from behind the 3-metre line.

Many other possibilities for shaping play exist. One of the simplest is manipulating the way in which points can be scored. Clearly, a game in which players can score points only with a dump will be very different from one in which they cannot use the dump to win a point. In the same way, a game in which players can win points only by hitting down the line will take on a specific character, whereas one in which they can gain points only by either deliberately hitting off the block or, conversely, making a successful block will shape and focus play in different directions.

Striking and Fielding Games

I know you are supposed to hit the white ball with the bat.
And then you run somewhere.
—Eddie Gaedel, 43-inch-tall baseball player
whose Major League career consisted of one
at-bat for the St. Louis Browns in 1951

● ● ● ● ●

Striking and fielding games take many forms, from rounders, the likely ancestor of both softball and baseball, to Finnish baseball to the peculiarly English game of cricket, which is now played in many countries worldwide. Interestingly, were it not for the American Civil War, cricket might now be a major game in the United States and baseball might never have progressed from the simple game of rounders!

Although pitching and bowling are both important elements of play, all of these games are fundamentally based around striking the ball into the opponent's territory and using the time gained to seize goals—bases—or score runs. The biggest problem with all of these games is that in a real game, players spend considerable time doing nothing. In a cricket test match, for example, players have been known to sit and

watch the action for more than two days while their teammates bat. Though inaction never reaches this extreme with baseball or softball, it is unreasonable to expect youngsters to sit around merely watching their peers and awaiting their turn to be involved.

The Loughborough group developed a solution to this problem by introducing the notion of sector games. Compared to cricket, in which the ball can be played through 360 degrees, both softball and baseball are already sector games. By reducing the sector further, to the angle between first and second base or between second and third, it is possible to play up to five or even six mini sector games on a large field (see figures 12.1a and 12.1b).

Although a primary focus of the Loughborough group was tactical awareness, these games

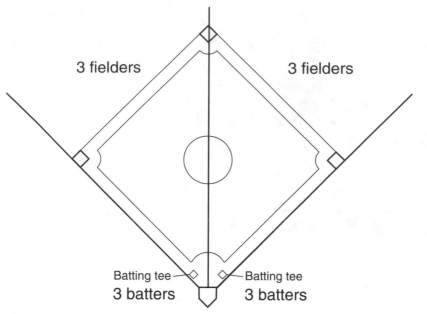

Figure 12.1a   The notion of sector games.

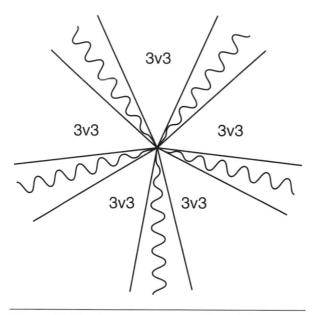

Figure 12.1b   Sector games involving 30 or more players.

can also be used simply to give large numbers of youngsters the chance to hit the ball, either off a tee or gently thrown, and to beat fielders positioned in the sector. With mini games involving three or four on a team, each player is continually involved, and opponents can rotate continuously.

With baseball and softball, the sectors extend out to home-run range with ground markings.

Markers indicate the distances the player has to hit the ball to score one, two, three or four runs. Each batter steps up for three consecutive hits—which means that each group must have several balls available—and tries to drive the ball past or over the fielders. Any ball caught costs the batter two runs, unless it is over the four-run line; then it is treated as a sacrifice fly and scores a single run.

The players keep score, and on the changeover the fielding team tries to score more runs than their opponents. In these games, while one batter is up, another teammate is getting the next ball ready on the tee while the third is acting as a combination feedbacker and commentator. If there are four on a team, the latter roles can be shared.

An instructor can easily introduce another level of complexity to these games. Simply add a rule that for any scoring hit to be valid, the batter must run and beat the ball to first base. This involves a slightly different organisational structure, but it makes the game more realistic while still retaining a high level of maximum individual participation (MIP).

With cricket the process is similar, but the sectors are now 45-degree arcs positioned to represent popular scoring zones for beginners. The one directly in front (see figure 12.2) is for the practice of driving over-pitched balls, and the one to the side (see figure 12.3) is for pulling or hooking short-pitched balls. Though both shots can be played off a tee, better players can use a lobbed ball for the drive and a thrown ball for the pull or hook. Now each batter receives six balls to hit because in cricket six balls represents an over.

As before, the sectors have markers at set distances to score—one, two, three or four runs, with six runs for a clean hit over the last line. Hits that are caught can be penalised any number of runs depending on the instructor's objectives.

In cricket, defensive play is also important, and a simple play practice can help players develop good technique in which the batsman

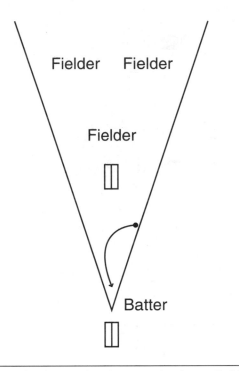

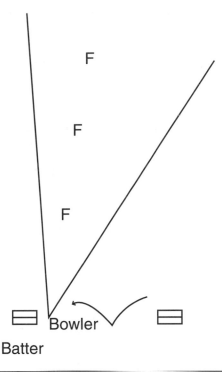

Figure 12.2 Sector for the straight drive. Fielders can position themselves anywhere and bowler (a teammate of the batter) lobs the ball for batsman to drive.

Figure 12.3 Sector for the pull shot. Bowler throws the ball to bounce up for batsman to pull or hook.

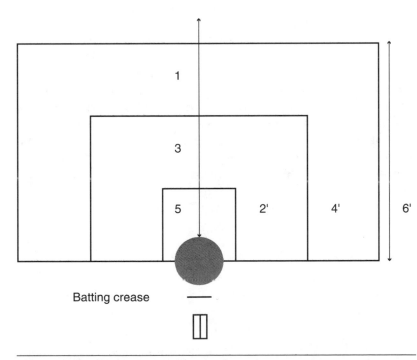

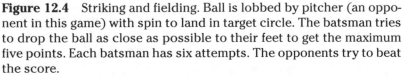

Figure 12.4 Striking and fielding. Ball is lobbed by pitcher (an opponent in this game) with spin to land in target circle. The batsman tries to drop the ball as close as possible to their feet to get the maximum five points. Each batsman has six attempts. The opponents try to beat the score.

plays with a vertical "straight" bat and "soft" hands. The batting crease is surrounded by a marked area as shown in figure 12.4. Now an opponent tries to lob spinning balls into a target area, forcing the batter to play correctly.

Though everyone usually gets to bat in baseball, softball and cricket, in the real game not everyone pitches or bowls. Despite this, youngsters love to aim at targets, and you can develop interesting targets of the kind shown in figures 12.5 and 12.6. Set these targets up in any free space and they will attract a lot of interest. They may also be the starting point for a lifelong interest in this aspect of sport.

The baseball pitching target can have either a cut-out area below the bat through which the ball must be pitched, or a plate of tin hanging down from the bat. The latter is especially popular

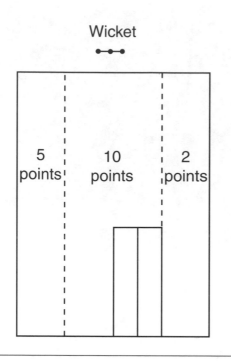

Figure 12.5 A cricket bowling target made of steel or solid wood is used. It is based on the "real" target zone; the regulation "wicket" is unrealistic and too small. Individuals or small teams compete in games of six balls to each player.

Figure 12.6 An example of an easily made wooden figure of a batter with a metal plate hanging on to the bat to represent the strike zone.

because a good pitch is obvious to everyone within hearing distance.

The cricket target is interesting because it is based on the real target area for effective bowling, which is far larger than the apparent target, namely, the wicket made of three stumps. While bowlers at every level love to hit the stumps, even in practice, the fact is that for bowlers at the highest level, the real target area is much larger than the regulation wicket. In fact, fast bowlers often make it fairly obvious that their target is the body of the batter and not

the wicket! The target can be made of steel or corrugated iron, which will take an enormous amount of punishment and still last a long while. Because of the size and weight of the target, it is best left in position in the practice nets.

While the sector games cover the catching and ball-stopping aspects of fielding, they do not cover throwing for accuracy. You can use the targets described previously for accuracy practice, but the challenge for sport educators in these games is to develop realistic and challenging play practices that emphasise this aspect of good play. The baseball game alluded to earlier in which the hitter has to beat the ball to first is one example of this kind of game. Many more are waiting to be developed!

Target Games

One of the advantages of bowling over golf is that you very seldom lose a bowling ball.
—Don Carter, U.S. bowler

● ● ● ● ●

In target games, technique and a good temperament are the most important elements in success. As always, the Play Practice approach to target games is based on the precepts outlined in chapter 5.

Golf

As one of the great games of the world, golf is the ultimate target sport. To hit a small ball long distances is challenge enough, but to get it close to a specific target—a small hole—while confronting the terrors of bunkers, trees, lakes or rivers in almost every possible weather condition appears almost magical. Fortunately, millions of people of all ages take up the challenge, and golf should be a part of any program of sport education where possible.

Golf's difficulty is also increased by the fact that in essence it is made up of two separate and distinctly different games. Striking a ball with a full swinging action using woods or irons comprises one of the games. The act of swinging a golf club has been variously likened to swinging a flail or hoe, or to an upright baseball swing. The primary requirement of this game is to develop a repeatable and accurate swing that hits the ball in the required direction.

The second game of golf is putting. Unlike the swing game, which is played largely in the air, the putting game depends on the player's ability to roll the ball accurately along the ground. The techniques within the two games vary greatly, so much so that even players of a very high standard may be considered masters of one but poor at the other. The two games are often taught in isolation. Swing coaching and practice usually take place at driving ranges, whereas many children's first experience of golf is at the local putt-putt.

For most students, a more complete mastery of the game depends on both a great deal of practice aimed at developing a repeating swing or putting stroke as well as the knowledge of when to apply particular shots. Fortunately, golf is well suited to the creation of mini games; indeed, it is possible to create play practices for almost any aspect of the game.

© Human Kinetics

The phenomenon that is Tiger Woods began hitting golf balls almost as soon as he could walk and is now well on his way to becoming the most successful player in history. He is also well on the way to accruing an immense fortune and is a role model for all those parents who believe that their children have the talent to emulate him. However it is important for parents to realise that his is probably a one in a billion talent which may never be equaled. So parents and coaches must ask themselves whether it is worth encouraging children to sacrifice their childhood and a vast range of other potential worthwhile careers in the hope that their child will be equally successful. One in a billion is fairly long odds!

The Play Practice approach is simple. From the very beginning, students, perhaps using seven- or nine-irons, hit toward or even onto a series of replica greens. These greens, which can be marked out with ropes or, better still, cut out on a playing field with a mower, should be the exact size and shape of famous par-three holes from golf courses around the world. You can, of course, reduce the distance between the tee and green to whatever length best suits a group. The actual hole can be any size the instructor wishes, but it should be significantly larger than a real one. Certainly, you should award special prizes for any hole-in-one!

You can also use modified target areas to help players develop a range of shots. For chipping practices, try placing hoops, cones or drawn targets on the green or other cut-out areas. The target areas can either offer a larger hole or define the area where a player should land a chip from off the green to run up near the hole. Bunker shots, which appear complicated, nonetheless lend themselves well to the use of Play Practice. In bunker play, the club should not actually strike the ball but instead should enter the sand behind the ball and lift both the ball and the sand on which it rests. How far behind the ball the club head should enter depends on the type of sand and whether it is wet or dry; these variables tend to make getting out of sand difficult because the decision-making element is greater than for most shots. Applying a Play Practice approach, however, simplifies many of the demands; for example, you can use the bunker sand to draw markings that show where the club should strike the sand to get the ball out. Markings may vary from simple lines or semi-circles to shapes or even faces drawn in the sand.

This approach can lead easily into the series of tests used in some special, unofficial tournaments for U.S. professional players. These tournaments are virtually a Play Practice approach to golf and include the following tests:

- Driving for distance
- Putting from set spots to get as close to the pin as possible
- A bunker shot from set spots to get as close to the pin as possible
- A short iron from set spots to get as close to the pin as possible

In the tests that require getting closest to the pin, distance is measured with a tape measure, although distance rings can be drawn. These tests can all fit into a relatively small area, and with a self-testing process, youngsters can work their way around them in pairs or small groups. Naturally, the instructor should record all performances with a view to improving them at a later date. In addition, you can hold "The Open" (e.g., the "Wodonch High School Open" or the "Detroit YMCA Open Golf Championship") at the end of a unit of work. Ideally it should take place on a real golf course, although a par-three course would be suitable. If neither is available, the test series just outlined would be appropriate—with suitable awards, of course.

Archery

Safety is a critical issue in terms of both the area where practice takes place and especially control of the firing area. The latter will be a function of the instructor's management skills, whereas the former depends simply on how much space is available. A rough guide is to allow 50 percent more distance than the maximum range of the equipment being used.

After introducing the safety rules and the basic elements of shooting technique, begin the Play Practice approach by having the students shoot for maximum distance rather than at targets. Though many might question this approach, there is little doubt that it has several advantages and that it works.

First, beginners will more readily appreciate the potential danger of a missile that can travel 180 metres (200 yards) or more. Second, as they gradually try to shoot farther, their technique will improve. They will begin to draw to the chin with correct finger positioning on the bowstring while maintaining a strong front arm—instead of the short draw, poor fingers and weak front arm that usually occur when aiming at close targets.

An added bonus is that the arrows will land at such an angle that they will not snake under the grass and get lost, as often happens when arrows are fired flat. This not only saves arrows and time spent looking for them but also ensures PPPP—plenty of perfect pertinent practice. Students are paired up: while one archer is shooting, the partner can provide feedback on one or two carefully defined aspects of technique. This instructional strategy can be used in many sports where students take turns.

The second practice involves firing high to drop the arrows into a horizontal target, such as the centre circle of a soccer field, from gradually decreasing distances. Volley firing—when the whole group releases its arrows at the same time on a given signal—is always a popular variation with children in this practice.

These practices shape the correct draw and help youngsters understand the relationship between a good draw, the release angle and the flight characteristics of the arrow. When the young archers have achieved a good draw in this way, the instructor can introduce regulation targets but again with a Play Practice twist. Secure large, colorful balloons to each target and award special prizes for every one hit. Naturally, other targets can be used, but for children little beats the dramatic bursting of a balloon.

One final variation is shooting at a moving target in the form of a cardboard box drawn slowly across the shooting area. Instructors can decide for themselves whether to paint a face or an animal on the box. Clearly, you can introduce regulation shooting and scoring at any point, but a culminating competition for the prized "golden arrow" will be sure to create considerable interest.

CHAPTER 14

Individual Sports

I sometimes think that running has given me a glimpse of the greatest freedom a man can ever know, because it results in the simultaneous liberation of both body and mind.
—Roger Bannister

• • • • •

One of the many advantages of Play Practice is that sport educators can apply the general principles across a wide range of individual sports. This chapter shows how it can be used to improve instruction in sports as different as track and field and snow skiing.

Track and Field

The varied and challenging events of track and field make up one of the great sports of the world. Every year millions of boys and girls and men and women in almost every country take part in track and field competitions that culminate every four years in the spectacle and drama of the Olympic Games.

Because each event makes different demands on the participant's physical and mental qualities, individuals of widely different abilities can find enjoyment and success in this sport. Recent years have seen a huge expansion in the range of individuals taking part in track and

field. People of all ages as well as individuals with a wide range of physical and mental impairments are able to participate in track and field right up to the Olympic level.

Although its popularity should give it an immense advantage as an educational and developmental activity, track and field rarely finds a place at the centre of the sport curriculum. All too often it is reserved for physically gifted children and enjoys status only as an interschool and interclub sport. There appear to be two reasons for this. The first is a mistaken belief that this sport demands great physical ability, dedication and mental toughness. The second is the misperception that track and field is a highly technical sport. Unfortunately, many texts reinforce these views by recommending adult training methods and techniques for children. Taught properly, track and field, along with gymnastics and swimming, should be central to any worthwhile program of sport education.

Courtesy of USC Spirit

Sergey Bubka is arguably the greatest field event athlete in the history of the sport. Born in the Ukraine, then a republic of the former U.S.S.R, Sergey was an enthusiastic player of both soccer and ice hockey as a young boy. However he demonstrated great all-round athletic ability from an early age and was encouraged to specialise in the pole vault by coach Vitaly Petrov at the Donetsk training centre. He went on to win six consecutive World Championships and to set innumerable world records both indoors and outdoors. In the process he revolutionised the technique of the event. However, many authorities believe that in his attempts to maximise his income by only improving the world record by 1 centimetre at a time, he missed the opportunity to completely fulfill his potential.

Play Practice and Track and Field for Children

Traditional methods of teaching track and field to youngsters have been based on two misconceptions. The first is that children should master the techniques of the sport in the same way they are expected to master the complex move-

ments of gymnastics. The second is that children can and will participate willingly in head-to-head competition against their peers in which a single winner emerges while the rest calmly accept their roles as losers.

I became brutally aware of both these fallacies early in my career in the swamp of reality. My students intuitively understood that in track and field no prizes were awarded for style; the essence of this sport was how fast, how high and how far. Equally important, they wanted to find out what they could achieve in these interesting challenges—without being exposed to the fear of losing, or, even worse, the opprobrium attached to finishing last.

Armed with limited knowledge and shaky instructional skills, I used a process of pragmatic tinkering and reflective analysis to develop what I came to call the "five-star approach to teaching track and field". This approach was initially driven by attempts to make cross-country running more palatable during the depths of the English winter when the playing fields became quagmires. Feedback from children quickly led to the use of a range of relatively short runs in which I recorded the time of every runner in the class. This in turn led to an emphasis on the individual performance of every runner and to the importance of doing one's best to improve.

The principles and methods I developed at that time led me to a similar approach in the teaching of track and field, where, with the addition of the concept of working models of technique, it provided a viable alternative to traditional methods. Eventually, these ideas led to a complete revision in the teaching of track and field in many countries; they also became the foundations of what was to become Play Practice. The relationship between the two becomes clear when we study the principles of the five-star approach to teaching track and field, which were first spelled out in the 1960s.

The five-star approach is based on the following tenets:

1. Children like to be challenged, but most of all they like to succeed and have their successes noted. They do not like to fail or be beaten, and they certainly do not want to be last at anything. Thus, one of the most important factors in the

learning process is early and continued success for each child. Even in the tough competitive sport of track and field, all children can succeed in indirect competition, in which each child strives to beat his or her own previous best performance, rather than direct competition, in which each competitor struggles to beat opponents.

2. Children like to see how fast they can run, how far they can jump or throw and how high they can jump or vault. They are much less concerned about how correctly they perform. **Teachers should never forget that correct technique, though important to ultimate performance, is only a means to an end and not an end in itself.**

3. The apparently complex events of track and field are closely related to, and have evolved from, the natural play activities of running, jumping and throwing. At the senior level these events are stylised forms of these activities that strongly emphasise the element of direct competition. With children it is important to retain the play element and eliminate direct competition as much as possible.

Using this approach, track and field is therefore regarded as a series of varied and enjoyable tests or challenges in which all youngsters can improve their performance and thus succeed. Increasing skill and fitness derived from participation enable children to experience the success and satisfaction of mastery and improvement throughout this vital early learning period.

If the track and field events are initially regarded as tests rather than as a series of complex movement patterns for children to master, the instructor's task is far easier. Very little knowledge is required to introduce the various tests of running, hurdling, long jumping and high jumping. The instructor should therefore introduce a working technique that enables children to do the following:

- Perform the event within the accepted rules. Even here, you can make some modifications to simplify the test without changing its essential nature.
- Master the basic elements of the test as quickly as possible
- Begin testing themselves almost immediately

- Develop a technique that is simple, sound and, most importantly, has the potential for continued development

The notion of introducing a working technique is critical to the success of this approach and parallels the way in which Play Practice modifies games to reduce their complexity. Nowhere is this better illustrated than in the pole vault, where, by introducing a working model of technique, it is possible to have children vaulting well above their own height after 30 minutes of practice in a sandpit.

The technical skill and knowledge needed on the part of the instructor to introduce athletics in this way is surprisingly small, and any committed sport educator can quickly build an enthusiastic and committed group of young athletes. Not only will they enjoy the challenges of this sport, they will also begin to improve the agility essential to success in many other sports.

The final element added to this innovative approach was the "five-star award scheme" devised by the brilliant and innovative Tom McNab, national coach for track and field in the south of England in the early 1960s. Tom had the idea of combining the teaching methods outlined previously with a points system. Children's performances were rewarded with certificates recognising levels from one star to five stars. This concrete recognition of their efforts had an immediate impact and became an invaluable motivational tool.

The scheme was immediately successful in Britain, and more than 20 other countries have since picked it up. The only downside has been a tendency for teachers to encourage children to specialise in just three events instead of selecting their best three performances from the entire range they have attempted.

Here it is vital to remember that track and field is a great sport in its own right. So while sport educators can use working models of technique to introduce children to the varied and interesting disciplines of athletics, they must be prepared to help children progress from the working model toward the advanced models that elite performers use. Naturally this will depend on the children's ability and interest and the time, facilities and equipment available. Most importantly, it will depend on the professionalism of the sport educator.

Clearly, making the transition from working to advanced models is easier in some events than in others. Ample evidence suggests, however, that in every school and community many youngsters possess the talent and desire to become competent performers even in events as complex as the hammer throw and the pole vault.

Though it may seem a daunting task at first, committed sport educators can improve their understanding of track and field, even if by studying one discipline at a time. In this way they will be able to grow with their students and be better able to help them realise their potential and in doing so perhaps change their lives for the better.

Because the primary emphasis in this approach is on personal performance and improvement, it is important to record each child's performance in every event. This is quite easily done by the instructor, by a helpful parent or by the children themselves. Naturally, every improvement must be noted and praised. You can produce small recognition certificates or, better still, award small prizes such as jelly beans and present them at the end of every session. Gradually replace these by an emphasis on the intrinsic feeling of satisfaction that comes from having done one's best.

The following basic plan can introduce track and field to youngsters between the ages of 10 and 14:

• While the group is warming up and preparing for the session, remind them of the importance of personal improvement and doing their best.

• Organise a time trial over a standard distance. The whole class can start at the same time in the 800 and 1,500 metres (half-mile and mile), and the teacher simply calls out each individual's time as he or she passes the finish line. In the 400 metre (440 yards), it is best to set the runners off in groups at 10-second intervals; the groups start as the instructor calls "Go," "Ten," "Twenty," "Thirty," "Forty," "Fifty," and so on, and they subtract this figure from the time called out to them as they finish.

• While the children are recovering from their effort, talk with them, praise their general performance and recognise all personal improvements if they have run the distance before.

• Introduce a new test. Start with the simpler events first. The following sequence is suggested:

1. The long jump. This is the most natural of the field events and hardly needs teaching at all. Simplify it further by using a 1-metre- (1 yard-) wide "takeoff zone" instead of the usual takeoff board, which even experienced athletes have great difficulty in hitting accurately. Encourage the children to use short approach runs, for this will give them sufficient speed and allow control at takeoff. At this stage, about all that you can tell them is, "Run fast and jump high!" Certainly, waste no time on in-the-air movements such as the hang or hitch kick. From the very beginning, try to give the youngsters an idea of approximately how far each jump is, with tape measures stretched from the takeoff zone through the pit.

2. The high jump. Bearing in mind that this event is structured by only one rule—the jumper must take off from one foot—this is again an easy test to introduce. Although any style of jumping off one foot is allowed, the old-fashioned scissors-style jump has many advantages. Despite the poor layout position over the bar, it is both simple and safe and provides good lift at takeoff. In fact, elite high jumpers use it as a primary training drill. Children who have special ability or interest can switch to the flop technique later on if suitable landing pads are available.

3. The hurdles. One successful approach is to start with hurdles—preferably elastic-top training ones—of the accepted height for the particular age group. Vary the distances between them.

4. The shot put. This is the safest of all the throws. Teach only the basic putting action in which the youngster pushes the shot away from the neck with a powerful punch of the shoulders and a driving extension of the arm.

Enhancing the Teaching of Athletics

When children are asked to nominate the most boring field event, they invariably choose the shot put. The following section illustrates how Play Practice can turn this supposedly boring activity into an enjoyable challenge in which youngsters are highly motivated to do their very best. It also illustrates the importance of good preparation and the simple, subtle but highly effective elements that make up really good instruction.

The process begins with ensuring that at least one shot of approximately the right weight is available for every two children. The second task is to select and mark out a suitable piece of ground for the activity. It must be "dead ground", that is, ground not usually or not often used for other activities. It is important that a border of some kind clearly define the limits of the area. Limiting the distance to 20 metres (about 22 yards) or less will put the group's efforts into good perspective. If the activity were turned round and the children faced a limitless field in front of them as they tried to throw or put, their efforts would seem puny. Limiting the distance is simple, subtle but effective.

The area is also marked in a way that conveys a sense of achievement to everyone. The first line is only 3 metres (about 3 yards) from the throwing line, and each child should attain that distance. If, on the other hand, the first line were set at 10 metres (about 10 yards), many children would be condemned to failure, no matter how hard they tried. Again—simple, subtle but effective!

The third element of preparation can involve the students. Ask them to make or find their own personal markers that they can use throughout the track and field unit for measuring run-ups as well as distances achieved. It can be something as simple as an old tennis ball or screwdriver painted brightly, or it can be something that they or a family member make especially for the unit. Naturally, a school can provide these markers, but the involvement of family or friends in the experience can be valuable.

After explaining and emphasising the safety rules, the practice can begin with the backward overhead throw with two hands. This commonly used training and warm-up activity is simple enough for beginners and introduces them to the importance of "legs first, trunk, shoulders, arms, wrist and fingers" in throwing a heavy implement. Depending on the time available and the instructor's interest and knowledge, this can be an excellent opportunity to examine the issues of strength, power, force, release speeds and delivery angle.

Each child takes three warm-up throws, during which time the instructor reemphasises the safety rules, and then each child takes three attempts in which the best distance thrown is marked. Measure the distance of the best attempt either by estimation or by using tape measures placed strategically in the throwing area. Now for the Olympic challenge! Tell the children that if they can beat their best throw to date, they "win a bronze medal in the Olympic shot put event!" If they succeed, they next try for a silver with the second throw; if not they try again for the bronze. Finally, on the third throw, those who have managed to improve twice already are "going for gold". Again, if they do not succeed, they continue to try for the appropriate level.

This approach generates considerable interest and quite a bit of fun. It then carries over to at least one of the progressions for teaching the actual technique of putting the shot. Experience suggests that it can completely change the attitude of young people to the challenge of throwing heavy weights.

5. The triple jump. This is also easy to teach as a test; it provides the immense satisfaction of jumping a long distance and offers great prospects of rapid improvement. Introduce it as a standing hop, step and jump, with the stress on the "dah-dah-dah"

rhythm once the children have mastered the correct foot pattern. With all these early attempts, give the youngsters an approximate idea of how far they are jumping.

6. The javelin. Taught properly and with stringent safety rules enforced, the javelin is not a dangerous event. Most youngsters will soon master the basic elements. As with the shot put, all throwing should take place from behind a scratch line with the landing area marked so that the children can see immediately how far they are throwing and note their improvements.

7. The pole vault. This is easy to teach if you have a large sandpit and some stout wooden staves or bamboo poles 2.5 to 3 metres (8 to 10 feet) long. Teach the children to hold the pole with the top hand 2.5 to 5 centimetres (1 to 2 inches) above their stand-and-reach height and with the bottom hand 45 centimetres (18 inches) lower. The thumbs of both hands should be uppermost, while the palm of the top hand should face the child while the bottom hand should be turned away. Then ask them to run about 30 feet to plant the pole into the sandpit, hang on and ride it as far down the pit as possible, telling them to "ride the pole on the same side as your top hand." As they gain in confidence and skill, suggest that they hold the pole higher and higher so that they can vault farther down the pit.

The next step is to put high jump standards on each side of the pit, set a soft crossbar at approximately 2 feet and ask the class to vault over it. Initially the skill they use is little different from the skill they needed to vault for distance, but as the bar is raised by 6-inch (20-centimetre) increments emphasise the need to pick up the legs and pull with the top hand so that the body is raised; finally, ask the children to turn and face back toward the run-up as they pass over the bar. Planting the pole in the sand eliminates the need for an accurate approach run and a skillful plant.

8. The discus. This is probably the most difficult and dangerous of the events to teach because the implement is so difficult to control.

First, teach the group how to hold the discus on the top joints of the spread fingers.

Next, have them practise rolling it along the ground as far and as straight as possible to learn how to release it correctly off the index finger. Finally, teach them the standing throw, flinging the discus out by a loose, sweeping horizontal arm pull that is initiated by punching the right side of the body around the left.

9. The hammer. It is highly unlikely that the test of hammer throwing will become an accepted part of any sport education program, but it is taught on a class basis to eighth-grade boys in some British schools using sandbag hammers. These are simple devices with a wooden handle, nylon rope instead of the usual wire, and a small sand-filled canvas bag replacing the metal ball. This makes them both safer and cheaper.

With all of these events, remember the criteria previously established for a working model of technique and bear in mind that children need only sufficient skill and knowledge at this stage to be able to perform the test within the rules—and with prospects of improvement. It is important to teach the basic rules of each event so the children know how to judge and measure correctly, and it is particularly vital to teach and continually reemphasise the safety rules.

If it is feasible, organise the youngsters into groups to test themselves in the events already introduced. As they master more tests, use smaller groups. Because of the problems involved with raising and lowering the high jump bar, if only one high jump area is available it may be convenient to base groups roughly on high jump ability.

During this period of group work it is possible to teach an event for which limited equipment is available. Rotate each group in turn to the teaching station while the rest of the class test themselves in known events. You can also use this time to give groups a chance to test themselves in the 100- and 200-metre (100- and 220-yard) dashes and in the hurdles when a shortage of stopwatches permits timing only a few children at once.

If time is available, organise an occasional continuous relay, with or without batons. With teams of 7 to 12 spread around a 400-metre (440-yard) track, these relays provide fun and hard running. Base the relays on running for a set time or for a specified number of laps.

The following sequence presents one way in which instructors can introduce track and field to beginners.

Introduce each event as a test.

Test the children by timing or measuring their performance in the event, or allow them to test themselves.

Record the performance in the test.

Retest again and again, recording each improvement and praising all improvements.

© Action Images

Marion Jones grew up in southern California and demonstrated remarkable all-round talent in baseball, basketball, track and field and gymnastics at an early age. After a stellar career in basketball at the University of North Carolina, she returned to track and field where she has established herself among the greatest of all female sprinters, winning three gold medals at the Sydney Olympic Games.

Play Practice and Cross-Country Running

Sport educators can use a similar approach to introduce cross-country running to the same age group. Here the tests consist of running courses ranging from 1,200 up to 3,000 metres (3/4 mile to 2 miles) over the most varied terrain in the area. Though road courses can be used, they are not recommended because of the possibility of damage the impact can cause to still-growing joints and bones.

It is important to stress that these runs are not races, but rather time trials in which every child succeeds as long as they do their best. No one wins a time trial, no one loses a time trial and, above all, no one finishes last in a time trial. Encouragement, praise and occasional criticism play an important part in maintaining interest and effort. It is vital to keep the less talented youngsters involved. The instructor must point out that all youngsters vary immensely in ability from one activity to another. Indeed, running ability varies with the distance run, as the youngsters well know, so it is only natural that some will run faster than others. Continually reemphasise in many different ways this fundamental idea of individual differences.

Before a group starts a run, remind them of the importance of doing their best, pacing their effort and listening to their time when it is called out to them in minutes and seconds as they finish. Let youngsters record their own times. Both at the finish and later on, the instructor has the opportunity to praise effort and improvement and to make personal contact with individual children. This approach to introducing athletics and cross country running has the following advantages:

• It gives all children a chance to grow fully as they experience the success and satisfaction that comes from improvement.

• It not only recognises individual differences but also encourages youngsters to accept them.

• It creates a highly favourable climate of opinion among the peer group that encourages the gifted youngsters to make full use of their talents. It exposes all children to these great disciplines and gives them a chance to discover an interest or talent that could form the basis of a lifetime of commitment and enjoyment.

• Initially, it requires little technical knowledge on the part of the instructor.

• Though it requires enthusiasm and good organisation, because no teaching method can be effective without these, it provides immense satisfaction for the sport educator.

Experience confirms that this approach leads to a very positive attitude toward both cross-country and track and field. It can also lead to very high performances in both sports. This was evident at Dr. Challoner's Grammar School in Amersham, England, which in a very short period became one of the most successful schools in the country in both. At a time when many schools would be happy to boast even one boy selected to represent their county at the English Schools Cross-Country Championships, the Dr. Challoner's team included in 1965:

John Gulson, 11th out of 360 runners from all over England in the senior race over 5 miles;

Jeremy Stagg, 18th;

Richard Melvern, 22nd;

John Newman, 24th; and

David Barnes, 94th.

In addition, the team included

Chris Murray, who finished 31st in the under-17 race;

Jeff White, 38th;

Andrew Parker, 46th; and

Chris Heppell, 97th.

In 1965 the six Challoners boys representing Buckinghamshire would have finished sixth out of 36 counties if their places had been scored as a team. Indeed, had John Newman managed to avoid the flu and been able to repeat his 24th position of the previous year, this school team would have finished third ahead of many large counties such as Essex, Surrey and Warwickshire.

The boys achieved this not because of intensive coaching or specialisation but rather because running developed as a part of the school's culture through the methods outlined in this chapter. John Gulson, for example, represented Buckinghamshire at soccer, cricket, basketball and athletics as well as cross-country running.

Play Practice and Elite Track and Field Athletes

Sport educators can use the principles of Play Practice to relieve the unrelenting regimen of training involved as athletes make the transition from talented adolescent to elite senior performer. This is important because compared to most sports, track and field has a poor ratio of training time to competition time; in some events, every second of an actual competition performance represents many hours of training. In addition, many elite athletes compete for only four months in their usual event and are then committed to heavy training loads for the remainder of the year.

During this training period, especially when winter sets in, it is difficult for them to produce performances that approach their best in their usual event. Poor weather conditions, limited competition and little incentive to perform well usually mean that they would perform below their best if expected to compete under these circumstances. This could be psychologically destructive, and the effort could also lead to unnecessary injuries. Yet it is important for them to test themselves regularly to assess progress during this period. This can be done by using simple field tests to introduce a strong element of competition to the training of athletes in many disciplines.

Coaches have used field tests for many years. They incorporate the principles of Play Practice and therefore bring the enjoyment of competition back into training. These tests are simply variations on the theme that all track and field events are merely challenges that test speed, power, spring, speed endurance, endurance and skill along with other valuable human qualities such as determination, self-control and intelligence. In fact, some challenges that are now regarded only as field tests, such as the standing long jump and standing triple jump, were once part of the sport of track and field and, along with the standing high jump, were included in the Olympic program. Indeed, the history of the sport is littered with many events that have either been eliminated from the sport altogether or, as with the pole vault, changed beyond all recognition by the impact of technology.

Some sport educators even believe that there would be many advantages to completely changing every four years the events that make up the sport of athletics. Doing this would quash a growing obsession with records, and the sport might begin a new and more dynamic life. Though this is unlikely to happen, it is certainly possible for an instructor to create a vast range of other events to use as field tests.

Using field tests has many advantages. The first is that athletes can compete year-round and therefore remain motivated. Because these challenges test the generic components of athletic performance events such as speed, power and spring, athletes from different disciplines can compete with or against each other in a wide range of different tests. This sometimes causes consternation among sprinters and jumpers as they discover, to their dismay, that throwers can often beat them in tests involving jumping, power and even speed!

When field tests are properly structured, athletes usually execute them with the intensity of a full competitive effort—especially if they are competing with friends or, even better, close rivals! This produces a training effect far beyond that of often repetitive drills, one that is often highly correlated with the needs of the athlete's usual event. As with the Play Practice approach to athletics for children, however, the emphasis is on indirect competition; the athletes compete with themselves and are continually striving to achieve personal best performances.

In these relatively informal competitions, which can take place on a regular basis during specific training cycles, athletes can also begin to improve their competition skills, which are based on a range of competencies such as the ability to visualise a successful performance, focus on key elements, concentrate to eliminate any distractions and then perform.

Ideally, a set of norms should be established for each event, similar to the scoring tables used for the multi events. As athletes see the various test results improving and their points moving up they become like decathletes, hungry for any improvement. They can more readily see the value of their training and begin to smell success in the upcoming season.

Field tests can provide valuable information to coaches in terms of an athlete's physical status across a whole range of parameters and can help pinpoint weaknesses. They can also provide some clues to technical problems. For example, in the pole vault many young athletes learn bad habits if they spend too much time vaulting on flexible poles early in their careers. A field test developed by coaches from the former Soviet Union can help determine the efficiency of the takeoff by comparing grip height off six steps with a stiff pole with an athlete's grip height using a full run and competition pole. In the same way, javelin coaches can compare the distance thrown with overweight and underweight javelins or throwing balls and use the information to indicate the relative status of technique and power.

Perhaps the final advantage of field tests is that they can predict probable performances in the real event as the training period winds down in preparation for real competition. R. Kismin and W. Ovtschinnov, distance coaches in the former Soviet Union, produced formulae based around 2 by 60- and 4 by 60-second runs for distance to accurately predict race times for the 800 metre and 1,500 metre, respectively. This information could help build runners' confidence and help them determine their racing tactics.

Usually, the greater the similarity between a test and the actual event, the better the test is as a predictor, but this is not always the case. For example, Victor Saneyev, three-time Olympic champion and world record holder in the triple jump, found an almost perfect correlation between his triple jump distances and the overhead shot throw and therefore "knew" when he was ready to perform well in the real event despite the apparently limited relationship between the two tests.

Because they can be conducted almost anywhere with very basic equipment, field tests can be useful in many ways. They can be especially valuable in identifying talented youngsters who have had very limited exposure to the real sport of track and field. For example, a simple ball-throwing test can identify potential javelin throwers far earlier than would be the case if youngsters had to first learn how to control and direct this implement.

Skiing

One of the major advantages of Play Practice is that sport educators can apply the fundamental principles to a wide range of sports to create more dynamic, effective and enjoyable learning situations. This is certainly the case with downhill skiing, where traditional methods of instruction have been bogged down by an overemphasis on the mastery of technique to the point where the joy and exhilaration of moving on skis is lost.

In fact, one of the major reasons behind the explosion of interest in snowboarding among young people may be that adolescents much prefer to go off and try the real thing, even at some cost in bumps and bruises, rather than be pinned down waiting for their turn to attempt the repetitive and boring technical practice typical of traditional ski instruction.

Given the constraints the average skier usually faces, such as cost and limited time to practise, it is critical to determine just how much a learner really needs to know to ski safely and enjoyably. As always, the Play Practice approach revolves around three simple questions:

1. Where are the learners now, and what do they want from the sport of skiing?

2. What is the fundamental nature of the sport?

3. How can we get individuals involved in the real activity as quickly as possible?

Traditional methods are based on a fundamental misconception about what most beginning recreational skiers expect from the sport. This misconception is a product of both history and the sociology of ski instruction, which is dominated by young men and women whose lives often revolve around competitive skiing. Clearly, if we view skiing in terms of racing down fixed courses marked by flags, the technical ability necessary to stay in control at high speeds—and avoid serious injury or even death—is of crucial importance.

The fact that most ski instructors are expert skiers first and teachers second has tended to lead to an overemphasis on the techniques needed to race down a mountain. Interestingly, even senior racers and instructors often argue for hours over relatively minor differences between national skiing styles.

Recreational skiers, however, do not spend much time racing down marked courses. They seem to prefer a "touring" approach where they select a route and its challenges to match their own technique and that of their friends. For them, technique is not an end in itself but rather a means to an end, so traveling safely and enjoyably on snow-covered slopes is more important than whether they use edging, carving or sliding techniques to deal with the terrain.

The implication of this is that instruction should not be based on the mere repetition of isolated techniques but should encourage learners to begin the process of learning to "read" both the slopes and the snow conditions. One of the most important aspects of performance in any sport is that the participant must understand his or her own capabilities and limitations. Nowhere is this truer than in recreational downhill skiing, with its ever-present threat to limbs and even to life itself.

It is crucial that from the very beginning, skiers learn to ski sensibly and safely on terrain they can cope with. Not only do out-of-control skiers risk their own safety, but they also threaten others on the slopes who are simply going about their business sensibly. This important aspect of wise skiing is highlighted in a section entitled "Saying No With Grace" in the excellent book *Skiing Out Of Your Mind* (Loudis, Lobitz and Singer, 1988). The authors remind us that it is not always easy to resist pressure from well-meaning friends.

A major problem most beginning skiers face is route selection. Beginners have difficulty not only applying the techniques they have learned but also deciding which terrain on any given slope offers them the greatest chance of success and enjoyment. Although most resorts apply a system of color coding ski runs for difficulty (e.g., green or red for beginners, blue for intermediate, black for advanced and "double black" for expert), no international standard exists. Many skiers, partway down a slope, realise to their dismay that they do not have the technical proficiency required to safely ski it. Therefore the ability to select terrain appropriate to the skier's technical ability becomes a critical skill. The implication of this is that instruction must move beyond the mere repetition of technique in isolation and should encourage learners to begin the process of learning to read both the ski slope and snow conditions. At the simplest level, the latter may involve simply learning to stay away from icy patches or deep powder, but with elite skiers it becomes vitally important to learn to avoid hidden obstacles when skiing off piste and above all, to stay away from slopes where avalanches are likely.

Ski instructors, especially those working with beginners, should therefore base their teaching on a "mini trek" around carefully selected terrain with many wide, gentle slopes. They can introduce and develop techniques and key concepts where necessary to deal with the terrain encountered. Again, Play Practice in action.

Clearly, technical ability is important in skiing, because the possibility of injury always exists. Therefore this trek should not merely be a wander across the snow. The route must be carefully planned to take advantage of terrain best suited to introduce and improve basic skiing techniques in a logical sequence. It should also incorporate an almost unnoticeable progression to more and more challenging slopes.

The selection of the learning environment is therefore a critical aspect of ski instruction. A simple example is the importance of the area selected for one of the very basic practices, a downhill run or schuss with skis parallel. Obviously, the slope needs to be just steep enough to allow some acceleration, but most importantly it needs a flat run-out where the novice can slow and stop without having to do anything special and certainly without having to dodge other skiers, pedestrians, dogs or snowmobiles. Similarly, using a gentle gully or couloir to practise turns can make learning this technique easier because the slide up the gully wall bleeds off speed and removes one of the major problems learners confront as they prepare to turn.

A trek approach has many advantages. Learners readily see the need for a particular technique to deal with a problem posed by a slope and will commit themselves more purposefully to mastering it. The varied challenges the terrain presents naturally varies the stimulus, keeping learners alert and motivated and giving them the fantastic sense of achievement that comes from moving around a mountain environment on skis.

One major advantage of using the mini trek is that it naturally introduces learners to the second component of skillful skiing, namely, the ability to read the terrain and pick a route that the individual can ski safely and enjoyably. This point cannot be emphasised strongly enough, because traditional approaches to ski instruction tend to equate "technique" with "skiing" and ignore the vital importance of skiers being able to select routes appropriate to their ability and confidence.

Instructors can make their students aware of the reasons for choosing a particular terrain; if a slope with a run-out has been selected, make the learners aware of this and tell them why. If you have obviously avoided certain terrain, point this out as well, and make sure learners are aware of the potential dangers or safety risks involved. On most slopes, terrain will usually vary in difficulty enough for a number of route options to exist. By using different-colored flags or slalom gates, instructors can mark out several routes of varying difficulty and learners can select their own routes. The instructor might point out the route options at the top and ask students to evaluate these options and describe where and how they will ski it. If a student encounters difficulty, the instructor should provide not only technical feedback but also feedback relating to the student's choice of terrain—was it too difficult, or did they try to apply the right technique in the wrong place?

In addition to carefully selecting practice terrain, ski instructors should go a step further and create safe and effective learning environments. If ski resorts can take the time and trouble to build special areas for hot dogging, boarding and aerials, then surely it is not too much to expect them to put as much effort into building suitable teaching stations.

Such stations might include a series of low bumps on a gentle slope positioned so that students learning to balance on parallel skis while moving down the slope could bleed off the speed they gained going down one bump by going up the next, so that they are always able to feel in control. Another possibility could be a created gully with the turning points built up by carefully sited and sculpted banks of snow.

Not only does this pay off in making it easier for beginners to master important techniques, it also demonstrates the commitment of the instructors involved to excellence in teaching. Ultimately, the Play Practice approach to the teaching of skiing takes the activity back to its roots, where it was simply the process of traveling across snow that was impossible to walk through.

C H A P T E R

15

Action Fantasy Games

All fantasy should have a solid base in reality.
—Max Beerbohm

● ● ● ● ●

The culmination of the Play Practice approach is to use action fantasy games to enhance practice in both individual sports and team games and therefore give all youngsters the chance to experience the magical moments Novak alludes to (see p. 6). The concept of action fantasy games evolved in an attempt to motivate groups of youngsters of varying ability to practise purposefully. The seminal influence came once again from the informal pickup games played around the world. In these games youngsters love to emulate their sporting idols and to take on their identities when playing. Indeed, the struggle to "be" a particularly favoured hero is often as hard fought as the game itself!

The concept is simple. The instructor presents a scenario such as this:

"It is two sets all in the Wimbledon final. Sampras, down 3 games to 4 in the final set, is serving at 15–30."

The youngsters choose who they wish to be— or toss a coin in the case of a dispute—and then play the match out.

or

"The United States, with the ball, trails Russia 90–86 in the women's Olympic basketball final with four minutes left to play."

Teams of three toss for the right to represent a country and then play the game out in a half-court format.

In this way, a sport educator can combine action fantasy games with mini games to create cameo situations in which young players commit themselves fully as they become immersed in the fantasy. There is little doubt that these games enhance the performance of young players, just as professional players step up their intensity in the last few minutes of a crucial game.

The sports chosen and the game situations highlighted can involve teams at any level from local leagues through national leagues, world series, test matches, world championships and the Olympic games. You can set the scenario in the future or re-create critical situations or periods from famous games of the past. In many ways these short fantasy games are very much like the simulations that elite coaches use to prepare their players for those same critical periods or situations that can occur in any game.

These fantasy games can stand alone as one-off situations or they can be part of a tournament. For example, they could be the initial round-robin tournament in a World Cup or Olympic games for soccer, where teams compete in pools of four for the right to advance to the next stage. At the conclusion of the pool stage, teams then move into the final stage and begin to play off in groups for positions 1 to 4, 5 to 8, 9 to 12, and so on. This could all be part of a festival of sport at the culmination of the unit or season.

The Evolution of Fantasy Games

As with other elements of Play Practice, the notion of action fantasy games evolved pragmatically as I looked for ways to help student teachers solve the never-ending problem of keeping large groups of children of varying ability "on task", i.e., positively involved in a practice activity. This problem is always exacerbated when a group is spread out, as is often the case in a game like tennis, and when the ability of a group ranges from absolute beginners to quite experienced players. However, it was made even worse by inexperienced teachers who, unaware of the importance of positioning and proximity, were often unable to watch the entire group.

The intrinsic enjoyment and challenge provided by fantasy games keeps children on task and gives an instructor the freedom to help those students who really need assistance. However, they can also be used to create stimulating mini games that replicate the situations which occur at the highest levels of play and so can be used to draw out even higher levels of performance from elite players.

When the first fantasy game was tried many years ago, the scene was set verbally with the players pretending they were playing matches in the World Table Tennis Championships. Children were given a list of world-class players whose names they could assume if they wished. In the first fantasy game, the score was set at 15–15 and the children simply played the game out. Depending on the final score of that game, for example, 21–19 or 21–15, they worked out an acceptable handicap and then agreed on the

starting score for the second game, such as 15–16 or 15–18, and also decided who would serve first. In the third game the score was again adjusted and the match finished.

Even this simple approach to fantasy games generated high levels of concentration and performance, particularly when combined with a tournament board that recorded the results of the "championships". Because games always started at 15–15, every point was important when playing to 21, so play tended to be very purposeful indeed! Other advantages were that games between individuals took far less time than playing a full game, and the scoreline was never embarrassing because even the poorest player had at least 15 points to start with! What was encouraging was the willingness of students to commit themselves to the fantasy and play out the games seriously.

Action Fantasy Game Cards

The next development was to use fantasy game cards as shown in figure 15.1. The information on the card sets the scene, and the children can either choose which player they want to be or they can toss a coin to decide. In either case, they play out the match as if it were a real championship. An additional benefit of using the cards is that the instructor is now free to help individual children who might be experiencing difficulty and who can benefit from one-on-one tutoring.

Instructors can use the action fantasy game concept to deal with some of the major problems encountered in teaching a game such as tennis, where youngsters are often dispersed over a large area and a wide range of ability usually exists. Surprisingly, it is often the more experienced players who quickly lose interest and begin to practise or play very casually. Their careless attitude rubs off on classmates nearby so that the quality of work from the whole group deteriorates. One method of dealing with this is to give the better players "coaching" roles, but this means that they are not always developing their own potential.

The solution is to make up a series of fantasy game cards based on great players playing in major tournaments, as shown in the accompanying examples. At the beginning of the session, children pair up and select a fantasy game card

Figure 15.1   Sample fantasy game card.

randomly from a box. After deciding who they are, they play out the game.

Adding Practice Tasks

The next step is to put a brief but specific practice task on the reverse side of each card that the player must complete before the match can begin. To maintain the fantasy element, set up these practice tasks as "the match warm-up," or as "practice just prior to a restart after a rain delay," "an injury," or even "a bomb scare." The cards can require the players to hit "forehand drives like Rafter or Anna," or to "keep the ball in play like Serena or Agassi," and can carry information about the way that player executes the particular stroke or task.

Creating Game Cards

The cards themselves can take many different forms but thick paper or stiff card of approximately 8 inches by 4 inches has been found quite satisfactory. Use different colors to denote different sexes or to distinguish cards for doubles, for example. Laminate the cards if possible to help them withstand the inevitable wear and tear. Ideally, keep the cards in a box clearly labeled for a particular sport, and cover the box with color photographs of the players or teams involved.

The fantasy games concept has been used extensively across the whole range of sports played in Australia, which takes in most of the games played around the world! Youngsters actually begin to take on the persona of their "star". As a result they are able to accept a lost game more cheerfully because they are not "personally" involved; as a result, games between individuals are played in much better spirits than would otherwise be the case. On some occasions, however, teams became so involved in the competition that examples of bad sporting behavior surfaced. Though this can be a negative aspect of the fantasy game approach, it can also give the teachers involved opportunities to deal with issues of critical importance to sport educators.

Using fantasy games at the beginning of a session encourages children to get ready quickly so they can start playing, although, as indicated previously, it is possible to build in a practice task that can be presented as an extended warm-up for the "match". For example, when the children randomly select a card from the appropriate box, if the fantasy game is facing them, they can immediately begin the game; but if a practice task is facing them, they must complete the practice task before they can start the game.

The element of chance involved makes this approach very acceptable to children, and they respond well to it. Another bonus is that when the majority of the players begin practising quickly and purposefully, the instructor is free to deal with the inevitable personal problems and minor organisational matters that arise at the start of any session.

The instructor can also use the cards variously during a session to keep the better players on task, as a reward for students who have worked particularly well at a practice task or to free the instructor to provide individual assistance. The fantasy game concept can be applied in many creative ways, and not only in the area of ball games, as the wonderful example below confirms.

An Example of the Fantasy Game Approach

In 1984, Sam White, an Adelaide student teacher, was required to teach a unit of work dealing with the maintenance of cycles and safe highway riding. To encourage purposeful and careful riding habits with a class of difficult boys, as well as to ensure perfectly maintained cycles, he created the "Tour de West Lakes", which was the name of the area around his school. Sam modeled his "race" on the world-renowned Tour de France and brought to the school as much information as he could find about this great sporting event.

Each lesson included a ride of several miles that made up a "stage" of the "race". To eliminate racing and its attendant dangers, Sam used the beautifully simple device of determining the finishing position and time randomly. As the riders finished each stage, they picked a card from a box that allocated a position and riding time so that the student who finished first might well draw a card that placed them last! This arrangement made actual racing pointless, and, when combined with a system of time penalties for traffic offences or careless riding, it ensured that the students rode sensibly and safely. Naturally, Sam also had a time bonus system for all bicycles that were well maintained.

Prizes were awarded for stage winners, and the race leader, as in the Tour de France, wore the famed yellow jersey. There were special sections for "sprints" and "hill climbs" as in the real tour, even though not a hill of any kind could be found within 15 miles of the school! Stage results were published and a well-organised presentation of prizes took place at the end of the "race". Though there is no research evidence to support this, we believe that few of the children involved will quickly forget this experience.

This section is dedicated to Sam, who was tragically killed while on his cycle preparing for a triathlon.

Sport Educator's Role

CHAPTER 16

Bench Coaching

You can see a lot by observing.
—*Yogi Berra*

• • • • •

At some point in their careers, many sport educators will find themselves coaching in the game, or what is commonly termed bench coaching. At the elite level, bench coaching is crucial to successful coaching, but it can be equally important for the sport educator working with young children. Bench coaching can have an impact, both positive and negative, far beyond a single game. This is because a competitive game can provide great opportunities for effective teaching. In a sense, a tough game provides the perfect learning situation; the players are focussed and want to win, the action is real, the learning is contextual and relevant and motivation is high to perform well. The challenge is to recognise and use every teaching opportunity that emerges both during the game and in subsequent practice sessions.

Eyeballing: Most Coaches' Basic Tool

Despite an increasing use of technology in elite sport, most coaches at junior level rely on their own powers of observation—intelligent eyeballing—to analyse what is happening on the field, and they can rarely expect more data than their eyes will give them.

Match Analysis

Match analysis, that is, a coach's ability to observe and understand what is happening in a game, is a significant component of bench coaching. Anecdotal evidence from a range of sports suggests that many, if not most, inexperienced coaches have minimal observation and match analysis skills. Perhaps this is best typified by the true story of an Australian rules football coach who decided to substitute a particular player because he had not had enough touches, only to discover, after some confusion and even more embarrassment, that they were playing with only 17 men, not 18. The player concerned had never taken the field and in fact had not even turned up for the game!

Clearly, some individuals do seem to have an almost uncanny ability to read a game and to make sound tactical decisions while under great pressure. Like many highly complex human capacities, however, the ability to analyse and understand what is happening in a game seems to be more intuitive than reflective. The challenge for researchers is to tease out the key elements of the process so that any enthusiastic sport educator can understand and master them.

A real game is a whirling, often chaotic ebb and flow of action with no instant replays, so a coach must absorb, interpret and react to continuous sequences of action, all the while remaining cool, calm and collected. This is a very complex process that has yet to be studied and analysed and is often studiously ignored, as is the case with the otherwise comprehensive coach-education programs that are part of most Australian sports. At the present time, competence in this area usually derives from intuition and experience rather than guided reflection. To a large degree it is based on knowing what to look for and identifying the critical elements in the continuously unfolding drama of a sporting contest.

The Need for a Template

Effective match analysis is based on a thorough understanding of the fundamental nature, strategy and tactics of a game. Ideally, coaches need a precise model or template of the game to give purpose and focus to their seeing. For lacrosse, soccer and some other invasion games, these are encapsulated in the principles of effective play detailed in earlier chapters; these provide the template necessary for intelligent observation and therefore help simplify the process of analysis. Because coaches have no time during a game to dig out half-remembered and undigested ideas on tactics, they must continually revisit and apply the concepts involved if those concepts are to be of real value.

With a template to provide a framework for overall observation, the coach can focus on other important factors, such as one-on-one match ups, the tempo of the game and specific patterns of play employed by the opposition. Without a structure provided by principles or rules, a coach is like a tone-deaf conductor who cannot read music trying to improve an orchestra. The principles or rules also provide a common tactical language that makes communication easier so players can more easily understand their role in the total team effort.

Scientific Match Analysis

Attempts to simplify the process of match analysis and to make it more scientific have led to various systems for the collection of hard data on player performance. At a basic level this involves the collection of information such as the number of individual possessions, effective passes, assists, shots at goal, scores, interceptions and turnovers in a game. These numbers are usually compiled by an assistant coach, a dedicated statistician or even a team of such observers.

Data of this kind can be valuable when it gives coaches a clearer picture of future opponents or when it makes the postmatch analysis of one's own team more objective, but it is not real-time, here-and-now data useful to a coach during a game. Even the far more complex data-collection systems outlined later cannot yet replace the coach's capacity for real-time analysis based on intelligent eyeballing.

However, systems that employ sophisticated computer programs are beginning to give coaches in some games access to real-time data. Coaches can use these to confirm the effectiveness of their own tactics or help predict the opposition's tactical responses. Given the importance of performance analysis, it is not surprising that even more advanced approaches to match analysis are being trialled. These combine game film, computers and physiological monitoring devices to allow coaches, or their sport scientists, to analyse virtually every aspect of play and player performance.

A major problem with scientific approaches to match analysis is that they are biased toward data that is easy to collect and often ignore crucial aspects of good play. Also, intangibles such as intensity or hustle are not easily measured but can change the course of a game as much by their psychological impact as by their objective value in gaining or retaining the ball. Perceptive coaches who value these elements of good play are gradually finding ways to quantify them and to factor them into any analysis of player performance. A good example of this comes from Australian rules football, where the number of what have been termed "sacrificial" acts are regarded as a clear indication of the players' commitment and determination. In basketball, diving to the floor to gain a loose ball would represent a sacrificial act because a risk of injury clearly exists in this situation.

The Three Phases of Match Analysis

Pregame analysis, or the scouting process, involves the observation and analysis of future opponents either in the flesh or through videotape. This analysis is essential at the higher levels of competition because it can give a coach invaluable insights into the strengths and weaknesses of future opponents and thus provide the key to victory. As was suggested earlier, computers are now being used in sports like volleyball to collect data and to predict the probable reactions of opposing teams and individuals to specific tactical situations.

Again, note that player performance and statistics, as well as specific patterns of play, can vary from game to game, so the team you scout may not be the same team you play against statistically or tactically. Remember, they will also be preparing—to play against you! A scouting coach may learn far more that is useful about an opponent by identifying their philosophy of play rather than merely gathering statistics, because the former is unlikely to vary much from game to game. Thus a scout must try to identify the crucial elements of an opponent's style and consider a whole range of issues, such as how they combine in attack, who their key playmakers are, who has the pace and agility to break down defences on their own. Do they press all over the field or do they retreat and counterpunch? How fast do they counterattack or fast break—and how fast do they recover in defence?

Finally, and perhaps most importantly, do they play with heart? Are they tough and resilient? Do they keep coming back when they get behind? Do they play it out until the final whistle? Among the most crucial issues are the philosophy and psychological makeup of their coach.

Though it may not be feasible to scout opponents at lower levels of play, the serious coach should be prepared to spend many hours involved in this process. In fact, watching many games at any level—but particularly at a level above the one you are working at—is essential if you are to quickly develop the observation skills necessary for effective match analysis.

Bjorn Borg, known as the "Iceman" because of his superb psychological control, was the greatest of the players who emerged through the Swedish "tennis miracle". The success of his game was based on great agility and fitness, a fierce determination and the ability to stay focussed at all times. This enabled him to compensate for the technical limitations in his method. Among his many great performances were five consecutive Wimbledon championships. As a young boy he played soccer, ice hockey and table tennis before specialising in tennis. Throughout his career he always paid tribute to the fact that his parents had never pressured him to play or to win.

Match Analysis During the Game

Match analysis during the game is probably the most difficult process in coaching, for a vast gulf exists between pre- or postmatch analysis and match analysis in the cauldron of a crucial game. Match analysis during the game is multilayered, and, as with the appreciation of anything complex, be it music, art or wine, the layers are usually peeled away only through thoughtful experience over many years. The process by which coaches progress from merely watching the action around the ball like a spectator to seeing and reading the whole game has yet to be studied in depth.

During the game a coach must be able to do the following:

- Watch the players of both teams in a relatively calm and dispassionate manner, even under intense pressure.
- Discern patterns of play and identify the contributions of individual players on both teams.
- See whether the team is attempting to carry out its game plan—and if not, why?
- Remain composed and decide what changes can be made to improve play.

Postmatch Analysis

Given the ready availability of video equipment, coaches at any level are remiss if they do not make every effort to film each game. At the highest levels of play, postmatch analysis of game film is virtually mandatory. Not only does it give the coach a chance to pick up details missed during the time compression of the game, it also gives players the chance to come face to face with their own performance. Combined with match statistics, game film can ensure that a very objective picture of player and team performance emerges. Even at the lowest level, postmatch analysis is critical because it gives a coach a specific focus for succeeding practices. It will also help players understand the reason for that focus.

It is important to use video replay of games positively, to highlight and reinforce successful aspects of play that you have emphasised in practice and that provide evidence that a team is beginning to achieve its goals, even when games are lost. The use of focussed video clips that highlight the performance of individual players is particularly valuable in that it forces them to accept their actual contributions. Human nature being what it is, very few players are prepared to be accountable when they have made crucial errors and find it far easier to put the responsibility on others. Video replays provide feedback that is very difficult to argue with.

*C*oaches must learn to see every game from the other team's point of view.

Think about an appropriate location for the postmatch analysis. The changing room must always be a place where hopes and expectations are high, so it is important not to conduct a postmatch analysis there immediately after the game when emotions are running high and when, after a loss, recriminations are likely to sour the atmosphere.

Precepts for Bench Coaching: The Basic Truths

The following precepts may help novice sport educators begin to understand the nature of bench coaching.

1. There are two teams out there—and two coaches. Like good chess players, coaches must learn to see every game from the other team's point of view; in effect, they must be coaching both teams if they are to anticipate opposition moves and predict likely responses. Coaches must accept that it is the opposition's task to make winning as difficult as possible and must actually enjoy the challenge this provides.

2. A competitive situation can bring out the best and the worst in both player and coach. The pressure to perform, to win or at least not lose, can affect even the most levelheaded individuals, who may lose their sense of perspective and say or do things they may long regret. If individuals find they cannot cope with this situation, they would do well to heed the old adage "If you can't stand the heat, stay out of the kitchen!"

A competitive situation can bring out the best and the worst in both player and coach.

3. Success or failure are determined more by the quality of training and preparation than by any changes made during the game. Coaches must keep the faith and believe in what they are trying to achieve and what they have done in training.

4. No matter who the opposition is or how well you prepare your team, players will make

mistakes, both forced and unforced. The manner in which a coach responds to these mistakes will influence them well beyond the individual game.

5. Improvement takes time. Getting children to play the way you want them to or developing a club culture does not happen overnight. Take a long view, and work systematically to achieve your goals.

6. Coaches must accept responsibility for their decisions and live with the consequences of their actions. To do this, they need a coherent philosophy of sport and of life, and they must develop the capacity to look forward and remain positive.

The Basic Process of Bench Coaching

The bench-coaching process begins when the whole team meets before the game and extends through until a brief postgame meeting. It is important to establish routines and expecta-tions in relation to each of the following elements.

Before the Game

A suitable arrival time and procedures, including a warm-up routine, need to be established, agreed upon and adhered to by all team members. This period allows the coach to check that all players have arrived fit and well, to remind them of the specific learning objectives for the game and to ensure that they are ready to play.

The pregame warm-up must be carefully planned to prepare players physically and mentally for the frenetic early moments of the game. It should gradually build in physical intensity and use game-situation drills and even some realistic tactical elements.

During the Game

Because it is difficult for a coach to watch everything that is happening in a game at the same time, observation must be focussed. The process involves an expanding and revolving

Bench coaching is an important aspect in the coaching role. Many split-second decisions are made during this time and the coach's reactions and attitudes become very important as they have a great impact on the players.

diagnosis as the coach continually asks himself or herself questions about what is happening in the game.

Are we focussed and in the game?

Is the opposition doing anything unexpected?

Are we responding quickly to changes of possession?

Are we carrying out our defensive tasks?

Are we supporting the ball player in attack—running hard into attacking positions?

Which team is controlling the tempo of the game?

Are we getting a good share of possession?

Who is our most dangerous opponent in attack?

Do we need to reorganise our defence?

Where do we have an advantage in attack? What are the opposition's weaknesses? How can we exploit them?

Clearly, the questions asked must reflect the performance level of the players. With a team of beginners, the coach may first look to see if players remember their basic team assignments or whether they are just chasing the ball wherever it goes. At the very basic level, the question may even be, "Are they playing in the right direction?" This is a revolving and expanding process because many of the same questions must be asked continuously throughout the game while others are added as the game progresses and the coach's coping ability improves.

Time-Outs

Time-outs provide opportunities to remind players of the key elements of the game plan, make tactical adjustments, give your players a breather, make multiple substitutions or change the tempo of the game. Coaches must view them as a time to look forward and give positive instructions about what needs to be done. In preparing for a time-out, coaches must organise their thoughts and be prepared to give their players precise, succinct information. Remember, by calling a time-out, you are also giving the opposition a chance to make changes, so you must be prepared for the adjustments they may make.

Quarter or Halftime Breaks

A coach who has been able to digest and interpret the lessons of the first period may be able to make some adjustments in tactics or personnel. Again, it is important to put yourself in your opponent's shoes and try to see the game from their point of view; it may be possible to anticipate changes they make, preempt them and so keep them off balance. In fact, it may sometimes pay off to make specific short-term tactical changes at this time to confuse the opposition players and cause them to quickly forget their coach's instructions.

Substitutions

With novice players, making substitutions is one area that will immediately reveal a sport educator's true philosophy. If every child gets an even run, no matter what the result, then clearly the coach is there for the players. If, on the other hand, the stars are allowed to dominate the playing time and the game, then questions must be asked. Obviously, as the level of play increases, this issue becomes one the whole group, players and coach, must address so that all involved have a clear understanding of how playing time is determined and why.

Reprinted, with special permission, of King Features Syndicate.

Coaches need a coherent philosophy of life and sport.

The Postgame Meeting

The postgame meeting should be brief and positive and based around the major learning experiences from the game. It provides a focus for subsequent practice sessions.

Summary

Competitive games should be viewed as high-level play practices that share the objective of improving playing performance in an enjoyable manner. Given the intensity with which winning is pursued at every level in some cultures, coaches may have trouble selling this view to many parents, but it must be done. Though there are many reasons why children drop out of sport, it is clear that unreasonable pressures to perform in competitive situations is a major factor. The sport educator must control this situation.

Sport educators working in a coaching role need a clear understanding of the way the rules influence the tactics and strategy of any game. It is interesting to note that the implications of major changes in the rules of a sport have sometimes gone virtually unnoticed for long periods. In 1906 American football was saved from self-destruction by major changes in the rules. It was not until six years later, however, in 1913, when Notre Dame convincingly beat the Army team at West Point using forward passes, many caught by the legendary Knute Rockne, that the full impact of those changes became apparent.

Sporting Behaviour

*True sport is always a duel: a duel with nature, with one's own fear,
with one's own fatigue, a duel in which body
and mind are strengthened.*
—Yevgeny Yevtuskenko

● ● ● ● ●

As chapter 1 suggested, sport is now fast approaching a watershed. The very real possibility exists that it will soon be torn apart by individuals or even nations bent on exploiting sport for their own ends.

This chapter cannot attempt to deal with all of the problems sport faces. It can, however, suggest a way in which sport educators may be able to ensure that competitive sport is a pleasant and fulfilling experience rather than war without the weapons. With competition comes pressure to win, and the focus shifts away from playing merely for the sake of the game. This pressure can affect an Olympic athlete who shoulders the expectations of an entire nation as well as a child who is the subject of a parent's ill-informed comments made while watching a junior competition. Whatever the source, pressure to succeed and win can lead to numerous problems and dilemmas that can challenge the integrity of everyone involved.

As mentioned earlier, sport educators are well

Reprinted, with special permission, of King Features Syndicate.

Pressure to win can come from many sources.

placed to defend the integrity of sport because by their every word and deed, they can demonstrate a philosophy of sport in action. To help coaches maintain their integrity in the face of the inevitable pressures that competition brings, this chapter provides a clear rationale for a philosophy of sport that both values sporting behaviour and, most importantly, does not disadvantage those who practise it. This proviso is of vital importance if coaches whose salaries depend on successful performance are to consider taking a more ethical position when dealing with the dilemmas they face daily.

While those who stand on the sidelines of sport moralising about ethical behaviour may well experience the satisfaction that comes from being "holier than thou", their views do little to improve the situation. For example, the French writer and former soccer goalkeeper Albert Camus (quoted in Green 1982, p. 138) stated that "integrity needs no rules." Though he is absolutely correct, this view ignores the reality of modern sport and leaves a gap between the ideal and the real that cannot be bridged.

Play Practice and Sporting Behaviour

As always, the Play Practice approach is pragmatic and is based on several principles. The first is that while sport can be valuable to society in many ways, it must always belong to the participants, a notion that Theodore Roosevelt expressed superbly: "The credit belongs to the man who is actually in the arena."

The second principle is that athletes should respect their opponents. As Robert Paddick (1988) stated, "It is obvious that to treat opponents as enemies in a situation valued for its own sake by all the players, all of whom are necessary for the continuation of the activity, is absurd, being a denial of the whole agreement for coming together—to play." (p. 3) This notion is picked up and expanded by Novak (1988):

Lucky the great athlete who has great competition. Unless another pushes him to new heights of achievement he will never know how good he might have been, for humans

The value of winning is only as great as the value of the goal reached.

cannot help falling short of heroic efforts when they are not called for…. In a real sense a great competitor is not the one against whom you compete, he forces you to struggle against yourself. (p. 346)

This leads naturally to the third principle, encapsulated in the Olympic motto, that striving to win is more important than winning. This concept is not easy for many coaches to accept, but, as any athlete knows, it is possible to win with a poor performance yet lose after a great one. Which experience is ultimately more satisfying, and which will contribute most to the athlete's continued improvement? As Gallwey (1977) states,

Winning is overcoming obstacles to reach a goal, but, the value in winning is only as great as the value of the goal reached. Reaching the goal itself may not be as valuable as the experience that can come in making a supreme effort to overcome the obstacles involved. The process can be more rewarding than the victory itself. (p. 123)

It must be stressed that the value of the contest depends entirely on the determination of all competitors to win. That struggle for victory can produce an aesthetic and enthralling event that elevates everyone involved, participants and spectators alike. A tight, intense contest gives all competitors the chance to improve their own performance, win or lose. As Gallwey says,

Like two bulls butting their heads against one another, both (athletes) grow stronger and each participates in the development of the other. (p. 123)

Conversely, any contest in which participants do not do their utmost to win becomes virtually meaningless, and they are guilty of conceivably the worst form of being a poor sport.

Clearly, cheating in any form negates the whole value of the experience. Not only are cheats dishonest but, importantly, they also miss the opportunity to improve that a fair but tough struggle provides. They are less well prepared for future opponents and consequently may never attain their full potential.

This may be too idealistic for many coaches to accept, particularly if their careers depend on their athletes' success. Thus, any philosophy of sport not only must represent an ethical position but, as suggested earlier, also should not disadvantage those who try to live by it.

Clearly it is impossible to deal here with all aspects of cheating in sport. Fortunately, at the junior level the major concern is the more overt forms of cheating that occur during a contest, such as what is often termed gamesmanship or intimidation, or simply all forms of being a poor sport. These can range from the use of racist comments to distract an opponent to deliberate attempts to injure key players on the opposing team.

Dealing With Poor Sports

As a coach, the key to dealing with poor sports is to encourage your players to stand above such things, to take the high moral ground and, most importantly, to turn their position into one that gives them the advantage. There is no better way to stop poor sports than to win by playing fairly. A study of sport psychology clearly shows that the ability to concentrate on the critical elements of performance without being distracted by any external factors is a key to success in sport. Athletes at the highest level must take this notion much further and focus so intensely that no conscious thought, including the chimera of winning, interferes with the uninhibited flow of action. Put very simply, if you have one eye on winning, you have only one eye to watch your opponent or the ball!

If you have one eye on winning, you have only one eye to watch your opponent or the ball.

Japanese exponents of the martial arts strive for kime, which means "to tighten the mind", and therefore exclude all extraneous thoughts, all fears and all distractions. When kime is achieved, performance flows free and uninhibited from the subconscious. Athletes in many sports now recognise that getting into this "state of flow" or "the zone" is the key to ultimate performance; this is when they can effortlessly release all of their ability. Phrases such as "playing unconscious" or "spacey" are becoming part of the language of sport and illustrate the importance of these ideas to high-level performers. There is certainly no place for emotion in the completely focused competitor for, as the samurai adage holds, "In battle as in life, anger will defeat you."

Novak provided the crucial conceptual link between effective mental preparation and good sporting behaviour when he said,

> To concentrate on the game is in a sense to be indifferent about one's opponent or oneself. It is to refuse to be distracted by wayward passions. If an opponent plays unfairly the sweetest revenge is not revenge but victory; one avoids striking back in kind in order to concentrate on the one thing necessary, perfect execution. Concentration on the game itself is the best safeguard against indulgence in ugly errant passions. It is the highest form of sportsmanship. It is not so much a moral as an ontological attitude. One isn't trying to "be good", but to act (play) perfectly. (p. 313)

Many great athletes have demonstrated this pragmatic approach to sporting behaviour in the past, and the highly successful Swedish tennis players of recent years appear to have adopted it as their credo. All sport educators should follow the same policy so that, while sports remain joyous contests instead of becoming spiteful battles, our standards of performance will continue to improve. Naturally, many who love sport believe that good sporting behaviour should be valued for its own sake and not for pragmatic reasons. However, unless it is possible to show that sporting behaviour can pay off, many competitors and coaches, perhaps too many, may reject the ethical considerations, and sport will increasingly lose its value as a humanising experience.

Because much of Play Practice is based on competitive but cooperative play, it is an ideal vehicle via which to explore these issues with young people. For example, children often play fantasy games with the furious intensity of world championships, and these games have the potential to generate all of the on-field aggression noted at the senior level. In turn, they provide a perceptive sport educator with ongoing opportunities to lead or initiate discussion about ap-

propriate sporting behaviour and about the fundamental nature of the sport experience. Of the many lessons that players can learn, one of the most important is that sport must always be about risk, victory and defeat, success and failure, mastery and mistakes. So a major responsibility for sport educators is to help their charges come to understand that, as the Olympic motto implies, the challenge is in the struggle, in honest participation. And that is enough!

> **O**ne of the most important lessons that can be learned is that sport must always be about risk, victory and defeat, success and failure, mastery and mistakes.

Another way in which sport educators can deal with this issue is simply to redefine winning. This was the major reason for the success of the five-star approach to track and field. In this most objective and apparently cutthroat of sports, winning and losing are clearly defined and obvious to all. But most people do not like to lose, and they certainly do not want to finish last. Yet when at least two people compete, the last position must be filled. With the five-star approach, the emphasis was switched from direct or head-to-head competition to what was termed indirect competition in which every individual competes against himself or herself to achieve personal bests.

Children love this approach, and track and field has flourished wherever it has been used. Naturally, if children wish to continue in the sport of track and field, they must be prepared to accept the notion of direct competition, but experience suggests that they can carry the personal-best philosophy into the competitive arena. Indeed, many of the great athletes, especially in the field events, have based their whole competitive philosophy on competing only against themselves and of completely ignoring the performances of their competitors.

Though it is less obvious, sport educators can apply this approach to other sports, including interactive team games, and it also ties in with both the Zenlike philosophy of samurai swordsmen and modern sport psychology. For example, in Australian rules football, one of the most brutal and physically competitive of all games, teams are now setting specific goals to achieve during a game rather than focussing merely on winning. Of course, their aim is always to win, but they believe that if they focus on achieving specific performance targets during the game, they *will* win. Interestingly, one of the key indicators is the number of "sacrificial acts", where players put their bodies on the line and in doing so risk pain or injury, a team records during a game. Previously, these acts were not recorded, even though a perceptive coach would have noted them. The importance of this particular aspect of play is that it reflects a team's commitment to getting or keeping the ball, and in this game commitment is everything!

In the same way, a basketball team that takes specific numbers of offensive and defensive rebounds, where commitment and desire are again as important as technique, will markedly improve its chances of winning. One consequence of this is that a losing team can come away from a game conscious of improvement or at least of achieving specific goals against a stronger opponent. This provides a far better basis for future development than the inevitable destructive criticism that is so often associated with defeat.

Finally, it may be worthwhile returning to the notion that losing can often provide a sounder foundation for later success than does winning. Malcolm Forbes captured this succinctly when he said, "Failure is success if we learn from it," while Thomas Watson Sr. averred, "Double your rate of failure.... Failure is a teacher, a harsh one but the best. So go ahead and make mistakes. Make all you can. Because that is where you find success. On the other side of failure."

Losing can often provide a sounder foundation for later success than winning.

Socrates warned that the unexamined life is not worth living. In an increasingly benign society, sport provides one of the few areas in which human beings can be tested in extremis and so experience those elemental feelings of exhilaration that make us searingly aware of our own existence. If all sport educators were to promote the idea that losing is a small price to pay for such experiences and that just to participate is to be a winner, sporting behaviour would flourish, and even more young people might join us in the joy of sport.

Postscript:
The Problem of Early Specialisation

One of the most serious crimes of our day is robbing children of their childhood.... To push kids to the brink of physical and mental exhaustion is absurd.
—Dr. Joseph Torg, sports physician

● ● ● ● ●

The essential theme of this book has been the importance of bringing the joy of play back to the sport experience for participants at every level. A simple extension of this is the notion that we should never distort sport for young people in the first place, and certainly we should never allow children's play to be stolen. For no matter how cleverly and fervently the arguments are put for preadolescent competitive sport, adults who encourage children to take on adult play forms, namely, organised sport, before they are ready are stealing children's play and denying them some of the experiences essential for a well-adjusted life.

When young people are forced to take on all the trappings and pressures associated with professional sport, their lives can become unbalanced. The end result can be the former high school sports star who is always looking back to long-ago moments of glory and is unable to escape from adolescence. Dennis Hopper captured this image brilliantly in the movie *Hoosiers,* in which he played the role of a former high school basketball player whose life disintegrated when he missed a crucial shot. It was a tragedy from which he had not yet recovered 20 years later.

Sadly, the problems do not end with the organised sport replacing children's play. There is a growing tendency to encourage young children to specialise in a single sport. Eight-year-old female gymnasts training for over six hours a day in many "developed" countries around the world is but one example.

In fact, one of the biggest problems sport educators face is the pressure to identify talented children and to encourage them to specialise in specific sports at an early age. In the drive for success it is easy to identify talented youngsters early and to push them hard in the belief that this is the only way to produce winning teams now or great players in the future. Because of the power of the sports entertainment business, many young people are easily encouraged to chase the ephemeral dream of a professional career.

This siren call can lead young people to neglect the studies that might give them a real opportunity to succeed in life, to sacrifice their childhood and even to use performance-enhancing drugs. Even worse, this desperate drive to succeed is counterproductive for thousands of children. This is confirmed by the numbers of junior athletes who retire prematurely because of what has been termed "psychological tiredness", a direct result of the pressure to perform in competition before they are mature enough to cope with winning, far less losing. These young people are then often lost forever to the sport in which they could have excelled. It might be more accurate to call this process "burnout" rather than "dropout".

Several studies have shown that early specialisation is at best unnecessary and at worst counterproductive. Among the most damning studies was one reported by Jess Jarver, an authority on talent identification in track and field. He detailed a project conducted in Finland where a 10-year development plan was initiated to find and develop potential Olympians in track and field. The most talented children were selected and provided with excellent coaching and subjected to intense training to prepare for national championships at the under-12 and under-14 levels. While the majority of the youngsters selected were still competing 10 years later and some had reached the national championship finals, not one of the top 100 children in the selected 12-year-old group had made the Finnish national team!

In 1985 a study by the Swedish Tennis Association suggested that early specialisation is unnecessary for players to achieve high performance levels in tennis. Among other things, this study found that the players who were part of the Swedish tennis "miracle" of the 1980s, including the great Bjorn Borg, were keenly active in a range of sports until the age of 14 and did not begin to specialise until about the age of 16. Many of these youngsters came from small rural communities where they had the opportunity to develop multiple talents and to compete with older players.

Interestingly, this study suggested that there was a disadvantage in learning to play in the larger clubs typical of cities and bigger towns; the cutthroat nature of early competition in these situations was seen to outweigh the benefits of better coaching. What was most significant was that many players who had been superior to the eventual elite while in the 12–14 age group had dropped out—been burned out—of the sport.

In addition to the problem of early dropout is the equally serious issue of the hundreds of thousands of young people who choose not to take part in organised sport in any form after a brief experience. Clearly this is a complex issue, and there are many reasons that young people opt out of such a culturally acceptable activity, but we know that it is not confined to elite performers.

It may be that the early selection of potential stars inevitably means early rejection for many youngsters who then choose not to take part. Even if this process guaranteed success for the chosen few it would still be impossible to justify, but it does not!

A recent study by Abernathy et al. of a group of 15 outstanding international players in a range of team games in Australia also suggests that early selection and specialisation may be unnecessary for youngsters who have the potential to become elite players. Their findings parallel those of the Swedish study and emphasise the importance of abundant free play and practice, involvement in multiple sports until the beginning of specialisation from age 12 to 14 and a commitment to excellence around the age of 16. Once again, small rural communities gave talented youngsters a good start, not least because they provided children an opportunity to play with adults. This study also found that although excellence was achieved only through a large volume of deliberate practice, the commitment was significantly lower (a mean of 3,939 hours) than suggested by earlier studies.

Interestingly, the Abernathy group's recommendations for the development of expert decision-making skills in team games are closely aligned with the principles of Play Practice. These include playing multiple sports to ensure a broad diversity of decision-making situations, because they believe that decision making does appear to transfer between sports. They also recommend the use of flexible rules and what they termed novel solutions, as well as ensuring that all youngsters are given a chance to take key roles. They also stress the need to value the process above the outcome.

Because thousands of hours of deliberate practice are necessary to attain high performance levels, the Abernathy group suggest that it is important to vary the practice environment as much as possible. This reaffirms what experienced coaches in many sports have been doing for many years. Interestingly, the players in this study accepted the fact that as they became more professional in their approach to training, the training became more boring and less enjoyable. Finally, the authors concluded that because skill can continue to improve over time, a need exists for training methods that provide a stimulus for ongoing skill development. It is interesting to compare the findings and recommendations of this study with the principles and methods of Play Practice, because the latter evolved through a process of reflective tinkering that has taken place over 40 years.

Despite all that has been said to date, there will always be parents and coaches who are tempted to risk the long-term futures of their children or charges in the hope of reaping some of the obscene financial rewards available to elite performers. Inevitably they will point to the exceptions, examples of the great players who began kicking, shooting or hitting a ball before they could walk, who began competing in a specific sport as early as it was possible to do so and who practised relentlessly to become successful.

They should be aware, however, that the July 2000 edition of *Pediatrics*, the journal of the American Academy of Pediatrics, carried a new and defining policy statement on the risks of early specialisation in a single sport. This policy states that children should be discouraged from specialising in a single sport before adolescence to avoid physical and psychological damage. They argue that the risks, which range from overuse injuries to delayed menstruation, eating disorders, emotional stress and burnout, outweigh the advantages of a possible professional career.

As Steven Anderson, chairman of the Academy's committee on sports medicine and fitness, said, "Waiting to specialise until the age of twelve or thirteen, when children are more emotionally and physically mature, helps ensure that they are pursuing an activity that really interests them rather than fulfilling a parent's or coach's dream."

Though the committee accepts that it would be unrealistic to call for a complete ban on specialisation, they recommend that their 55,000 member pediatricians and pediatric specialists be on the lookout for problems to ensure that children are not overwhelmed or burned out. Another member of the committee reviewing this issue, Thomas Rowland, a pediatric cardiologist, said that "there was concern about the extremely intensive sports play which begins at the age of five, where the child's whole life becomes oriented toward sports success and victory. There's an intuitive feeling that this is not appropriate." He continued, "When you look at the statistics of how many of these kids who are being pushed are going to make it, it's well under 1 percent." As was evident from the Finnish study, even well-thought-out talent identification and development programs may have even less success than this.

Recall the example from chapter 1 that detailed the way in which Chinese female swimmers were prepared to "eat bitterness" if by doing so they could be successful for a few months. Clearly this process has nothing to do with sport education; it is simply the exploitation of young people by coaches to whom they have entrusted their bodies and their dreams. When, as was the case in the former East Germany, this abuse is compounded by the systematic use of performance-enhancing drugs, a situation exists that no civilised nation should tolerate.

Finally, those parents and coaches who still believe that the risks to children are worth the potential reward should realise that they are starting a miniature "arms race". No matter how early they start their children in a sport, surely someone, somewhere will start their children earlier and work them harder. Reports of talent identification programs for potential gymnasts in China suggests that the Chinese are now targeting and testing three-year-old children! It will surely not be long before the cloning of talented athletes begins.

Before we react with righteous indignation, however, we must remember that in a totalitarian nation, where the end always justifies the means, every citizen is expected to sacrifice himself or herself for the good of the state. In such countries sport coaches may have little choice but to follow the party line no matter the cost to individuals, including children. In the same way, we may react in horror to stories of the exploitation of young children in the sweatshops of Asia, which produce much of the sporting equipment we use and the sports clothing we wear. In both cases the thought of children being raped of their childhood is almost enough for many of us to attempt to do something to stop it.

But freed as we are from the overwhelming pressure that comes from the power of the state or from abject poverty, what will be our excuse if we steal the dreams of young people and use them for our own ends?

The final word here must go to Michael Novak, who in *The Joy of Sports* captures stunningly the essence of sport and its place in our culture. He writes,

> *Sports are not merely entertainment, but are rooted in the necessities and the aspirations of the human spirit. They should be treated with all the care and intelligence, care and love the human spirit can bring to bear. It is a corruption, not only of sports but of the human spirit, to treat them as escape, entertainment, business or a means of making money. Sports do provide entertainment, but of a special and profound sort. They do depend upon a financial base, and it is not wrong that they should repay investors and players decent returns. Yet sports are at their heart a spiritual activity, a natural religion, a tribute to grace, beauty and excellence. We ought to keep the streams of the spirit running clean and strong.*

This must surely be the rallying cry for all those individuals to whom this book is dedicated.

Bibliography

Abernathy, B. et al. 2000. Developing expert decision-making skills. University of Queensland *In Sport.* Unpublished study.

Almond, L. 2000. The evolution of the Games for Understanding approach. (personal communication)

Almond, L., D. Bunker and R. Thorpe. 1983. Games teaching revisited. *Bulletin of Physical Education* 19(1):3–35.

American Academy of Pediatrics. 2000. Intensive training and sports specialization in young athletes. *Pediatrics* 106(1): 154-157.

Bronowski, J. 1973. *The ascent of man.* London: British Broadcasting Corporation.

Campbell, M. 1996. *Ultimate golf techniques.* Surrey Hills, Australia: RD Press.

Cohen, J.M. and M.J. Cohen. 1980. *The Penguin dictionary of modern quotations* (2d ed.). Harmondsworth, Middlesex, England.

Collins, H. 1996. *Collins: Concise Dictionary of Quotations.* Glasgow: Harper Collins.

Cox, M. and D. Gould. 1990. *The Swedish way to tennis success.* London: Weidenfeld and Nicolson Ltd.

Cozens, F.W. and F.S. Stumpf. 1953. *Sports in American life.* Chicago: University of Chicago Press.

Editors of Sports Illustrated. 1971. *Sports Illustrated basketball.* Philadelphia: Lippincott.

Gallwey, T. 1977. *Inner tennis.* New York: Random House, Inc.

Green, J. 1982. *Dictionary of contemporary quotations.* London: Pan Books.

Green, J. and D. Atyed. 1982. *The book of sports quotes.* London: Omnibus Press.

Hines, B. 1983. *A kestrel for a knave.* London: Penguin.

Ian, J. 1975. At seventeen, on *Between the lines.* CD, Sony Music, 1987.

Jones, K. and P. Welton. 1978. *Soccer skills and tactics.* New York: Crown.

Laban, R. 1948. *Modern educational dance.* London: McDonald and Evans.

Loudis, L., C. Lobitz and K. Singer. 1988. *Skiing out of your mind: The psychology of peak performance.* Huddersfield, England: Springheld Books.

Mosston, M. 1966. *Teaching physical education: From command to discovery.* Columbus, OH: Charles E. Merril.

Novak, M. 1988. *The joy of sports.* Lanham, MD: Hamilton Press.

O'Donnell, L. 2000. Cycle of success sentences stars to burnout. *The Australian,* February 14.

Paddick, R.J. 1988. The relevance of Olympism to modern sport. ACHPHER Biennial Conference.

Pepper, F. 1985. *Handbook of 20th century quotations.* Aylesbury: Hazell Watson and Viney.

Schon, D. 1987. *Educating the reflective practitioner.* San Francisco: Jossey-Bass.

Siedentop, D. 1983. *Developing teaching skills in physical education* (2nd ed.). Palo Alto: Mayheld Publishing Company.

Siedentop, D. 1994. *Sport education: Quality P.E. through positive sport experiences.* Champaign, IL: Human Kinetics.

Silberman, C. 1970. *Crisis in the classroom.* New York: Random House.

Steinhaus, A.H. 1963. *Towards an understanding of health and physical education.* Dubuque: Brown.

Taylor, R. 2000. A sporting chance at life. *Adelaide Advertiser,* September 13.

Wade, A. *The F.A. guide to training and coaching.* London: Heinemenn.

Watson, D. 1998. A demi god called Don. *The Australian,* August 27.

Index

Note: Figures are indicated by an italicized *f* following the page number.

About the Author

Alan Launder has been deeply involved in sports for more than 50 years as a competitor, teacher and coach. In that time he has worked in Great Britain, the United States and Australia. Since 1973, he has been a senior lecturer at the University of South Australia, where he helped to develop a four-year degree course in physical education—teacher education that became a model for programs in other countries. He won the 1992 Rothmans Prize in recognition of his ability to develop and communicate innovative ideas in sport education. The paper that won the prize, "Coach Education Towards the 21st Century", has had a great influence on the coach education programs of many Australian sporting federations.

Alan holds senior coaching qualifications from Great Britain and Australia in soccer, cricket, basketball, track and field and table tennis. In 1984, he was a coach of the Australian track and field team at the Los Angeles Olympics. In 1986 and 1988, he was the head coach of the Australian team at the World Junior Championships. In 1991, 1993 and 1995, he was a coach of the track and field team at the World University Games. Most recently he has served as a consultant to the Australian Track and Field Coaches Association and to the Australian Lacrosse Association as they reinvented their coach education programs.

Alan regards his major career achievement to be the development of the philosophical and pedagogical principles that underpin the "Five Star Award", an innovative approach to teaching track and field that has been adopted by more than 20 countries.

In his spare time, Alan's hobbies are sporting art, travel, snow skiing and fine wine. He lives with his wife, Jennifer, in Salisbury East, South Australia. He has two sons, David and Richard, and three grandsons, James, Mitchell and Matthew.